Records of the Three Kingdoms in Plain Language

Records of the Three Kingdoms in Plain Language

ANONYMOUS

Translated, with Introduction and Annotations, by
Wilt L. Idema and Stephen H. West

Hackett Publishing Company, Inc.
Indianapolis/Cambridge

19 18 17 16   1 2 3 4 5 6 7

For further information, please address
  Hackett Publishing Company, Inc.
  P.O. Box 44937
  Indianapolis, Indiana 46244-0937

  www.hackettpublishing.com

Cover design by Rick Todhunter
Composition by William Hartman

Library of Congress Cataloging-in-Publication Data

Names: Idema, W. L. (Wilt L.) translator. | West, Stephen H., translator.
Title: Records of the Three Kingdoms in plain language / translated, with
    an introduction and annotations, by Wilt L. Idema and Stephen H. West.
Description: Indianapolis : Hackett Publishing Company, Inc., 2016.
Identifiers: LCCN 2016009481| ISBN 9781624665233 (pbk.) |
    ISBN 9781624665240 (cloth)
Subjects: LCSH: Chinese drama—Translations into English.
Classification: LCC PL2658.E5 R45 2016 | DDC 895.1/2008—dc23
LC record available at https://lccn.loc.gov/2016009481

Contents

Records of the Three Kingdoms in Plain Language

Acknowledgments

We would like to thank Professor Oki Yasushi for helping us acquire relevant Japanese materials and translations, Liu Lidan for her help in assembling the manuscript and glossary, and the anonymous readers who provided valuable comments on the original draft.

A Note to the Reader

The Introduction to this narrative provides historical and cultural context for the text and some general consideration of its structure and themes. These are not entirely necessary to get the general gist of the story. You will find them helpful, however, in placing the *Plain Tales* within its cultural and generic context. Should you decide to move immediately to the story itself, you should be aware of the following guides to help you understand it better.

Measurements: A *li* is approximately one-third of a mile; a Chinese foot is approximately thirty-two centimeters or roughly ten inches. A Chinese pace or step is equal to a modern double pace, approximately five feet.

Names: Each of the characters is identified by one of sometimes several names. We have chosen to retain the original variety of names for the simple reason that Chinese does not use pronouns in addressing the self or others, preferring to refer to people by their rank within the family, their official title, or their social status. China was, and is, a strongly hierarchical society, in which age, status, and gender carry weight. Names are thus not just designators of people, but are also indexical to their status vis-à-vis the speaker. For instance, Liu Bei, the major figure of the text, is known by several designations:

Liu Bei is a combination of his surname Liu and given name Bei. This name is only used in official documents or in historical retrospect, for instance by the narrator. It would be unthinkable to call a person by his given name in normal contexts.

He also has a familiar name, Xuande, a public-use name given in later childhood and used by superiors, close friends, and family members. Even the narrator uses this name when he wants to establish an authoritative sense of intimate knowledge when describing Liu Bei's activities, or wants to create a sympathetic bond between the audience and the character, inviting them into that circle of supposed intimacy through the use of this name.

Liu Bei is also called variously the Vanguard, the District Protector, the Magistrate, or such-and-such general. This of course designates his role in a military or civil bureaucracy. This is the normal form of address between members of the civil or military institutions.

In addition, Liu Bei is referred to as the First Ruler, since he would become the first ruler of the Shu-Han, which he and Zhuge Liang eventually established. This was a way to distinguish him from his son, the second and last ruler of the Shu-Han, who is designated as the Young Ruler or Later Ruler.

Finally, after his kinship to the royal family was confirmed by checking his lineage against the Imperial Geneology, he was called the Imperial (Younger) Uncle. This name occurs only after this incident takes place in the narrative, and is used primarily by his colleagues when they speak about him to a third party.

Likewise Guan Yu (surname and given name) is known as Yunchang, his public-use name, Zhang Fei as Yide, and Zhuge Liang as Kongming. Zhuge Liang is also known as the Reclining Dragon, a sobriquet often understood as his Daoist name.

It is a feature of the text that upon first appearance, the given and public-use names are usually provided, along with the civil or military title, and any sobriquets will be stated and explained.

Background-highlighted text: These are found in the original printed edition of the work and are reproduced here, using a black box holding white text. The function of these highlights is not always clear; they may be related to either printing convention, as markers within the original story, or otherwise some sort of signal to the reader (perhaps even artifacts from the oral cycle itself). They often seem to denote what might be considered a particularly famous or well-known episode. They may introduce poems, following episodes, and they may occur at the beginning of a phrase or interrupt what would be considered a complete thought. We have retained them as what were obviously important features of the original text.

Table of Major Dynasties

SHANG ca. 1460–1045 BCE

ZHOU 1045–256 BC

    Western Zhou 1111–771 BCE
    Eastern Zhou 770–256 BCE
    Spring and Autumn 722–476 BCE
    Warring States 475–221 BCE

QIN 221–207 BCE

HAN 206 BCE–220 CE

    Western Han 206 BCE–9 CE
    Eastern Han 25–220

THREE KINGDOMS 220–266

    Wei 226–266
    Wu 222–280
    Shu-Han 221–264

WESTERN JIN 266–316

NORTHERN AND SOUTHERN DYNASTIES 386–589

SUI 581–618

TANG 618–907

FIVE DYNASTIES 907–960

SONG 960–1279

    Northern Song 960–1127
    Southern Song 1127–1279

LIAO 916–1125

JIN 1115–1234

YUAN 1260–1368

MING 1368–1644

QING 1644–1911

Table of Important Reigns, Reign-Periods, and Dynasties

WESTERN HAN 206 BCE–9 CE

XIN 9–23

EASTERN HAN 25–220

Guang Wudi	25–57	
Mingdi	57–75	
Zhangdi	75–88	
Andi	106–125	
Shundi	125–144	
Chongdi	144–145	
Zhidi	145–146	
Huandi	146–168	
Lingdi	168–189	
Shaodi	189	
Xiandi	189	Yonghan
	189–190	Zhongping
	190–194	Chuping
	194–196	Xingping
	196–220	Jian'an
	220	Yankang

WEI 220–266

Wendi	226–227	Huangchu
Mingdi	227–233	Taihe
	233–237	Qinglong
	237–239	Jingchu
Gaogui xianggong	254–256	Zhengyuan
	256–260	Ganlu
Yuandi	260–264	Jingyuan
	264–266	Chengxi

SHU-HAN 221–263

Zhaolie di	221–223	Zhangwu
Houzhu	223–238	Jianxing
	238–258	Yanxi
	258–263	Jingyao
	263–264	Yanxing

WU 222–280

Dadi	222–229	Huangwu
	229–232	Huanglong
	232–238	Jiahe
	238–251	Chiniao
	251–252	Taiyuan
	263	Shenfeng
Houguan hou	252–253	Jianxing
	254–256	Wufeng
	256–258	Taiping
Jingdi	258–264	Yongan
Guiming hou	264–265	Yuanxing
	265–266	Ganlu
	266–269	Baoding
	269–272	Jianheng
	272–275	Fenghuang
	275–276	Tiance
	276–277	Tianxi
	277–280	Tianji

HAN-ZHAO (known as HAN from 304–318) 304–329

Liu Yuan	304–307	Yuanxi
	308	Yongfeng
	309	Herui
Liu Cong	310	Guangxing
	311–315	Jiaping
	315	Jianyuan
	316–318	Linjia
Liu Can	319	Hanchang
Liu Yao	318–329	Guangchu

WESTERN JIN 266–316

Introduction

During its heyday in the second part of the first century, the mighty empire of the Han 漢 (206 BCE–220 CE) ruled over a dominion that stretched from present-day northern Korea to present-day northern Vietnam and from the coasts of the Yellow Sea to the oasis towns of Central Asia. But, in the middle of the second century, the empire began to unravel. Inside the empire, dissent in the court weakened the power of the central government, and outside the capital, the growing power of local magnates did the same. The dynasty barely survived the huge rebellion of the Yellow Scarves[1] religious movement, and then only at the cost of ceding all military power to the dictator Dong Zhuo 董卓 (d. 192), who moved the capital from Luoyang to Chang'an to bring the court even more fully under his control. When the imperial court then called upon provincial governors to extirpate Dong Zhuo, they did so, but a decades-long civil war followed as the governors, each more powerful than the imperial government, contested to become the supreme power.

Eventually the empire was carved into three. The northern part of the empire, ruled from the cities of Ye and Xuchang in Hebei, became the domain of Cao Cao 曹操 (155–220); the southeast, under the sway of Sun Quan 孫權 (182–252), was headquartered in modern-day Nanjing; and the southwest was ruled from Chengdu by Liu Bei 劉備 (161–223), a distant relative of the imperial family of the Han. When, upon the death of his father, Cao Cao's son Cao Pi 曹丕 accepted the orchestrated abdication of the last emperor of the Han and established the Wei 魏 (220–265), Liu Bei and Sun Quan too, respectively, assumed the imperial title as emperors of the (Shu-)Han 蜀漢 (221–263) and the Wu 吳 (222–280) dynasties.[2] These three concurrent dynasties are usually referred to as the Three Kingdoms (*Sanguo* 三國).

The wars that resulted in the foundation of the Three Kingdoms soon became the stuff of legend, and thanks to novels and ballads, plays and prints, movies, television dramas, and computer games, the names of the generals who fought these battles are household words in China and beyond to this day.[3]

---

1. Adherants wrapped their heads in yellow headscarves in order to distinguish themselves from government soldiers. In most studies on Chinese history in the West, they are called "Yellow Turbans"; the name, however, is a misnomer since these scarves bore no resemblance at all to the turbans worn by peoples of the Middle East or South Asia.

2. For a convenient survey of the political history of this period, see Mansveld Beck (1986) and De Crespigny (1991a). For a detailed biography of Cao Cao, see De Crespigny (2010).

3. For an English-language introduction to Three Kingdoms culture, see Besio and Tung (2007). For extended surveys in Chinese, consult Guan Siping (2009); Shen Bojun and Tan Liangxiao (2007); Zhu Yixuan and Liu Yushen (1983). See also Kim Bunkyō (1993).

The Three Kingdoms in History and Legend

From an early date—at least one thousand years ago—the three-part division of the empire has been considered karmic retribution for the ungrateful treatment of three able generals by Liu Bang 劉邦 (256–195 BCE), the founder of the Han dynasty. In the chaos following the collapse of the Qin 秦 (221–207 BCE), the first dynasty to unify China as an empire, Liu Bang had only been able to vanquish his formidable rival Xiang Yu 項羽 (232–202 BCE) because of the assistance of his councilors and generals. Once he had defeated all his internal foes, however, he became suspicious of his former allies, now all enfeoffed as powerful princes, and had three of them—Han Xin 韓信 (d. 196 BCE), Ying Bu 英布 (d. 195 BCE), and Peng Yue 彭越 (d. 196 BCE)—murdered by his wife, the notorious Empress Lü 呂后 (241–189 BCE), who grasped all power upon his death.

Records of the Three Kingdoms in Plain Language (*Sanguozhi pinghua* 三國志平話), the thirteenth-century popular account of the epic battles resulting in the empire's tripartition translated in this volume, opens with an account of the underworld judgment concerning Liu Bang and his wife on one side and the three meritorious generals on the other side. When Liu Xiu 劉秀 (6 BCE–57 CE) reestablished the Han dynasty following the short-lived usurpation of Wang Mang's 王莽 (45 BCE–23 CE) Xin 新 dynasty (9–25), he allows residents of his new capital Luoyang to enjoy the imperial park. While reading historical accounts of the Qin and the founding of the Han in the park, Sima Zhongxiang 司馬仲相, a student, is filled with indignation at Heaven's injustice. In a dream he is called to the underworld to judge the case of the murdered generals and sentences them to be reborn as Cao Cao, Sun Quan, and Liu Bei, whereas Liu Bang and his wife will be reincarnated as the last emperor of the Han and his empress.[4] As a reward for his keen judgment, Sima Zhongxiang will be reborn as Sima Yi 司馬懿 (179–251), whose descendants supplant the Wei dynasty of Cao Cao's descendants. Sima Yi establishes the Jin dynasty (266–419) and reunifies the empire by conquering first the southwest ruled by Liu Bei's son and next the southeast ruled by a grandson of Sun Quan. The conclusion of our thirteenth-century account points out, however, that the unification of the empire by the Jin was only short-lived and that in the early part of the fourth century once again a Han dynasty was established.[5]

---

4. This story also circulated independently in many adaptations, both as a story and play. See Li Fuqing (1997b, 52–60); Ogawa Yōichi (1982, 78–81); Ōtsuka Hidetaka (1998); Zheng Zhenduo (1961, 171–76). As time went by, later versions increased the number of reincarnations.

5. In the early years of the fourth century the Jin dynasty was wracked by civil war. It then survived for another century in the south, while northern China was ruled by various mostly ethnically non-Chinese dynasties, such as the Han-Zhao dynasty (304–329) founded by Liu Yuan 劉淵 (d. 310).

Stable bureaucracies may leave neat archives but fighting armies seldom do. From the very beginning the accounts of the events of the final decades of the Han and of the half-century or so of the Three Kingdoms have been embellished by gossip and legend, which make it difficult to establish the full truth of what happened in all detail. Many incidents were transmitted in multiple and at times contradictory accounts. The major canonical account of the collapse of the Han and the foundation of the Three Kingdoms is Chen Shou's 陳壽 (233–297) *Records of the Three Kingdoms (Sanguozhi* 三國志).[6] This work presents the history of the period from 184 to 280 not as a continuous narrative, but through a collection of biographies. While Chen Shou devotes one chapter to the biography of Liu Bei, many other biographies are grouped together. For instance, the biographies of Zhang Fei and Guan Yu are included in one chapter together with the biographies of the generals Ma Chao 馬超 (176–222), Huang Zhong 黃忠 (d. 220), and Zhao Yun 趙雲 (d. 229). Chen Shou had originally served Shu-Han, but when he compiled his history, he was in the service of the Jin dynasty. For his account of Wei and Wu, he could rely on existing materials, but the small number of chapters on the Shu-Han dynasty is from his hand. His text is known for its sparse language and the moral evaluations of the characters. Although Chen Shou had originally compiled his history as three independent works (the *Records of Wei,* the *Records of Wu,* and the *Records of Shu-Han*), these works were later combined into a single text.

In the fifth century Pei Songzhi 裴松之 (372–451) wrote a detailed commentary that incorporated more than 240 sources, providing *Records of the Three Kingdoms* with not only more details than Chen Shou's terse account but also often alternative versions.[7]

The first known printed edition of the *Records of the Three Kingdoms* dates from as early as 1003. Later in the eleventh century, a detailed annalistic chronicle of the events during the century from ca. 180 to ca. 280 appeared from the hand of the great historian Sima Guang 司馬光 (1019–1086) in his *Comprehensive Mirror for Aid in Government (Zizhi tongjian* 資治通鑑), which covered Chinese history from the fifth century BCE to 960 CE.[8] This huge work gave rise to many abridged versions in later centuries, each with its own emphasis and each reflecting the historical debates circulating at the time of their compilation.[9] But neither Chen Shou's *Records of the Three Kingdoms* nor Sima

---

6. Cutter and Crowell (1999); De Crepigny (1970); Ng and Wang (2005, 94–98).

7. The final decades of the Han dynasty are also covered in Fan Ye's 范曄 (398–445) *Documents of the Later Han (Hou Han shu* 後漢書).

8. De Crespigny (1969; revised edition De Crespigny [1996]) and De Crespigny (1989) provide translations of the annals for the years 157–220. See also Ng and Wang (2005, 147–55).

9. One of the issues that were hotly debated was whether the Wei or the Shu-Han had to be considered the orthodox successor dynasty of the Han. Sima Guang had treated the Wei as such,

Guang's annalistic chronicle, nor its abbreviated versions, provided a continuous narrative of this era.

Whereas canonical historiography considered the Wei dynasty the orthodox successor to the Han dynasty, popular opinion increasingly favored Liu Bei and his Shu-Han dynasty as the legitimate heir.[10] The popular imagination glorified the sworn brotherhood of Liu Bei and his two friends, the impulsive and violent Zhang Fei 張飛 (d. 221) and the invincible and arrogant Guan Yu 關羽 (d. 219). Guan Yu had acquired divine status by the sixth century and would eventually become one of the most powerful gods in the Chinese pantheon.[11] Liu Bei's advisor and field marshal Zhuge Liang 諸葛亮 (181–234) was depicted not only as an inspired strategist but also as a master of magical arts.[12] As the story continued to develop over the centuries the account of the wars became increasingly focused on the initial cooperation of Cao Cao and Liu Bei and their later enmity. In the process Liu Bei became the embodiment of dynastic virtue and his opponent Cao Cao the evil mastermind (or "crafty brave" *jianxiong* 奸雄 as he is called in Chinese).[13] While we have considerable anecdotal evidence for the popularity of Three Kingdoms lore during the Tang dynasty (618–907), there are no independent texts on this subject among the ballads and prosimetric narratives from the eighth to tenth centuries discovered at Dunhuang.[14] Among these latter manuscripts, the war between Liu Bang and Xiang Yu at the founding of the Han is the most popular historical subject,[15] and we also find one story on the early adventures of Liu Xiu, who reestablished the Latter Han empire.[16] By the middle of the eleventh century, however, Kaifeng, then the capital of the Northern Song dynasty (960–1127), had professional storytellers who specialized in narrating the "events of the Tripartition."[17]

---

but the great Neo-Confucian philosopher Zhu Xi 朱熹 (1130–1200) treated Shu-Han as such in his rewriting of the *Zizhi tongjian* as *Tongjian gangmu* 通鑑綱目.

10. For a survey of twentieth-century studies on the development of Three Kingdoms lore, see Wang Lijuan (2007, 1–20).

11. Diesinger (1984); Duara (1988); Haar (2000); Hansen (1989, 88–90); Louie (1999); Moore (2003); Yang (1981). In Chinese, see Li Fuqing (1997a); Liu Haiyan (2004); Ōtsuka Hidetaka (1995); Wang Lijuan (2007, 213–364); Zeng Yongyi (2003, 509–28).

12. Henry (1992); Tillman (2002b). In Chinese, see Chen Xianghua (1990); Yan Chunxi (2003).

13. Kroll (1976).

14. Mair (1989).

15. For a French and English translation of one of these texts, see Mirabile (2003).

16. For an English translation of this story, see Waley (1960, 53–56).

17. Idema and West (1982, 27–28). In the process of oral transmission the story was enriched with many "epic motives" and "epic situations," which are analyzed in great detail by Li Fuqing (1997b, 65–97). The topics discussed include the sworn brotherhood of Liu, Guan, and Zhang, and the animals slaughtered when they swear their oath; Liu Bei's triple invitation of

At the same time the intellectuals of the time widely and heatedly discussed the leading personalities and events of that era.[18] All of these developments merged in a narrative account that was published in the early fourteenth century as *Records of the Three Kingdoms in Plain Language*. This fast-paced tale was to remain the most popular account of the legend for the next two centuries,[19] was widely utilized by playwrights in the fourteenth and fifteenth centuries,[20] and then was finally supplanted in the early sixteenth century by the much more detailed *Popular Exposition of the Records of the Three Kingdoms (Sanguozhi tongsu yanyi* 三國志通俗演義), also known as *Romance of the Three Kingdoms (Sanguo yanyi)*. The epic narrative of this later 120-chapter "novel" has remained immensely popular to this very day, not only in China, but also in other East-Asian countries such as Korea.[21]

Plain Tales

Records of the Three Kingdoms in Plain Language was printed as part of a series that included at least four other titles and may have included more. The five preserved titles are nowadays collectively known as the *Five Completely Illustrated Plain Tales (Quanxiang pinghua wuzhong* 全相平話五種). This series

---

Zhuge Liang and Zhuge's role as advisor; the berserker warrior as exemplified by Zhang Fei; the specific weapons of the heroes such as the Guan Yu's curved-moon blade; the heroes' mounts, such as Guan Yu's horse Red Harrier; and the battle scenes. In his analysis of these epic motives Li Fuqing not only draws widely on Chinese materials from Chen Shou's *Records of the Three Kingdoms* to modern folktales, but also on the rich literature in Russian on the epic traditions of Central Asia.

18. McLaren (2006; focusing on the discussion on Liu Bei); also see McLaren (2011, 2012). For the Song dynasty discussion on Zhuge Liang, see Tillman (1995, 1996, 2002a, 2004, 2007); Shen (2003). One of the most famous and popular literary works of the eleventh century, Su Shi's *Red Cliff Rhapsody (Chibi fu* 赤壁賦), is a meditation on Cao Cao's defeat at Red Cliff. For an English translation, see for instance Owen (1996, 292–94). Also see Owen (1996, 579–80) for his translation of Su Shi's "Meditation on the Past at Red Cliff" (*Chibi huaigu* 赤壁懷古), one of his most famous lyrics. For a comprehensive selection of anecdotes and poems related to Three Kingdoms lore from the fourth to the fourteenth centuries, see Zhu Yixuan and Liu Yushen (1983, 1–239); for a comprehensive selection from the Ming and Qing dynasties, see Zhu Yixuan and Liu Yushen (1983, 526–944).

19. On the originality of *Records of the Three Kingdoms in Plain Language* as a structured narrative and its focus on Liu Bei and his supporters (especially Zhang Fei and Zhuge Liang), see Tu Xiuhong (2009).

20. Idema and West (2012).

21. For English translations see Brewitt Taylor (1925); Roberts (1991). For discussions and analyses of the novel, see Hsia (1968, 34–74); Plaks (1987, 361–490). Chinese scholars disagree over the extent to which the novel is indebted for its qualities to the plain tale. See Han Weibiao (2007).

was published by the Yu 虞 family of Jianyang in the Zhizhi period (1321–
1323) of the Yuan dynasty (1260–1368).[22] Apart from *Records of the Three
Kingdoms in Plain Language* the series includes *A Completely Illustrated Plain
Tale: The Book of King Wu's Campaign against Zhou* (*Quanxiang pinghua
Wuwang fa Zhou shu* 全相平話武王伐紂書), which deals with the founda-
tion of the Zhou dynasty in the eleventh century BCE;[23] *A Completely Illustrated Plain Tale: Yue Yi's Attack on Qi—The Final Collection of the Springs and
Autumns of the Seven States* (*Quanxiang pinghua Yue Yi tu Qi qiguo chunqiu houji*
全相平話樂毅圖齊七國春秋後集), which deals with the wars between the
northeastern states of Yan and Qi in the early decades of the third century BCE;
The Completely Illustrated Plain Tale of Qin's Conquest of the Six States (*Quanxiang
Qin bing liuguo pinghua* 全相秦併六國平話), which carries the alternative title
of *A Biography of the First Emperor of the Qin* (*Qin Shihuang zhuan* 秦始皇傳);
and *A Completely Illustrated Plain Tale: A Sequel to the Book of the Former Han*
(*Quanxiang pinghua Qian Hanshu xuji* 全相平話前漢書續集), which carries
the alternative title *Empress Lü Executes Han Xin* (呂後斬韓信) and begins
with Liu Bang's final victory over Xiang Yu, continues through the murder of
the three meritorious generals, and ends with the extermination of the Lü clan.

Five Completely Illustrated Plain Tales has been preserved in only a single
copy that is now kept at the Naikaku Bunko (Cabinet Library) in Tokyo. In
the twentieth century it has repeatedly been reproduced in photographical
editions,[24] and recently the original text has been put online in high-quality
images. All individual texts in the collection are also available in modern typeset
editions,[25] while a collective critical and annotated edition has been provided by
the contemporary scholar Zhong Zhaohua 鍾兆華.[26] For his edition of *Records
of the Three Kingdoms in Plain Language* he has also utilized *A Brief Account of
the Tripartition* to collate the text. The single surviving (slightly damaged) copy
of *A Brief Account of the Tripartition* is kept in the library of Tenri University
in Nara, Japan; this edition too is nowadays easily available in reproduction.[27]

A series that is very comparable to the *Five Completely Illustrated Plain
Tales* is the *History of the Five Dynasties in Plain Language* (*Wudaishi pinghua*

---

22. After this text had been separately reproduced in Japan in the early 1920s, by 1930 it had
also been reproduced by the Commercial Press in Shanghai. Jiangsusheng shehui kexueyuan
(1990, 26).

23. For a full translation of this text see Liu (1962, 6–75).

24. For instance Anonymous (1956); Anonymous (1971).

25. Anonymous (1959); Ding Xigen (1990).

26. Zhong Zhaohua (1990). See also Zhou Wen (2009). *Records of the Three Kingdoms in
Plain Language* is also available in two Japanese translations: Nikaidō and Nakagawa (1999);
Tatsuma Shōsuke (2011).

27. For facsimile editions, see for instance Anonymous (1990a, 1990b, 1999).

五代史平話), which consists of five plain tales, each recounting the history of one of the five short-lived dynasties that ruled northern China during the years from the demise of the Tang 唐 in 907 to the foundation of the Song 宋 in 960.[28] In this case, each of these five plain tales is divided into two parts, of which the first recounts the early career of the founding emperor, while the second part is devoted to the rapid decline and fall of his dynasty. We encounter a similar contrastive structure in *An Anecdotal History of Proclaiming Harmony* (*Xuanhe yishi* 宣和遺事).[29] This work has been transmitted both in a two-part and in a four-part edition, but in both cases the first half of the work is devoted to the luxurious and irresponsible behavior of Emperor Huizong (r. 1101–1126), while the second half describes his sufferings at the hands of the Jurchen following their conquest of northern China and capture of Kaifeng. The only text that is also classified as a plain tale but is not divided into parts is *A Brief Account of Xue Rengui's Conquest of Korea* (*Xue Rengui zheng Liao shilüe* 薛仁貴征遼事略).[30] This anonymous work, which has been preserved in one of the surviving chapters of the *Grand Compendium of the Yongle Era* (*Yongle dadian* 永樂大典) of 1407, narrates the heroic deeds of the common soldier Xue Rengui during the campaigns of Emperor Taizong of the Tang against the state of Koguryo during the second quarter of the seventh century.[31]

The titles mentioned in the preceding two paragraphs have been grouped together as "plain tales" by modern historians of Chinese literature upon their rediscovery in the early twentieth century.[32] As is clear from their titles these works all provide accounts of exciting periods of Chinese history; written in simple prose including some vernacular elements, they tend to be of modest

---

28. For a modern typeset edition of this text, see Anonymous (1954a). This edition is based on a photolithographic edition produced in 1911 of a copy of a thirteenth-/fourteenth-century printing of the text. The text is incomplete. For a brief discussion of this text, see Lu Hsun (1959, 144–47).

29. For a modern typeset edition of this text, see Anonymous (1954b). An English translation has been provided by Hennessey (1981). See also Hennessey (1984).

30. For a modern typeset edition of this text, see Zhao Wanli (1957). See also Idema (2007).

31. The *Yongle dadian* has only partially been preserved. From its table of contents we know that this huge compilation contained a substantial section devoted to *pinghua* but these chapters have been lost. The story of Xue Rengui also appears in a fourteenth-century drama, *Xue Rengui Returns Home Clad in Brocade* (*Xue Rengui yijin huanxiang* 薛仁貴衣錦還鄉), translated and introduced in West and Idema (2014, 138–95).

32. Some scholars also treat *The Nine Remonstrances of the Duke of Liang* (*Lianggong jiu jian* 梁公九諫) as a plain tale. This text features the infamous Empress Wu Zetian 武則天 (624–705) who intends to appoint her nephew Wu Sansi 武三思 (d. 707) as the crown prince, and the intrepid statesman Di Renjie 狄仁傑 (607–700), who urges her to reappoint her own son as crown prince and reinstitute the Tang dynasty. This text is included in Ding Xigen (1990), which, however, does not include *A Brief Account of Xue Rengui's Conquest of Korea*.

size.[33] The examples of the genre often only survive in single copies, as these texts had been replaced in the public's favor from the sixteenth century onward ✳ by the far more extensive "historical novels" that were compiled in the Ming dynasty (1368–1644). When these plain tales were rediscovered in the twentieth century, they were primarily discussed as forerunners of the vernacular fiction of the Ming. The pioneering scholars of traditional vernacular fiction identified the plain tales as promptbooks of the professional storytellers of the Song dynasty (960–1279), or claimed that these texts were based on such promptbooks. When *Records of the Three Kingdoms in Plain Language* was first reprinted in China in the late 1920s, its preface claimed: "This must derive from a script that had been transmitted from teacher to pupil by itinerant storytellers."[34] Because some modern genres of storytelling go by the homophonous name of *pinghua* 評話, this identification seemed obvious.[35] But in Song

---

33. Other genres of printed vernacular narrative from the late Song to the early Ming rely more heavily on verse: "poem-stories" (*shihua* 詩話) are divided in short chapters, each concluding on a poem spoken by one of the characters in the story; "ballad-stories" (*cihua* 詞話) tell their stories in a continuous alternation of prose passages and passages written in seven-syllable ballad-verse; and "ballad-texts" (*ciwen* 詞文) are completely written in ballad verse. Other prosimetrical genres of period include "all keys and modes" (*zhugongdiao* 諸宮調) and "precious scrolls" (*baojuan* 寶卷).

34. Jiang Dianyang (1996, 746). Crump (1951) combines this view with the suggestion of Zhang Zhenglang (2004; originally published in 1948) that the plain tales derive from the commentaries on the sets of poems on historical subjects by late-Tang authors such as Hu Zeng 胡曾. In Hsia (1968, 35–36) the expectation that plain tales should reflect the superior artistry of the best professional storytellers of the Song capital cities results in a very negative opinion on *Records of the Three Kingdoms in Plain Language*. This plain tale is, in his words, "atrocious in style and often transcribes the names of places and persons in wrong characters. Events are narrated most sketchily and history itself is reduced to a contest in magic, cunning, and prowess. . . . It is possible that the publishers . . . had entrusted the task of compilation to a hack of little learning and less writing ability. Based on the promptbooks of provincial storytellers, it could not have represented the art of storytelling among its famous practitioners in the capital cities. But with all its uncharacteristic crudities, this version must have conformed to their repertoire in one respect at least: the application of the theory of moral retribution to the workings of history." Having summarized the opening scene of the underworld judgment Hsia concludes by noting that the later novel "does away with all this kind of didactic nonsense." Hsia's negative view of *Records of the Three Kingdoms in Plain Language* very much echoes the verdict on this text by Zheng Zhenduo (1961, 170–71; 186–90; originally published in 1929). For recent studies that treat the plain tales as the promptbooks of storytellers, see Gao Mingge (1986, 1–18) and Xiao Xiangkai (1997, 44–99).

35. For a summary of twentieth-century Chinese scholarship on plain tales, see Ji Dejun (2002, 15–29). Tan Fan et al. (2013, 136–44) relies heavily on Gu Qing (2005). Gu points out that the term *pinghua* is not encountered before the Yuan dynasty. He treats the term as both a designation of a genre of literature and a form of storytelling, even though evidence for its use in that latter sense is very meagre for the Yuan. For a bibliography of studies on *Records of the Three Kingdoms in Plain Language*, see Nikaidō and Nakagawa (1999, 314–18).

sources storytelling on historical topics is called "narrating history" (*jiangshi* 講史), and while we know the names of many of its practitioners, we know next to nothing about the characteristics of this genre. We also don't know whether the professional storytellers used promptbooks or not, and if they did what these promptbooks would look like.[36]

More recent scholarship has started to question the close relation between plain tales and (hypothetical) promptbooks. Not only are many plain tales relatively well printed (with carefully planned and executed continuous top-of-the-page illustrations in the case of the *Five Completely Illustrated Plain Tales* and *A Brief Account of the Tripartition*),[37] many of them also heavily rely on works of canonical historiography for their own text. It has been suggested therefore that these texts in their preserved printings should first of all be considered popular reading materials for a literate audience who might not have the scholarly inclination, time, or energy to work their way through the voluminous works of canonical historiography or simply might prefer a good read.[38] In Chinese publications this audience is often described as "common townspeople" (*xiao shimin* 小市民) but probably the audience was much broader. Full sets of the dynastic histories and other works of canonical historiography were not always easily available even after the invention of printing and still must have been quite expensive. Many literati as well as military officers and members of the nobility, educated merchants, and gentlemen farmers may have been among the readers. During the Yuan, when the vernacular was widely used in government documents, the readership may also have included members of the Mongol elite and its Central-Asian allies. As far as their content is concerned, it is obvious that the plain tales rely not only on written sources but also take many of their materials from an oral tradition of some sort or another, but to what extent we can identify that oral tradition exclusively with the activities of the professional storytellers of the eleventh century and later is not clear,[39] because plays

36. Many modern scholars writing on storytelling of the Song dynasty apparently believe that storytelling in Song and Yuan times must have been comparable to storytelling as a low-class popular entertainment of late-imperial and Republican times, but as printing was still much less developed, drama was in its infancy, and vernacular fiction had still to be invented, it appealed to a very broad segment of the population, up to the emperors. See Guan Siping (2009, 115–16).

37. For a discussion of these illustrations, see Hegel (1998, 172–76). Mair (1988, 3–6) suggests the existence of a kind of storytelling using pictures as the origin of this format.

38. Hegel (1998, 22–26); Idema (1974); Lu Shihua (2009); Luo Xiaoyu (2010). Ji Dejun (2002, 61 note 1) points out that the many homophonic substitutions for complicated and/or rare characters that had been decried by earlier generations of scholars may well have facilitated reading for many contemporary readers.

39. Many scholars who treat the plain tales as the promptbooks of storytellers first use the plain tales to reconstruct the characteristics of Song-dynasty storytelling, and then conclude that the plain tales reflect these characteristics. Basing himself on a broad comparison with other epic

on episodes from the Three Kingdoms saga also were popular on the early stage
and in other forms of entertainment such as shadow theater.[40]

Records of the Three Kingdoms in Plain Language

Among the plain tales *Records of the Three Kingdoms in Plain Language* stands
out for a number of reasons. The first of these is its length: it is the longest of
the plain tales.[41] The second is that despite its length it contains no direct bor-
rowings from canonical historiography; while its protagonists and their adventures can of course be traced to canonical historiography, it does not copy or
paraphrase the language of these texts for its descriptions of events. This also
means that its language is consistent in register throughout. Whereas other
plain tales may switch from simple but pure classical Chinese to a very vernacular style depending on their sources, the language of *Records of the Three
Kingdoms in Plain Language* is written throughout in a simple semi-classical
language full of repetitions, except for the poems and letters that are quoted in
the text, which are in classical Chinese. It should also be stressed that this is one
of the rare texts to have been preserved in two different editions. Apart from
the edition as part of the *Five Completely Illustrated Plain Tales*, the text has also
been preserved in an independent edition entitled *A Brief Account of the Tripartition* (*Sanfen shilüe* 三分事略). The latter edition looks very much like a later
and cheaper reprinting of *Records of the Three Kingdoms in Plain Language* but
carries a date that would suggest it was printed in the late thirteenth century
(1294 or 1295).[42] While some scholars are willing to accept this date, others

---

traditions and modern Chinese traditions of storytelling, Li Fuqing (1997b, 120) concludes
that "the theory that *Records of the Three Kingdoms in Plain Language* is a direct record of storytelling is not correct."

40. Idema and West (2012, xvi–xvii); Chen Xianghua (1995, 364–74).

41. If *A Completely Illustrated Plain Tale: The Book of the Han* on the wars between Liu Bang
and Xiang Yu would have been preserved alongside *A Completely Illustrated Plain Tale: A Sequel
to the Book of the Former Han*, their combined length would have easily surpassed that of *Records
of the Three Kingdoms in Plain Language*. This would correspond to the great popularity of episodes from this period on the Yuan stage. See Idema (1990).

42. The date of printing is not necessarily the date of composition. Xiao Xiangkai (1997, 52)
considers *Records of the Three Kingdoms in Plain Language* a work of the eleventh century, but
does so because this is the period for which we know of the existence of storytellers specializing
in "the events of the Tripartition." Other scholars have proposed a later date (the Jin dynasty,
1115–1234) or even an earlier date (the Tang dynasty). The current text of *Records of the Three
Kingdoms in Plain Language* can only date from the twelfth century or later, because it includes
a text by the famous Song dynasty statesman and poet Su Shi 蘇軾 (1036–1101). Lu Shihua
(2009, 128) argues that the present text of *Records of the Three Kingdoms in Plain Language* can
only date from the Yuan dynasty (1260–1368) because it includes a *qu*-song but that may be
too strict. Some scholars who date the composition of *Records of the Three Kingdoms in Plain*

insist that *A Brief Account of the Tripartition* must have been printed at a later date, some suggesting as late as the fifteenth century.[43] Those who put their trust in the earlier date suggest that both *A Brief Account of the Tripartition* and *Records of the Three Kingdoms in Plain Language* may be reprintings (one low quality, the other high quality) of an even earlier, now lost printing of the text.[44]

We should not expect *Records of the Three Kingdoms in Plain Language* to provide us with a comprehensive account of all Three Kingdom narratives that were available at the time of composition. The author made a selection in view of his own conception of the narrative as a whole. This is clear because on occasion certain events are only referred to in the text, but not narrated in detail.[45] This is further underlined by the existence of *The Story of Hua Guan Suo* (*Hua Guan Suo zhuan* 花關索傳), a prosimetric epic on the life of Hua Guan Suo, a son of Guan Yu, who is mentioned only once in the *Records of the Three Kingdoms in Plain Language*.[46] This text, which also dates from the period 1250–1450, does provide accounts of some episodes that also occur in the *Records of the Three Kingdoms in Plain Language*, such as the oath in the Peach Orchard and the death of Guan Yu, that are quite different. The early Yuan-dynasty playwright Guan Hanqing 關漢卿 (c. 1240–c. 1320) in his play on the deaths of Zhang Fei and Guan Yu, which has been preserved in a fourteenth-century printing, provides an account that corresponds closely to the version of the tale that is provided in *The Story of Hua Guan Suo*, indicating that this tradition of the tale most likely goes back to at least the thirteenth century.[47]

Language to the Yuan dynasty read the text's support for Liu Bei and its negative characterization of Cao Cao as an expression of Chinese patriotism and anti-Mongol sentiment. See for instance Hu Shiying (1980, 727); Zhang Bing (2005, 61–66). Kim Bunkyō (1993, 89–93) has pointed out the problematic nature of such an interpretation by reminding us that Liu Yuan, whose Han dynasty (304–329) is hailed as a revival of the earlier Han dynasties in the final pages of the *Records of the Three Kingdoms in Plain Language*, was not ethnically Chinese but belonged to the Southern Xiongnu. See also Kim Bunkyō (2008).

43. Jiangsusheng shehui kexueyuan (1990, 28–29).

44. Luo Xiaoyu (2010, 140–49).

45. Luo Xiaoyou (2010, 150–51). The most obvious example is the summary account of the "Meeting to Discuss Heroism," which is encountered early on in the second part. We only learn that Liu Bei is so scared that he drops his chopsticks, but not what scares him to such an extent. From other sources we know that it is Cao Cao's declaration that he only considers Liu Bei a hero on a par with himself. Zhou Zhaoxin (1995a, 312–15).

46. For a typeset edition of *The Story of Hua Guan Suo*, see Zhu Yixuan (1997, 1–67). For an English translation, see King (1989). Also see Inoue (1989).

47. For an English translation of Guan Hanqing's *In a Dream to Western Shu* (*Xi Shu meng* 西蜀夢), see Idema and West (2012, 296–315; a translation from the corresponding pages from *The Story of Hua Guan Suo* may be found at pp. 367–73). Also see Ueda Nozomu (1995) on Yuan and Ming stories not included in the plain tale and the novel.

The *Records of the Three Kingdoms in Plain Language* is divided into three parts or "scrolls" (*juan* 卷). In this case each of the three sections has a unique emphasis. The first begins with the judgment of Sima Zhongxiang and then proceeds with a description of the origin of the rebellion of the Yellow Scarves, setting the stage for the action to come. The story then switches to the introduction of the three sworn brothers Liu Bei, Zhang Fei, and Guan Yu. They first establish their merit by fighting the Yellow Scarves, and later contribute to the war against Dong Zhuo and the latter's adopted son Lü Bu 呂布 (d. 198). During this period they enjoy the support of Cao Cao, who will step into the vacuum created by the death of Dong Zhuo to become the most powerful man in northern China. By the beginning of the second part, Liu Bei is invited by the last emperor to join a plot against Cao Cao. But Liu Bei and his sworn brothers are quickly defeated and dispersed. While Guan Yu agrees to serve with Cao Cao, Liu Bei seeks the protection of Yuan Shao 袁紹 (d. 202), but leaves him to seek his fortune in Hubei. In the meantime Zhang Fei has established himself as a highwayman in Old City, and it is there that the sworn brothers meet each other again. From there they move on and Liu Bei becomes the prefect of Xinye thanks to the magnanimity of the governor of Jingzhou, his distant uncle Liu Biao 劉表 (142–208). While at Xinye, Liu Bei manages to attract Zhuge Liang as his main advisor and field marshal. When Cao Cao begins a southward push, Liu Bei eventually concludes an alliance with Sun Quan, who controls the Jiangnan area, and together they inflict a devastating defeat on Cao Cao at the battle at Red Cliff. This is all due to the superior tactics of Zhuge Liang and of Sun Quan's advisor Zhou Yu 周瑜 (175–210), who is constantly bested by Zhuge Liang's brilliance, and who eventually dies of spite when he realizes he can never match it.

The third part starts with a description of Zhou Yu's failed attempt to conquer the area of the modern province of Sichuan. This is followed by the account of Liu Bei's conquest of this region. Following the death of Guan Yu and the loss of Jingzhou, the death of Zhang Fei, and the death of Liu Bei during a failed attempt to take revenge for the death of Guan Yu, the majority of this final section focuses on Zhuge Liang's attempt to maintain the independence of the Shu-Han regime. To do this, he carries out southwesterly campaigns against non-Chinese tribes and northeasterly campaigns against the Wei dynasty. Following the death of Zhuge Liang, the Shu-Han dynasty is eventually conquered when Liu Bei's son decides to surrender to the enemy rather than organizing a final, all-out defense of his land.

In this way each part of *Records of the Three Kingdoms in Plain Language* has its own set of characters, its own central conflicts, and its own geographical focus as the action moves from northeast China to central China and on to southwestern China. On closer reading it would appear that each part can be subdivided into a limited number of story cycles, even though these are not marked as such in the text.[48] For the benefit of our readers we have inserted subheadings of our own making.[49] These should not be confused with the "content signposts" that irregularly appear in the original Chinese text. In the original Chinese edition these signposts are highly visible as they are printed in relief, in white in a black box, a format we reproduce in the current translation.[50] The fact that these signposts occur in some sections of the text in close proximity and at other places are not found at all for long stretches of text suggests perhaps that the full text of the *Plain Tales* may have been partly composed by utilizing preexisting versions, each with their own conventions of presentation.

The heterogeneity of the source materials used in the different parts of our text is also suggested by the variations in the use of a limited set of stereotypical narratorial phrases. These run the gamut, from "our story now divides in its telling" (*hua fen liang shuo* 話分兩説, five times in Part I) and "our story now divides in two directions" (*huafeng liangtou* 話分兩頭, once in Part III, none in Part II), to a simple "speak of/explain" (*shuo* 説).[51] The most common phrase is "let us now talk about something different" (*queshuo* 卻説). This can be used to simply begin another line of the story, but it is often used, like the classical narrative marker *chu* 初, to mean "let us go back to talk about . . ."; that is, to go back in time and tell what happens to a character involved in the same event during a simultaneous time period. Another common narratorial address is "later speak of/and then speak of" (*houshuo* 後説). This appears not at all in Part I, six times in Part II, and fifteen times in Part III. This is perhaps the most interesting of narrative markers, in the sense that it often introduces what were possibly well-known and major scenes (that are left unexpanded in the text). While it may simply function as a temporal phrase, "and then . . . ," there is a directness to it that seems to imply a direct command, "Now go on and tell about incident X."

---

48. Børdahl (2013, 41–42) points out that the expressions *queshuo* 卻説 and *shuo* 説 (see "A Note on the Translation"), which often mark shifts of topic, are, in some cases, preceded by an empty space in the text of the *Sanguozhi pinghua* as if to highlight the beginning of a new chapter or paragraph. But not all occurrences of *queshuo* and *shuo* are marked in this manner, however, and close scrutiny suggests that these empty spaces should rather be considered as belonging to the category of those empty spaces used to set off the beginning and end of lines of verse (such poems are often used to conclude a major episode).

49. Cf. Ashida (1974, 411).

50. There are three places in the text where the signpost either lacks the black box or is otherwise embedded in the text.

51. These set narratorial phrases are in Western scholarship often called "storytellers' phrases" and are seen as a relic of the origin of vernacular Chinese fiction in professional storytelling. For an exhaustive study of use of the phrases in early vernacular literature, see Børdahl (2013).

What the difference in use and frequency betrays is something that is apparent in many colloquial texts: they are conglomerate and often a mixture of circulating tales that are not composed from beginning to end, but copied or adapted from available sources. The fact that Part I uses essentially different forms of direct narrator address may seem only a preference, but it is definitely related to the fact that the narrative episodes in Part I are much more detailed and complex than in the other two parts; the flow of the narrative itself is much more unified and does not demand the constant narrative prods to move the story along. This difference between Part I and the following two parts is also reflected in the use of the phrase, "this is named" (*mingyue* 名曰). This term is used only once in Part I to designate the name of a pavilion; in Parts II (ten times) and III (eight times), in addition to being used to identify place names and names of material objects, it is also used to introduce or stipulate the names by which famous episodes are recounted: "This is called 'the Single Sword Meeting,'" or "this is called 'Beheading Cai Yang in Ten Beats of the Drum,'" and so on. These phrases, in turn, are also associated with the hurried pace of, particularly, Part III, and the quick movement from event to event without any narrative ligatures except the intrusive voice of the narrator himself.

Throughout its three parts the narrative of *Records of the Three Kingdoms in Plain Language* is focused on action and dialogue; extensive description and analysis are rare. The most commonly experienced emotions are joy and anger, and when such emotions are mentioned they tend to be extreme. In its characterization *Records of the Three Kingdoms in Plain Language* lays great stress on Liu Bei's descent from the imperial house of the Han, even though at the beginning of the story he lives in very reduced circumstances, making a living by plaiting straw sandals.[52] Liu Bei is a fine fighter himself by all accounts, but the anonymous author of *Records of the Three Kingdoms in Plain Language* prefers to stress Liu Bei's qualities as an administrator: each time that he serves in an administrative position, the population is said to benefit greatly from his rule and venerate him accordingly. Liu Bei likewise often remains passive in the story, sometimes to the extent of sulking rather than moving to action. In the middle section, he rarely makes a move without the assent of Zhuge Liang. His sworn brothers Guan Yu and Zhang Fei are primarily characterized as formidable warriors. Both men have impressive physiques—one is tall and the other is stout—but whereas Guan Yu is the very embodiment of righteous virtue,

---

52. Li Fuqing (1997b, 97–114) analyzes in considerable detail how the description of physical features and clothing is used to indicate status and character. Shōji Kakuitsu (1991) provides a survey of the bewildering variety of names by which the main characters are indicated and their use in the text, as well as the curse words and invectives that are used to describe them. He notes that only the physical features of Liu Bei and his closest associates are described, and that only they are allowed to recite poems to express their innermost feelings.

Zhang Fei is an impetuous drunk who brooks no authority. If Guan Yu has a
fault, it is his overweening self-confidence and irascibility, whereas Zhang Fei is
distinguished by his love of an honest fight and his somewhat paradoxical hor-
ror at the tactics of mass destruction by fire and water as employed by Zhuge
Liang and Zhou Yu. In *Records of the Three Kingdoms in Plain Language* Zhuge
Liang is very much portrayed as a Daoist wizard who combines his superior
tactical and strategic insights with a variety of magical skills. Liu Bei's qualifi-
cations as a ruler are underlined by highlighting his humility in thrice inviting
Zhuge Liang to join his staff, and Zhuge Liang will reciprocate when he supports Liu Bei's unworthy son with unwavering loyalty until the day of his death.
As Liu Bei's political star rises, he attracts an ever-increasing number of heroic
warriors to his cause, each with their own character and ambition.

In the first part of *Records of the Three Kingdoms in Plain Language* Cao Cao
is the most effective general in the struggle against the evil dictator Dong Zhuo
and his adopted son Lü Bu, and he is eager to ensure himself of the service of
Liu Bei and his sworn brothers for this purpose. But once Liu Bei sides with the
emperor against Cao Cao, the latter becomes his implacable foe. As the most
powerful warlord on the North China plain who has exterminated all his opponents there, Cao Cao is distinguished by his ruthless quest for power. While
he at times also may display an unexpected magnanimity, it is not enough to
permanently win over Guan Yu when the latter briefly serves under him.[53]
Despite their individual qualities the generals who serve under Cao Cao all pale
in comparison to him and to Liu Bei and his sworn brothers. Only after the
fall of the Wei dynasty will Zhuge Liang have an opponent worthy of him in
Sima Yi, even though the latter attains his successes by his refusal to give battle.

Both Liu Bei and Cao Cao look down upon Sun Quan for his lowly background (his father was a melon grower in Changsha),[54] but the successive generations of the Sun family, based in Jiankang (modern-day Nanjing), securely
dominate the Jiangnan region, and can rely on the services of loyal and capable generals such as Lu Su 魯肅 (172–217) and superior strategists such as
Zhou Yu.

The sixteenth-century novel will mostly follow the characterizations of
Records of the Three Kingdoms in Plain Language but also make its own changes,
partly because of its desire for a closer adherence to canonical historiography.[55]

---

53. *Records of the Three Kingdoms in Plain Language* shows no interest in Cao Cao's qualities as
a poet. Cf. Diény (2000). It does, however, ascribe a number of poems and songs to Liu Bei in
order to strengthen his characterization.

54. Zhuge Liang's opponents will also often put him down as a mere farm boy, a "country hick"
or "village cowherd." Even Liu Bei may be cursed as "a starving peasant" or a "crafty barbarian."

55. Yang (1980). While the novel in outline follows the plain tale it also drops a few episodes.
From the first part of the plain tale the novel omits three episodes that highlight the heroics of

For instance, Zhuge Liang becomes more of a dignified Confucian scholar and loses some of his magical skills. On the other hand, the novel greatly expands its description of Cao Cao's fiendish character.[56] At the same time the sixteenth-century novel would greatly develop the description of the battle of Red Cliff and turn Zhuge Liang, against all fact, into the mastermind of Cao Cao's greatest defeat.[57]

As *Records of the Three Kingdoms in Plain Language* is very much a tale of continuous warfare and vicious politics, female characters play only a limited role. But women, and men's relationships to them, are more important to the narrative than it would appear at first sight. The central female character in the first part is Diaochan 貂蟬.[58] Both Dong Zhuo and and his adoptive son Lü Bu are bewitched by her charms, to the extent that Lü Bu is willing to murder his adoptive father in order to regain his former consort. Later in the first part, Lü Bu causes his own downfall when he comes to a realization about the meaningless nature of conquest and fame, ignores his generals' pleading, and retreats to spend all his time to dally in pleasure with Diaochan. While it is quite common to see women as distractions from a man's public life, this is one case where it is clearly not lust or the machinations of an evil woman, but a kind of happiness that turns Lü Bu into her constant companion when he realizes the fruitless nature of vainglorious pursuits. This part of *Records of the Three Kingdoms in Plain Language* shows how a tempting woman can destroy the fictive kinship of adoption in the case of Dong Zhuo and Lü Bu. Diaochan is really only a

---

Zhang Fei; from the second part it omits Zhou Yu's failed attempt on the life of Liu Bei at Yellow Crane Tower; and from the third part it omits the rebellion of Pang Tong 龐統 following his appointment as magistrate of Liyang 歷揚. See Sun Kaidi (1965, 114; originally published in 1934).

56. Plaks (1987, 407–76) provides a detailed discussion of the major personalities in (various versions of) the novel, and consistently contrasts their characterization in the novel with that in historiographical sources and in *Records of the Three Kingdoms in Plain Language*. While scholars agree that *Records of the Three Kingdoms in Plain Language* had a formative influence on the later novel, the novel did not directly borrow from the text of the plain tale. In this respect *Sanguo yanyi* is different from the many other historical novels of the sixteenth century that often copy verbatim large sections of earlier plain tales.

57. For those who have read the novel, the plain tale's description of the battle at Red Cliff is quite disappointing. When discussing *Records of the Three Kingdoms in Plain Language*, Lu Hsun (1959, 163–66) quotes its account of the battle and comments: "The brevity and crudeness of the language are reminiscent of a prompt-book, for the story-teller would fill in the bare outline with dramatic details to entertain the audience. But the fact that this book has illustrations shows that it must have been printed as reading material."

58. Wang Lijuan (2007, 63–212) provides an exhaustive study of the various versions of the legend of Diaochan.

pawn, a player in the chess game of ruthless men and patriots; she is not evil, but is pliable to the demands of men.

The second part contrasts this weakness by demonstrating how, in the case of Liu Bei, Guan Yu, and Zhang Fei, the fictive kinship of a sworn brotherhood can withstand such temptations. When Guan Yu is serving under Cao Cao, the latter tries to bring him over to his cause by offering him ten beauties, whom Guan Yu refuses to touch. At this time Guan Yu also finds himself in charge of Liu Bei's wife and concubine and, whereas other men might perhaps take advantage of this situation, Guan Yu behaves most properly and avoids all suspicion.[59] The second part of *Records of the Three Kingdoms in Plain Language* also shows us the example of possessiveness in Zhou Yu who, though happily married, is stirred into action by the desire to save his young wife from the clutches of the lecherous Cao Cao. These two examples, one positive and the other problematic, create three distinct male types: Lü Bu and Zhou Yu are driven by desire and Guan Yu is uniquely oblivious to female charm. At the same time, the second part also presents us with models of virtuous womanhood as foils to Diaochan. At decisive moments Sun Quan repeatedly receives wise advice from his mother, while his younger sister, who is married to Liu Bei in a plot to slay him, proves herself in the end a loyal wife who is willing to turn against her own family in order to save Liu Bei's life.[60]

When we reach the third part of *Records of Three Kingdoms in Plain Language* women almost disappear from the narrative. When Guan Yu arrogantly turns down a marriage proposal from the Sun family, he sets in motion developments that will lead eventually to his own death. And, when Liu Bei feels obliged by their oath of brotherhood to take vengeance for Guan Yu, his campaigns result in both his and Zhang Fei's deaths. When Liu Bei places the particularistic homosocial bond of brothers over dynastic interests (which are, after all, about successions of heirs), the resulting barrenness is embodied by his son and successor who prefers to cavort with eunuchs.[61] In the eyes of our

---

59. Lü Bu and Guan Yu are linked by the fact that the latter acquires Lü Bu's superb horse, Red Harrier. They are contrasted in some stories that show Guan Yu beheading Diaochan.

60. As a result, her final failed attempt to return to her own family and subsequent suicide strike one as out of character.

61. Liu Bei's preference for his generals over his family is foreshadowed in the famous episode of Zhao Yun saving his son during Cao Cao's campaign against Liu Bei and Sun Quan. As Liu Bei's troops flee from Cao Cao's advancing army, Liu Bei's dependents are separated from their guards. When Zhao Yun risks his life to find them, he can rescue Liu Bei's infant son. When he presents the child to Liu Bei, as narrated in the second part of the plain tale, the father dashes it to the ground because it has endangered the life of a fine general. In *The Story of Hua Guan Suo* the prevalence of the sworn brotherhood over all other ties is highlighted by the detail that Zhang Fei and Guan Yu (who are married, in contrast to Liu Bei who is single at the time) kill each other's dependents in cold blood so none of them will have any second thoughts.

anonymous author the perfect marriage may well be exemplified by Zhuge Liang. Only on the eve of his death do we learn that he had been married all along when he instructs his wife to make sure that their muddleheaded son does not seek an official career. The only conspicuous female character in this final part of the plain tale, in fact, is the divine maiden who informs Zhuge Liang of his impending death. Many heroes in traditional vernacular fiction meet with such divinity, but as a rule such a meeting takes places at the beginning of their career when the goddess instructs them in the martial skills and military tactics that will ensure their career.

The last female character to make her appearance in *Records of the Three Kingdoms in Plain Language* is the evil Empress Jia 賈, whose conspicuous abuse of power and lasciviousness ensure the speedy disintegration of the Jin dynasty, thus echoing the evil machinations of Empress Lü that were the ultimate cause of the dismemberment of the Han empire. The adulterous Empress Jia, who despises her disabled husband, also echoes the character of the wife of school teacher Sun 孫 whose expression of disgust at his disease causes him to attempt suicide, after which he discovers the heavenly book that will inspire the rebellion of the Yellow Scarves. As a proper marriage is described as the "correct beginning" (*zhengshi* 正始) of a well-ordered society, these disruptive women embody the chaos that will engulf the empire.

Conclusion

Compared to the later novel on the same theme, *Records of the Three Kingdoms in Plain Language* is in many ways a much simpler text. But we should not simply read the plain tale from the later perspective of the *Romance of the Three Kingdoms*. The plain tale covers far fewer episodes than the later novel, and many of the episodes that are covered are dealt with in a very cursory way. If the plots of the individual episodes are not always as complicated as those in the later novel, however, they are often more natural and convincing. The language is clear and straightforward, and the story moves at a fast pace. In its own time the plain tale presented its readers with a novel and exciting account of the events of a fabled period of Chinese history, and its long popularity should cause no surprise. Even today, we believe, *Records of the Three Kingdoms in Plain Language* merits translation as a good read and as an introduction to fascinating aspects of traditional and contemporary Chinese culture.

A Note on the Translation

For our translation, we have used the original Yu Family printing, which is available in high-quality images from the Digital Archives of the National Library of Japan.[1] The text is large and for the most part extremely clear. We have keyed our translation to the original text; the original page numbers will appear within single square brackets. The aim of working from the original was to avoid the pitfalls that have plagued photographic reprints of the original, which are invariably blurred (also because they are reduced in size), as well as the miscopyings and mispunctuations one finds in modern typeset editions. We have referred often to Zhong Zhaohua's emendations to the text, and we have followed his changes when they seemed logical. Because he provides a complete list of changed characters and words, readers who want to delve further into the language of the text should consult his diligent work.

There are two types of word errors, generally, that stem from the original text: mistranscriptions of characters and the use of homophonic variants. The mistranscriptions are of various types. This is due in part to the fact that the text uses full-form characters as well as short-form characters (many of which are in use today in the simplified characters of the People's Republic of China), and to the fact that when the text was cut in the woodblocks, there was probably a gap between the writer of the text and the cutter, who was probably illiterate. Many mistakes are due to sloppy copying (*ai* 艾 for *wen* 文, for instance). The homophonic variants really do not pose much of a problem, if we remember we are dealing with a story cycle (not a text) that adapts the conventions of oral performance; as long as the pronunciation is accurate (when heard or read), it is completely understandable.

Much of modern textual work on the *Plain Tales* has been involved in trying to rationalize the words, phrases, and events of the narrative on the basis of the different versions that precede it in historical sources, or postdate it in other fictional forms. This is stimulated by a desire to restore the tale to some hypothetical and virtual form of historical accuracy. While checking against other sources can occasionally unearth information that will help with understanding events, more often than not it proves a useless enterprise: the *Plain Tales* are not works of historical scholarship. Furthermore, the audience for which it was created was no more interested in "real" history than audiences who watch films or read books that are fictional re-creations of historical eras. The "feel" of reality was enough, and as agents within a fictional text, the characters are

---

1. http://www.digital.archives.go.jp/

not obliged to operate by the rules of real history, whatever they may be. In this sense, the *Plain Tales* are a fine read against the grain of historical accuracy that is so valued in Chinese narrative. Rich in the use of formal elements of the historiographical tradition (dates, home area, public office) the actual facts of these elements are often wrong.

建安虞氏新刊

新全相三

至治新刊

國志平話

漢曰大丈夫生於世當如此非乃快哉鐵校東民
於途廢之中縛夫子倒懸之患見如此切齒命與子絕
雜當有不平之心
裏驚　　却說張飛一日飲了二兄同今步小巷子裏
劫掠居民財奪人妻女倘若職來財貪不能作
主玄德曰似此若何飛曰咱同喝不善燒主報典義兵
閣家來見燕忘念奔來見人特來見人若來見主公有商
攔往飛因念人至公家見主公把門人至左前史有商議的
欲與主公有議的事見飛即隨身日交請來見有一人在衛前
利於毋曰燕主賜飛事把門人曰今公有幹飛曰令有一人在衛前
黃巾賊區天下偽若來此中央備却不路砂來燕
便賊來何懼友德并闊公言曰此幸有理即便上馬
京燕主曰食然如此机府摩天矣倉廩无桑兼其粮草
萬諸匡人交誰人爰其顧曰飛曰便招得此義族其受
署有此小家財可膽每人燕主曰令便招得此義族其受
誰寫此頭曰飛曰公家有一人姓劉名雀守正起人義族爲首者
山靖王劉勝之後其人尖的龍準鳳目耳垂過肩手
乘過膝可爲頭目燕主即特別冷正起人義族爲首者
乃劉玄德少下關雲長張兵毒糊方閣歇殺不

[1a] *Newly Printed by the Yu Family at Jianyang*
New and Illustrated: Records of the Three Kingdoms in Plain Language
Newly Printed in the Zhizhi Period

Newly Printed in the Zhizhi Period:
The Completely Illustrated Plain Tales,
Records of the Three Kingdoms, Part I

East of the River was the land of Wu, Shu's was among the Streams,[1]
And Cao Cao, brave and heroic, held fast the Central Plain.
It is not that these three divided up the sub-celestial realm—
They returned to take vengeance for their murders.

Sima Zhongxiang's Karmic Dream

Long ago there was a certain Liu Xiu, a man of Whitewater Village down in
Dengzhou, Nanyang; he was known as Wenshu, and his imperial name was
August Emperor Guangwu of the Han.[2] Now *Guang* means the rays of the
sun and moon that shed their light into the subcelestial realm; *wu* is "might,"
and it was the way by which he had won the world. This was why he was called
Guangwu, "shining might." He built his capital at Luoyang and had ruled there
for five years. Then, on a particular day, as he wandered at leisure he went into
the Imperial Park. Once he got inside there were rare trees and exotic flowers
and his pleasure of viewing them knew no end.

The emperor asked his high officials, "Must we be indebted to Wang Mang
for this garden's construction?" His eunuchs replied, "This has nothing to do
with Wang Mang. It is in fact due to the pressure put on the common folk to
transplant, buy, take cuttings, and graft these flowers. We owe everything to
the labors of the people of Luoyang, the Eastern Capital."

---

1. That is, modern Sichuan ("Four Streams"). We have followed the practice that the word
"River" when standing alone and capitalized refers only to the Yangzi River.

2. On the revival of the Eastern Han and Emperor Guangwu, see Bielenstein (1986).

"Transmit Our edict," said Guangwu, "Tomorrow is the Festival of Clear and Bright, the third of the third month,[3] so put this up on a yellow plaque: 'We will enjoy the pleasure of this garden with the common folk.'"

When the next day arrived, the Hundred Surnames all enjoyed the flowers inside the Imperial Park, and they occupied all of the kiosks and halls.

Suddenly a single student came on the scene. In a white robe, a horn-studded belt, a gauze cap, and black boots—his left hand swinging a pot of wine; his right carrying an earthen bowl; and his back bearing his zither, sword, and book basket—he came to enjoy the sights of the Imperial Park. But he got there late and all the kiosks and halls were so full there was no place to sit. Our young burgeoning talent went straight ahead for a hundred paces or so and saw a cypress that would block the wind. And there he put his wine pot and earthen bowl down on the lush and green carpet of grass and unslung his sword, zither, and book basket. He settled himself down and poured some wine into the earthen bowl. After one drink he was thirsty for more, and he drank three more bowlsful, one after the other. Before you could snap your fingers, he was already half sloshed.

As soon as one bowl of Bamboo Leaf[4] pierces through his heart,
Two peach blossoms appear on his face.

Now what was the name of our burgeoning talent? His surname was Sima, and he was known as Zhongxiang. Because he became a bit dejected while sitting there, he played a tune on his zither, and when done, opened up his book box and [1b] took out a book. He opened it to read, and reached the part about how the doomed Qin had pushed roads across the Five Ranges in the south,[5] built the Great Wall in the north, filled in the Great Sea in the east, and in the west had constructed the Epang Palace, and how it had buried the scholars and burned the books. When Zhongxiang saw this, he could not suppress his fury and violently cursed, "The First Emperor was a ruler without the Way. Had I, Zhongxiang, been the ruler, of course I would have ensured that the common people of the whole world were overjoyed!" He also said, "The First Emperor oppressed the common people until eight or nine out of every ten died, none were given a decent burial, and the stench offended Heaven and Earth! Since

---

3. The third of the third month celebrates the *Shangsi* sacrifices, an ancient ablution rite that had, by this time, become primarily a festival to celebrate spring's return and enjoy the blessings of the season.

4. A conventional name for high-quality rice wine.

5. The First Emperor of Qin had dispatched some five hundred thousand penal laborers into the modern area of Guangdong and Guangxi to build roads, passes, and posthouses in the territory occupied by the Viet peoples. This was one of the four massive cardinal-point construction projects supposedly undertaken by the First Emperor.

the Lord of Heaven made the First Emperor a ruler, even he must have some blind spots. Now in the south the First Emperor feared that Xiang Yu had already turned against him at Langya and then, in Xuzhou, Liu the Third[6] of Feng in Pei had 'roused righteous men' to revolt. Blades and weapons suddenly sprang up throughout the world—troops suffered the hardship of belting on armor, and people suffered the misery of dirt and ashes."

As soon as he had said this more than fifty men, clad in brocade gowns and flowery caps, suddenly emerged from behind a trellis of wild-roses and marched over to him. At the head were two rows of eight men in purple vestments and golden belts, with ivory tablets and ravenblack boots. One official of some rank or another, with a purple and gold fish[7] hanging from his belt, addressed him as follows, "At the behest of the Jade Emperor we request Your Majesty to accept these six major ritual gifts." Zhongxiang saw that another person was holding a golden-phoenix plate, on which six objects had been placed.[8] These were the Equal-to-Heaven Cap, the Coiling-Dragons Robe, the Without-Worries Shoes, a scepter of white jade, a belt made of jade, and the precious sword of authority. After he was persuaded to do so, Zhongxiang accepted all of these objects and immediately put them on; he then sat down, holding the white-jade scepter in his hands.

The eight men told him, "This is not a proper place for Your Majesty to sit." They had barely finished speaking when, all of a sudden, among those fifty men in their flowery caps several lifted up and brought over a dragon-phoenix palanquin which they put down in front of him. "May Your Majesty ascend the chair!" Zhongxiang lifted the hem of his yellow gown, ascended the chair and sat in a dignified manner. The eight men divided themselves into two rows to head the cortege, while behind him the fifty with flowery hats surrounded him in a dense group. They walked all the way to a palace hall that was covered with glazed tiles, and someone said, "We invite our king to dismount."

He ascended the hall and saw a Nine-Dragon Throne. Zhongxiang sat down there in a dignified manner to receive congratulatory hurrahs of "Long live our Majesty," and when that was done, the eight men addressed him as follows, "Your Majesty knows the crimes of Wang Mang: he killed Emperor Ping with poisoned wine, executed the infant Ying, did in the empress, and cleaned out their palace apartments, killing who knows how many palace beauties.[9] These

---

6. Liu Bang; the name used here refers to his earliest days before he was on the road to the imperial throne. He was called either Liu the Third (the third in the rank of his male cousin cohort) or Liu the Youngest. He was from the small village of Feng in the County of Pei.

7. In the Tang and Song dynasties officials of rank five and higher wore fish-shaped tallies at their belts.

8. These are the traditional six accoutrement of an emperor.

9. This violates a prohibition about not killing people you usurp.

were his crimes. Later he established the house of Xin and became emperor. He took on the adult name Great Lord. [2a] But eighteen years later Liu Xiu from Whitewater Village in Dengzhou in Nanyang rose in righteous rebellion, smashed that Wang Mang, and snatched the empire back again. He deposed Wang Mang, who is now banished and locked away in a courtyard. Currently, His Majesty Guangwu occupies the throne. For his ministers he has in support the lords of the twenty-eight fixed constellations and the four Dipper stars to serve him as generals and commanders. Guangwu is the Great Thearch of Purple Tenuity.[10] Now a sky cannot have two suns; a people cannot have two rulers. But you, our king, have here accepted this appointment. Yet you have neither troops nor generals. Not only do you lack wisdom and cunning, you don't even have the strength to truss up a chicken. If Guangwu learns about this, leads his troop and officers and appoints a grand marshal, you think he'll let you off?"

Zhongxiang asked, "My ministers, what would you have Us do?"

The eight men said, "Your Majesty should try out the Nine-Dragon Throne but if you look up at the plaque below the eaves, you'll see this is definitely not the Major Audience Hall with its nine bays."

When Zhongxiang looked up, he saw a red-lacquered plaque with four golden characters as big as dustpans: "Hall for Avenging Wrongs." Zhongxiang dropped his head and pondered the meaning but couldn't figure it out. So he asked, "My ministers, We do not understand what this means."

The eight men replied, "Your Majesty, this is not the world of light, but that of the shades. A moment ago when you were reading about the doomed Qin in the Imperial Garden, you vilified the First Emperor and complained about the intentions of Heaven and Earth. Your Majesty, is it not said that those who follow the Buddha are reborn above into paradise, but those who do not are reborn below into hell? Just consider the people who lived in the times of Yao, Shun, Yu, and Tang: they deserved to be rewarded, just as the people of Jie and Zhou deserved to be slaughtered.[11] Our king does not understand the meaning in all of this: a ruler without the Way has a people who have committed a karmic sin. This is precisely by design of the Lord of Heaven. By vilifying the First Emperor you displayed your resentment toward the Lord of Heaven.

---

10. This is a circular area that surrounds the Pole Star, and is the heavenly analogue to the imperial seat. It is called Purple Tenuity partially because the current Pole Star was not visible as a pole star in the earliest days of astronomy; while they understood that there was an axis, there was also this tenuous area circumscribed by the wobbling axis.

11. Yao, Shun, Yu, and Tang are exemplary good rulers from Chinese earliest history. Yao ceded the throne to Shun because of his virtue; Shun in his turn ceded the throne to Yu. Yu founded the Xia dynasty and was succeeded by his own son. Tang founded the Shang or Yin dynasty, which later succeeded the Xia. Jie and Zhou are two prototypical bad last rulers. Jie was the last ruler of the Xia dynasty and was responsible for its collapse, and Zhou was the last ruler of the Shang dynasty.

The Lord of Heaven ordered us to summon Your Majesty and make you the Lord of the Underworld in the Palace for Avenging Wrongs. If you can pass sentence on these underworld cases without any partiality, he will make you the Son of Heaven in the world of light, but if you judge them wrongly, you will be banished to the backside of the Mountain of Darkness and never again see human form."

Zhongxiang said, "Which cases do I have to judge?"

The eight replied, "Your Majesty, you only have to transmit your sagely order and there will be people who submit a statement and make an accusation."

"Well, I'll do as you say." When he transmitted his sagely order, there was indeed a man who loudly shouted, "I've suffered a wrong!" In his hand he held a single-page writ of accusation.

When Zhongxiang [2b] had a better look he saw a man with a golden helmet on his head, wearing golden chain-mail armor, dark red battle dress, and shiny black boots.[12] Blood flowed from his neck and stained his gown below. He kept on shouting, "Injustice" and "I've been wronged." When Zhongxiang accepted his written statement and unrolled it on his desk to read it, it turned out to be a case from 205 years past. "How in the world do you think I can pass sentence on such a case?" And he swept the documents from his desk. But the person lodging the accusation said, "I am Han Xin. I suffered at the hands of Gaozu of the Former Han. I hail from Huaiyin and achieved the rank of King of the Three Qi. I accumulated ten great merits. I pretended to construct a trestle road as a diversion so I could secretly cross Chencang and chase Xiang Yu to Raven River, where he wound up slitting his own throat. But while I made this major contribution to the establishment of the Han, Gaozu never even thought about 'carrying the axle, pushing the wheel, or speaking an oath.'[13] He pretended to go off on a visit to Yunmeng and had Empress Dowager Lü trick me into going to Weiyang Palace where I was slain by a blunt sword. I died through injustice, so please act on my behalf!"

A startled Zhongxiang exclaimed, "What should I do?"

"Your Majesty," replied the eight men, "if you cannot quickly decide a case like this, how can you ever become a Son of Heaven in the World of Light?"

Before their words ended, he heard yet someone else shouting, "I, too, have suffered an injustice." He saw a person with unbound hair and a red headscarf, dressed in a green robe under willow-leaf armor, and wearing shiny black boots. In his hand was a writ of accusation, and every single word that came out of

---

12. The text says "polished green," but refers to highly polished black boots that have an oily sheen, in precisely the same way people use the term "green hair" to refer to oiled and shiny black hair.

13. All signs of great respect and gratitude shown by a ruler to his generals. The axle and the wheel refer to the axle and wheel of the carriage in which the person so honored is riding.

his mouth was "injustice" or "wronged." When Zhongxiang asked him for his name, he replied, "I am Peng Yue. I was appointed King of Great Liang and was one of the liege lords under the command of Gaozu of the Han who, together with Han Xin, established the Han. But when peace finally reigned throughout the world, there was no further need for me either. I was tricked into coming to the capital where I was minced into a meat paste and fed to the liege lords throughout the empire. That is the wrong I have suffered."

Zhongxiang accepted his statement.

Then he saw yet another, also holding a statement in his hand who shouted that he too had suffered injustice. Zhongxiang saw that this man wore a lion-head helmet, a green battle dress under dragon scale armor, and green boots. When asked for his name, Bu replied, "I am a vassal of Gaozu of the Han, and my name is Ying Bu. I was appointed as King of Jiujiang. The three of us— Han Xin, Peng Yue, and I—established the empire of Han: twelve emperors who have reigned for more than two hundred years. Such was our great merit! But in a time of peace they had no use for me either and Gaozu cunningly betrayed the three of us, tricked us into entering the palace, and had us all killed. Such are the wrongs we have suffered. May Your Majesty act on behalf of the three of us."

The emperor grew furious [3a] and asked the eight men, "Where is that Gaozu of the Han?"

"Your Majesty has only to summon him," they replied.

"Do that now," said the emperor.

They transmitted his sagely order and summoned Gaozu of the Han. In no time at all the latter arrived in front of the steps and threw himself prostrate on the ground. Zhongxiang interrogated him as follows, "The accusations of these three people are all the same. Han Xin, Peng Yue, and Ying Bu established the empire of the Han, but you cunningly accused them of rebellion and had them killed. What kind of principle is that?"

Gaozu replied, "The Yunmeng Hills have thousands of sights, so I went there to amuse myself. Empress Lü was temporarily in charge of the country and I have no idea whether these people rebelled or not. Please summon the empress dowager and we'll see what the truth is."

When the empress dowager had been summoned, had made her bows below the steps, and had wished Zhongxiang a myriad years, he interrogated her as follows, "When you were temporarily in charge of the country, you cunningly accused these three men of rebellion and intentionally slew these meritorious officials. What should be your punishment?"

The empress dowager glared at Gaozu and said, "Your Majesty,[14] when you had become lord in charge of the mountains of rivers and of the altars of earth

_____

14. Now speaking to Han Gaozu.

and grain,[15] I said to Your Majesty, 'At present peace reigns, so why are you so unhappy?' And your sagely intent was thus expressed, 'You don't know what's bothering me. The Hegemon-King had a roaring and booming voice but these three men pursued him until he slit his throat at Raven River. These three are like sleeping tigers—what shall We do once they awaken? Now We will leave for Yunmeng to amuse ourselves, leave you to temporarily act as emperor, and you can trick these three into coming to the palace where you can do away with them.' Your Majesty, why don't you confess to this now instead of blaming everything on your lowly handmaid?"

Zhongxiang asked Gaozu, "These three men did not rebel but were deliberately murdered. Why don't you submit a confession?"

"Your Majesty," said Empress Lü, "it's not my word alone. There is still another witness."

When Zhongxiang asked who that was, she said, "That would be Kuai Che, also known as Wentong. If Your Majesty summons him, you will get to the bottom of it."

After Kuai Wentong was summoned, arrived at the hall, and finished his dutiful ritual obligations, Zhongxiang asked, "Did these three men rebel? You are the witness!"

Wentong replied, "There is a poem that describes this. The poem goes,

> How pitiable, that lord of Huaiyin—
> Capable of sharing the anxieties of Gaozu:
> The Three Qin were rolled up like a mat,
> And Yan and Zhao vanquished in a snap.
> At night he dammed up a river with sacks of sand;[16]
> In daylight he decapitated the rebel vassal.[17]
> But because Gaozu was neither firm nor resolute
> Empress Lü decapitated the liege lords all.

After each of their confessions had been taken, Zhongxiang wrote a memorial to inform the Lord of Heaven. The Lord of Heaven immediately dispatched a

---

15. All metonymy for the state.

16. This refers to Han Xin's strategy in the battle at the Wei River (濰水), where he lowered the level of the river by damming it with sandbags; afterward he forded the depleted river and attacked his rival Long Ju (龍且.); he then staged a retreat, and when the opposing forces chased him, he loosed the sandbags, drowning a considerable number of his foes. See "The Marquis of Huai-yin, Memoir 32," in Sima Qian (Ssu-ma Ch'ien) (2008, 87).

17. Zhong Zhaohua (1990, 402 note 46) takes this as a reference to Xiang Yu, who actually slit his own throat when surrounded.

divine warrior in golden armor who presented him with the divine ordination[18] to carry out the will of Heaven. That edict of the Jade Emperor read:

For Zhongxiang to note:

Gaozu of the Han betrayed his meritorious ministers, so We will have these three men share the empire of the Han: Let Han Xin take as his share the Central Plain and become Cao Cao; let Peng Yue become Liu Bei in Sichuan; let Ying Bu take as his share the area east of the River and, as King Wu of Changsha, become Sun Quan. Gaozu will be reborn in Xuchang and become Emperor Xian, and Empress Lü will become his wife, Empress Fu. Let Cao Cao occupy the Moment of Heaven, imprison Emperor Xian, and kill Empress Fu to take revenge. East of the River let Sun Quan occupy the Advantages of Earth—all those many mountains and rivers! Let Liu Bei in Sichuan occupy the Harmony of Men. Liu Bei will be able enlist the courage of Guan Yu and Zhang Fei, but he will need a man of cunning and strategy. Let Kuai Wentong be reborn in Jizhou (which is Langya Commandery) as Zhuge Liang, also known as Kongming. His name in the Dao will be Master Sleeping Dragon and he will build himself a hermitage and live on Sleeping Dragon Ridge in Dengzhou in Nanyang. This place will be where lord and vassals unite and together establish their state. They will proceed to Yizhou in Sichuan where they will establish their capital and reign as emperors for over fifty years. Let Zhongxiang be reborn in the world of light as Sima Zhongda. He will gather in all three kingdoms and rule alone over the sub-celestial realm.

Thus ends the verdict of the Lord of Heaven.

The Origin of the Yellow Scarves[19]

Now we will speak about something else. Right now, in the year in which Emperor Ling of the Han has ascended the throne, bronze and iron both rang out. The emperor, startled, asked his high ministers, "Has such a thing ever happened in past?"

---

18. Literally, "Document of Buddhist ordination." In early colloquial texts, this can mean simply a divine document.

19. In Western historical scholarship this movement is usually described as "Yellow Turbans." As described later in the narrative, adherents of the movement wore yellow headscarves to distinguish themselves from government troops. Their headdress was, however, quite different from the turbans worn in the Middle East and South Asia.

The Prime Minister Huangfu Song stepped forward from the ranks and replied, "This has happened twice from the ancient times of Pangu to the present. Long ago in the Spring and Autumn period, when the Son of Heaven, who was King of Qi, ascended the throne, bronze and iron rang out for three days and nights. The King of Qi then asked his great ministers, 'What good or bad fortune is foretold by this ringing of bronze and iron?' He asked three times but all of the high ministers were silent. The King of Qi was furious and summoned the grandee Ran Qing, 'You are a grandee, why is it you cannot explain this? I will set a term of three days for you; you must reveal the fortune it signals, good or bad.' The King of Qi did in fact not receive his ministers in audience for three days.

"But, when Ran Qing returned home, he was deeply depressed and unhappy. A family tutor at his mansion noticed the sorrowful expression on his face and asked the grandee, 'Why are you so unhappy?' The grandee answered, 'Teacher, I will tell you. All the bronze and iron in the world are ringing, and when my lord and king asked me whether this predicted good fortune or bad, I truly had no idea. Now the King of Qi has given me a time limit of three days, and if I do not come up with an answer I will be charged with a crime.' [4a] The teacher replied, 'This is easy!' The great grandee exclaimed, 'If you know the answer, you will be appointed to office and receive a substantial reward. What of the fortune, good or bad, of this affair?' The teacher replied, 'It doesn't predict any good fortune or bad. It only predicts that a mountain will collapse.' 'How do you know?' The teacher explained, 'Bronze and iron are the offspring of the mountains and mountains are the progenitors of bronze and iron.'

"The great grandee Ran got the meaning and immediately went to court to report to the King of Qi. The latter assembled his ministers, and grandee Ran stepped forward from the ranks and reported, 'The ringing of bronze and iron does not predict any fortune, good or bad.' The King of Qi asked, 'What?' He replied, 'It predicts that a mountain will collapse.' The ruler asked, 'How do you know?' And he reported, 'Bronze and iron are the offspring of the mountains, and the mountains are the progenitors of bronze and iron. It is neither lucky nor unlucky.' The King of Qi was highly pleased and promoted Ran Qing to higher office and rank, to be held by his sons and grandsons without interruption. Only a few days after Ran Qing had reported to the throne, one of the peaks of Flowery Mountain collapsed. So, Your Majesty, this affair does not predict good fortune and does not predict misfortune."

It was no more than a few days after he had finished speaking that a memorial arrived from Yunzhou, stating that a hole had appeared at the foot of Mt. Tai, as big as a cartwheel and of unknown depth. The court dispatched an emissary to investigate whether this was a lucky or unlucky event.

Let us now talk about something else. At some distance from this hole there was a mountain house, the mountain retreat of Old Master Sun. The Old Master had two sons, the elder of whom took charge of the farm, and the younger of whom studied his letters. He was going to be schoolteacher Sun, but he suddenly contracted leprosy: all his hair fell out and his body never stopped oozing pus and blood. The stench offended his father and mother, and that's why they built him a thatched hut more than a hundred paces behind the farm.

His wife brought him his food each day. Now one day, his wife brought him food early in the morning. It was the third month of spring and when she arrived at the door of his hermitage and saw the full extent of his illness, she could not bear to look at him. Covering her mouth and nose with her hands, she gave him his food but leaned away from him.

The schoolteacher heaved a sigh and said, "A wife is supposed to share your house when alive and your coffin when you're dead. But—if even my wife can't stand me when I'm alive, how much less can others? What's the point of living even a day longer?"

After he had finished speaking and his wife had gone away, he came to the conclusion that he should find a place to die. He took the crutch he used in his illness, and put on his pus- and blood-stained shoes. After going twenty or thirty steps straight north from his hut, [4b] he saw a hole. He put down the staff, took off his shoes, and straightaway jumped into it. But inside the hole it seemed like someone carried him on his back and laid him on the ground. He completely lost consciousness. After a long time, he suddenly came to and opened his eyes to have a look; straight above him he saw one dot of blue sky.

The schoolteacher said, "A moment ago I was desperate to kill myself, I never expected I would escape death!"

After a time in utter darkness, he gradually saw a bright light straight north of him. About ten paces after he started walking in that direction, he saw a staff of white jade. But when he tried to take hold of it, it turned out only to be two leaves of a gate standing ajar. When he pushed that grotto gate open with his shoulder, it was as bright as day. He saw a stone mat and sat down on it to rest for a while. Tired, he lay down on the stone mat and fell asleep. But when he suddenly stretched himself out, his feet touched something soft. And when he arose with a start, what did he see? Doomed to an end was the four-hundred-year-old empire of Han, just because this schoolteacher reached this very spot!

The schoolteacher saw a huge python, a motionless coil—from fat head to tapered tail—three foot tall. Immediately that python escaped into the grotto. The schoolteacher followed the snake inside the cave, and although he didn't see the snake, he did see a stone casket. He lifted the lid of the box with his hands and found one scroll of text. He took it out and read it from beginning to end. It turned out to be a text to cure all 404 diseases. It made no use of the eight kinds of eight herbs of the Divine Husbandman. It did not involve refining, matching, or curing with heat. Nothing was turned into pills or powders. No activants were used to get it down. On every page were prescriptions for cures; for every kind of symptom all you needed was a cup of water over which the correct incantation had been spoken—you would be cured as soon as you swallowed that! When he came to the passage on leprosy, the method prescribed was a famous prescription for treating the disease of our schoolteacher. When he saw this, he was filled with joy. He took the heavenly book with him, left through the grotto gate, and sat down on the stone mat.

Now our tale divides again. When the wife of the schoolteacher brought his food again, she couldn't find the schoolteacher. She came back and informed her father-in-law and he immediately set out with the elder son and others to search. When they came to the hole, they saw his staff and his pus- and blood-covered shoes. The father and mother, elder brother, and wife circled around the pit, weeping. After some time they could hear someone calling from the pit. They fetched a rope and lowered it into the hole with a branch at its end to save the schoolteacher. When he appeared from the pit and father and son saw each other, they were deeply moved. [5a] When they were done crying, the schoolteacher said, "Father, don't be sad and anxious anymore. I found a heavenly book that will cure my symptoms." They immediately returned to the farm together. He took one cup of pure water and swallowed it into his stomach when he finished reciting the incantation. His leprosy was immediately cured, and his hair and skin went back to their original state! Later, no matter the distance, people came to seek treatment and every one was cured. They offered him as a contribution for his services cash and goods worth more than twenty thousand strings[20] and he ordained roughly five hundred or more disciples.

One of these was called Zhang Jue. One day he took his leave from his teacher, "My old mother back at home is advanced in years, so I request a leave of absence in order to take care of her."

The schoolteacher replied, "When you leave I will give you a book with famous prescriptions, so it doesn't matter if you don't come back."

The teacher instructed Zhang Jue, "With these famous prescriptions you will cure all complaints and diseases in the empire; but never ask people for money. Abide by my words."

After Zhang Jue had left his teacher and returned home, he treated diseases in all places he passed through; everyone was cured but he never asked for money. Zhang Jue said, "If I cure you, all of your young and adult males will follow me as my disciples—there is no claim on the old."

---

20. Traditional Chinese copper coins were round with a square hole. Larger amounts were counted in strings of nominally one thousand coins.

Zhang Jue roamed through the four directions and ordained more than a hundred thousand disciples. He recorded their surnames and names and their places of registration, and also the cyclical year, month, and day of their birth. "If I want you for a mission, when that written notification arrives report with the speed of fire. And all of my disciples must abide by the meeting time. Anyone who does not come upon receiving the notification will certainly die. All those who do not follow me will be visited by disaster!"

So suddenly, on that day the Yellow Scarves rose in revolt against the Han, Zhang Jue's notifications were dispatched throughout the whole world and within a few days his disciples had all arrived at Zhang Family Village, thirty *li* to the east of the capital of Guangning Commandery in Yangzhou Prefecture. Zhang Jue and two of his nephews gathered the whole in this village, and when they had all assembled, he shouted, "You two younger brothers bring them over here!"

The two younger brothers brought out four bundles, and when these were opened in front of Zhang Jue, they were filled with yellow scarves, which they distributed to the troops and the captains wore . . . Yellow Scarves. Zhang Jue instructed his troops as follows, "Today the empire of the Han dynasty is bound to end and I am bound to rise. If one day I will be lord, the greatest soldiers will be appointed as princes, the lesser ones will be appointed as marquises, and even the bottom rung will be appointed as prefects."

When this meeting was over, they had no armor or weapons at all. In the beginning they all wore soft battle clothing and carried only rakes and [5b] clubs. But the leaders, Zhang Jue and the two others, led these one hundred thousand men and first took Yangzhou to provide battle dress and armor, bows and swords, saddles and horses, and all other weapons.

Setting out with their army, they started from Guangning Commandery in Yangzhou Prefecture. Whenever they came upon some village, they took that village; whenever they came upon some district, they took that district—they took countless counties and prefectures. Whenever they came to a place, whole families were enlisted in their rebellion. Those who did not comply were either killed, conquered, or enslaved. Occupying two-thirds of the Han empire, the Yellow Scarves had amassed three hundred sixty thousand people in total.

Here our tale divides. One day Emperor Ling of the Han received his ministers in audience and deliberated with the high ministers, saying, "Now the Yellow Scarves number three hundred and sixty thousand in total. What is to be done?"

Huangfu Song stepped forward from the ranks and reported, "This humble minister now makes this request, 'Your Majesty, if you will accept my three conditions, the Yellow Scarves will disappear by themselves.'"

When the emperor asked which three conditions, he replied, "The first condition is that you promulgate throughout the empire an edict of pardon for all violent criminals who rose in rebellion and gathered in the mountain forests, who attacked and plundered fortified cities; secondly for all those who killed or harmed imperial officials, attacked or robbed granaries and storehouses, and wounded or harmed the common people; and thirdly for all those who are willing on their own initiative to leave the Yellow Scarves to become good subjects of the state—but should they not leave the Yellow Scarves, they will be slain along with their whole family."

The emperor said, "We will follow your proposal and on the day the proclamation of pardon arrives, all will be pardoned and forgiven."

Huangfu Song also reported, "At present the troops of the Han dynasty are weak, their officers few, whereas the Yellow Scarves are so powerful in numbers they cannot be defeated. Your Majesty can summon a volunteer army throughout the empire, promising them high office and great rewards. You should also appoint a grand marshal, and provide him with blank patents of office[21] and great rewards for the troops. 'When great rewards are offered, men of courage will come forward.'"

When the emperor asked, "Who should be the grand marshal?" the answer was, "If there is someone else who can be grand marshal, then hand the seal of office to him, but if there is no one else, I myself will go."

The emperor said, "Well, then you take the seal."

He provided him with blank patents of office and treasure, and made him commander of the one hundred thousand men of the Imperial Guard. He gave a royal order, "Even though you lack the Simurgh Conveyance,[22] act at your own discretion, as if it were Us in person."

After Huangfu Song had received the golden seal and had become grand marshal, he took his leave of the emperor and left the court leading his army.

The Oath in the Peach Garden

Here our tale divides. A poem reads,

> The dangerous tilt of the house of Han was surely serious,
> The rebellious chaos of the Yellow Scarves spread all over the East.
> If it hadn't been for the lawless deeds of these bandit traitors,
> How could those "true beams to support heaven" have ever appeared?

---

21. To be filled out at the proper time with the proper number or wording.

22. The imperial chariot; i.e., the symbolic status of the emperor.

The story goes that there was a man named [6a] Guan Yu, also known as Yunchang. He hailed from Xieliang in Puzhou in Pingyang. From birth he had the eyebrows of a god and the eyes of a phoenix, a curly beard and face like purple jade; he was nine feet, two inches tall[23] and loved to read the *Springs and Autumns* and *Zuo's Commentary*. When he studied the biographies of rebellious vassals and evil sons, he was filled with a furious hatred. He killed a district magistrate because the latter coveted wealth and loved kickbacks and greatly harmed the common people. Fleeing for his life he became a fugitive and went to Zhuo Commandery.

> If he would not have fled for his life, drifting and roaming about,
> How would he have met friends who prized righteousness over gold?

The story goes that there was a man named Zhang Fei, also known as Yide, who hailed from Fanyang in Zhuo Commandery, in the princedom of Yan. From birth he had the head of a panther and round eyes, the jowls of a swallow, and the whiskers of a tiger; his body was more than nine feet tall, and his voice resounded like a huge bell. He came from a very rich family. Because he was idly standing outside, he saw Lord Guan pass through the streets: his physique was extraordinary, but his clothes were in tatters—he was not a local man. So he stepped forward and greeted Lord Guan with a bow, which the latter returned.

Fei asked him, "Sir, where are you going? And where are you from?" As Lord Guan was being questioned by Fei, he saw that Fei too had an exceptional physique, and said, "I hail from Xiezhou in Hedong. Because the local magistrate treated the people most cruelly, I killed him. Not daring to stay in my village, I came to this place to seek safety." When Fei heard this tale, he realized that Lord Guan had the ambition of a true man, and invited him to a wineshop. Fei ordered up some wine, "Bring us two hundred coins worth of wine." The owner brought it promptly.

Lord Guan saw that Fei was a serious person. As they were talking and speaking, they were in complete harmony. When the wine was finished, Lord Guan wanted to buy the next round, but he had no money with him and looked uncomfortable about it. Fei said, "How could that be?" And he ordered the owner to bring more wine. The two of them toasted each other, and as they were talking found themselves in such harmony that they resembled old friends. Indeed:

> The day that dragon and tiger meet with each other
> Is the time when lord and vassal happily unite.

---

23. When heroes are described in the text, they are given outlandish size, strength, and build. It is doubtful that Guan Yu was actually 2.2 meters or 7' 3" tall.

Let us begin to speak about a man named Liu Bei, also known as Xuande. He hailed from Fanyang in Zhuo Commandery and was the worthy seventeenth-generation great-grandson of Emperor Jingdi of the Han and a descendant of Liu Sheng, the Quiet Prince of Zhongshan. From birth he had a dragon face, an aquiline nose, the eyes of a phoenix, the back of Yu, and the shoulders of Tang;[24] his body was seven feet, five inches tall, and his hands hung down below his knees. When he was speaking, joy or [6b] anger never showed on his face, and he loved to befriend heroes. As a child he had lost his father; he lived with his mother and made a living by weaving mats and plaiting sandals. At the southeastern corner of his house a mulberry tree grew above the fence. It was more than fifty feet tall. If you had a look at it from close up you saw the various layers of leaves resembled the canopy of a little carriage. Passersby all marveled at the exceptional nature of this tree, which was bound to produce a man destined for greatness. When Xuande was still a child he would play below this tree with other children in the family, and say, "I am the Son of Heaven, and this is the Great Audience Hall."

When his uncle Liu Deran noticed him uttering these words, he said, "Don't wipe out our family with light-hearted words!"

Deran's father was Yuanqi, and Yuanqi's wife said, "He has his own family. Chase him away from our gates."

"But," said Yuanqi, "If our family has such a boy, he is surely no common person. Don't speak such words!" When the boy turned fifteen, his mother had him travel and study, and he studied at the house of Lu Zhi, the former prefect of Jiujiang, whom he honored as his teacher. But Lord Liu did not like the study of books very much; he loved dogs and horses and fine clothes, and was fond of music.

On this day, after he had plaited his sandals and gone to the market and had sold them, he also came into this wineshop to buy a drink. When Guan and Zhang saw the extraordinary physique of Lord Liu and his thousand kinds of indescribable blessings, Lord Guan offered him a drink. When Lord Liu saw that these two people also had exceptional physiques, he was very pleased and did not reject the offer, but took the cup and promptly drank it. When he had finished it, Zhang Fei offered him a cup, which he also accepted and finished. Fei invited him to sit with them, and after they had finished three cups of wine, the three of them stayed together as though old friends united in harmony.

But Zhang Fei said, "This is no place for us to sit. If you two gentlemen have no objection, let's go to my place and have a drink." When the two of them heard this, they promptly followed Fei to his house. In the back there was a peach orchard, and in that orchard there was a little pavilion. Fei thereupon

---

24. Yu was the mythic founder of the Xia dynasty (twentieth–sixteenth century BCE); Tang was the founder of the Shang dynasty (fifteenth–eleventh century BCE).

invited the two of them and brought wine to the pavilion, where the three of them happily drank. While they were drinking, each told his age: Lord Liu was the eldest, Lord Guan was the next, and Fei was the youngest. And so the eldest became the eldest brother, and the youngest the youngest brother. They slaughtered a white horse in sacrifice to Heaven, and killed a black ox in sacrifice to Earth. They did not find it necessary to be born on the same day, but they vowed to die on the same day. The three of them would be inseparable in walking, sitting, and sleeping. They swore to be brothers.

Lord Liu saw that the situation of the Han dynasty was as perilous as piled-up eggs: robbers and bandits arose in swarms and the common people suffered distress. [7a] He said with a sigh, "Should a real man live like this in this world?" Time and again they discussed how they could save the common people from this terrible situation, and how they could free the Son of Heaven from his powerless situation. They saw traitorous ministers ignore orders and bandits manipulate power, and were filled with indignation!

> Because dragon and tigers are filled with love and righteousness,
> Evil sons and slanderous ministers are startled from their sleep.

Let us speak now instead about that one day Zhang Fei informed his two elder brothers, "At present the Yellow Scarves rebels are spreading everywhere, plundering the people's money, and stealing their wives and daughters. If these rebels come here, I may be very rich, but I won't be able to do anything about it."

Xuande said, "So what should we do in such a situation?"

Fei said, "The best for us is to inform the Prince of Yan and hire some volunteer soldiers. Then what do we have to fear even if these rebels show up?"

Xuande and Lord Guan said, "Such an action makes sense." And so they got on their horses, left Zhang's home, and came to discuss the situation with the Prince of Yan.

In a snap of the fingers they had reached the steps before the palace of the Prince of Yan, but when they dismounted, they were barred from entering by the gatekeeper. Zhang Fei said, "I've come here for the very purpose of seeing the prince as I have something to discuss with him."

The gatekeeper replied, "Just wait here for a while and let me inform the prince." The gatekeeper reached the front of the main hall and stated, "There's someone outside the palace who wants to discuss something with you, my prince."

The Prince of Yan said, "Ask him in." Zhang Fei immediately followed the gatekeeper into the hall, and the Prince of Yan granted Zhang Fei a seat.

The Prince of Yan asked, "What is your business?"

"The Yellow Scarves," replied Zhang Fei, "are now spreading all over the world. Should they come to this city and it is completely unprepared, wouldn't they trample the capital of Yan to dust?"

The Prince of Yan replied, "That may be so, but the government storehouse is without money and the official granaries are empty, so I lack the food and fodder to provision an army. And who could be their leader?"

Zhang Fei said, "Even though I am only a lowly subject under your command,[25] I do have a bit of family property that can be used to provide for troops."

"But," replied the Prince of Yan, "even if we could summon some volunteers, whom could we appoint as their leader?"

Zhang Fei said, "There's someone staying at my place whose name is Liu Bei and he is also known as Xuande. He is a descendant of Liu Sheng, the Quiet Prince of Zhongshan. This man was born with a dragon's nose and a phoenix's eyes; his ears hang down below his shoulders and his hands hang down beyond his knees. He can be the leader."

The Prince of Yan immediately issued an order to raise the flag for summoning volunteers. Their leader was Liu Xuande, and under him served Guan Yunchang, Zhang Yide, Mei Fang, Jian Xianhe, and Sun Qian. [7b] Within a month they had summoned an army of three thousand five hundred volunteers.

The Campaign against the Yellow Scarves

The Prince of Yan was out one day with Liu Bei training troops on the parade grounds. When the Prince of Yan inspected them he saw that all of the troops and officers they had raised were strong and each of them was dauntingly brave. The Prince of Yan was very pleased. But at the main gate someone showed up who reported, "Disaster!"

Youzhou Commandery summoned braves who raised buckle and spear:
  The mutinous Yellow Scarves had come to seek out their own deaths.

When the Prince of Yan asked, "What kind of disaster?" the answer was, "Right now the Yellow Scarves are only a hundred *li* from this city and have come to take Youzhou."

The Prince of Yan said, "Leader of the volunteers, what shall we do?"

---

25. A tentative rendering of 某雖有上部下民, which we understand as an equivalency of 某雖是上部下民.

"My lord, don't worry," said Xuande, "I want to lead this army out to defeat the Yellow Scarves." Having said this, Xuande took his leave of the Prince of Yan and led the troops they had raised thirty *li* out of the city where they stationed themselves.

Xuande sat down in his tent and asked, "Who dares go forth to find out the strength of the bandit troops?" Before he had even finished speaking Zhang Fei, in front of the tent, spoke out, "I will. I want to go alone!"

Xuande replied, "Go, brother, but be careful!" When he had said this, Zhang Fei mounted his horse and left the camp.

In no time at all, Zhang Fei returned and dismounted from his horse in front of the tent, and reported, "Right now the Son of Heaven has sent out the grand marshal, Huangfu Song, with a writ of pardon. If there are any who have committed a crime, but who will summon troops and buy horses and dare defeat the Yellow Scarves, they will be given the seal of vanguard. And once they will have annihilated the Yellow Scarves, they will be appointed to office and given rewards. Brother, so my proposal is this: here we rely only on the lord of a single commandery, so it would be much better to join the grand marshal of the Han and spend our efforts on behalf of the state. Fighting in the east and extirpating in the west, conquering in the south and campaigning in the north, we will manifest our merit in the present and leave a name for the future."

When Xuande had heard Zhang Fei's words he was very pleased and immediately led the men under his command out of camp to welcome the grand marshal.

When the grand marshal arrived at the tent, he said, "Now the Son of Heaven pardons all of you for the crime of raising an army of volunteers. If you defeat the Yellow Scarves, you will be promptly given high office and rich reward." After he said this, the grand marshal granted Xuande a seat. Guan Yu, Zhang Fei, and the others were just about to depart.[26] And when the grand marshal noticed the heroic looks of Xuande, Guan, and Zhang, he was greatly pleased. "With such heroes as these, I see the Yellow Scarves traitors as no more than grass or weeds." The grand marshal immediately told Xuande to assume the seal of vanguard and then dispatched fast riders to go and determine [8a] the strength of the Yellow Scarves.

When the spies returned they reported, "The major force of the bandit troops are in Xiqing Prefecture in Yanzhou, and their five hundred thousand men are stationed in two places. Three hundred thousand are in Yanzhou. In Apricot-Forest Village, thirty *li* from Yanzhou, two leaders, called Zhang Bao and Zhang Biao, are in charge of the other two hundred thousand." The grand

---

26. Zhong Zhaohua (1990, 380) emends "about to depart" (待去) to "stood in attendance" (侍立), although the original text very clearly writes the former phrase.

marshal ordered the vanguard to lead fifty thousand troops to assess the real situation in Xiqing Prefecture.[27]

"I don't need fifty thousand," replied Liu Bei. "Using only the three thousand five hundred men now under my command, I will go first to Rencheng District and there make camp." The grand marshal's major force followed behind and also made camp in Rencheng District.

The grand marshal once again asked his officers who would be willing to go and find out the actual situation and persuade the bandits to surrender. Liu Bei said, "I am the vanguard now and I want to go." He was immediately provided with proclamations of pardon. When Liu Bei had been provided with these pardons, he took his leave of the grand marshal and led his own troops to the eastern gate of the district capital of Rencheng, where he made his way across the river to go to Ban Village. Xuande asked, "How far is it from here to Apricot-Forest Village?" "About fifteen *li*." Xuande then asked his troops, "Who can take this proclamation of pardon to Apricot-Forest Village and invite Zhang Biao to surrender?" As soon as he had finished speaking, Zhang Fei replied, "I want to go." "How many troops do you need?" "I don't need any," Zhang Fei replied, "I will go alone. I'll take the proclamation of pardon to Apricot-Forest Village and invite Zhang Biao to surrender."

So Zhang Fei departed, a single rider on a single horse. When he reached Apricot-Forest Village, soldiers guarding the gate tried, but were unable, to block his way and he proceeded straight to the commander's tent in the middle of the army, where he halted his horse and rested his lance across his saddle. Over fifty people were seated in that tent, and the one sitting in the middle was Zhang Biao. Around the tent over five hundred men readied their lances. Zhang Biao and his men were all surprised and Zhang Biao asked, "Who are you? Perhaps a spy?" Zhang Fei replied, "I am not a spy. I am a simple soldier in the vanguard command of the grand marshal of the Han. I didn't come here for any private business, but I bring you the sagely edict of the emperor and a proclamation of pardon. Even if you have committed the most defiant of crimes, plotting rebellion, or have killed officials appointed by the Son of Heaven, you will all be pardoned. If you join the Han, take off your Yellow Scarves, and raise the flags of our state, your sons will be ensured an appointment and your wife will be ennobled, and you will receive a high office and great rewards. But if you don't join us, you will all be slaughtered."

When Zhang Biao heard this, [8b] he was furious and ordered his underling to immediately set to . . . and they all came forward at once to try and stab Zhang Fei. He paid them no heed but firmly closed his fingers on the end of his eighteen-foot lance and twirled it in a circle so none of these troops could

---

27. This is one among many anachronisms in the text. Xiqing Superior Prefecture (襄慶府) did not come into existence until the Song dynasty, when it supplanted Yanzhou prefecture.

approach him. Who knows how many lances and bucklers of the bandit troops he snapped? The bandit troops in the camp cried out, and, frightened and scared, scattered on their own. On his single horse Zhang Fei moved at liberty through the bandit army and not a single one dared oppose him. Then the bandit troops heard the sounds of gongs and drums, and Zhang Biao saw someone report at the tent, "Your Majesty, a disaster!" Zhang Biao asked, "What kind of disaster?" "The vanguard of the Han has been divided into six companies of five hundred men each. With their bronze drums banging wildly, banners waving and troops yelling, they have captured the gate and are bursting into the camp." Zhang Biao led his troops as fast as he could in a mass flight to Yanzhou. The Han troops followed in hot pursuit for over fifty *li*.

Xuande then collected his troops, returned to Apricot-Forest Village, and made camp. He ordered his soldiers to guard the gates of the camp and then he checked on his officers. When he asked how far his troops had chased those bandit troops, the answer was, "They all entered the city of Yanzhou. The old and young were abandoned and we killed them all." Xuande then sent a report to the grand marshal and told him to hasten to Apricot-Forest Village. When the grand marshal saw the report, he was very pleased and immediately led his troops to Apricot-Forest Village. Liu Bei received the grand marshal and they sat together in the tent for a banquet.[28] The grand marshal issued an order, "All of the the troops of the vanguard and the officers and leaders under the command of the grand marshal shall be rewarded."

As they were banqueting, a spy arrived before the tent to report, "Zhang Biao just entered Yanzhou and has combined his troops with those of Zhang Bao; they have a huge force." When the spy had finished, the grand marshal issued an order, "Who dares take Yanzhou?" "I want to go," Xuande replied. The grand marshal was very pleased, "Since the bandit army is huge in numbers, and 'a few are no match for a crowd,' you should take some additional troops with you." But Liu Bei said, "I don't need many troops. It will suffice to take only a mixed troop of brave soldiers under my command." "Then go," replied the grand marshal, "but be careful."

Xuande immediately took his leave from the grand marshal and, provided with proclamations of pardon, rushed off to Yanzhou. At a distance of some ten *li* from Yanzhou he made camp. Xuande asked, "Who will take these proclamations of pardon and invite Zhang Biao and Zhang Bao to surrender?" Zhang Fei replied, "I want to go!" Xuande asked, [9a] "How many troops will you need?" "I will not need a single one," Zhang Fei replied, "I will go alone." But Xuande said, "I'm afraid something might go wrong. You should take five hundred troops with you." "No need," said Zhang Fei, and he repeated, "No need."

---

28. The reader will notice a large number of banquets in the text. These are normally ritual occasions for greeting people, for celebrating victories, etc.

Liu Bei said, "Then take a few less." Zhang Fei then said, "I am summoning those of you who willingly volunteer. If you follow me, the sons and grandsons of those who attain success will enjoy a state salary forever." At his first call, he got seven men and seven horses; at his second call he got three men and three horses; and at his third call he got two men and two horses, so all together they were thirteen, and he said, "This is enough."

Zhang Fei led the thirteen to Yanzhou, bearing the proclamations of pardon. When they arrived outside the city wall, Zhang Fei had a good look at the wall and moat, and the war towers and battle sheds on the wall. "Deer antlers" had been buried deep in the earth[29] and the moat had been dredged. On top of the wall he saw "rolling logs"[30] and catapult stones were everywhere; the draw-bridge was drawn up and the slide gates were lowered. From outside the city wall Zhang Fei loudly called out, "Who's up there? Let's talk!" After he spoke, a group of soldiers on the wall engaged in conversation with him, and asked, "Who are you, soldier?" Zhang Fei replied, "I am Zhang Fei, a soldier of the vanguard general under the command of the grand marshal of the Han." And he asked the man on the wall, "Who are you?" "I am the captain that holds Yanzhou, Zhang Bao." Zhang Fei said, "I am now bringing proclamations of pardon. If you surrender, you will be pardoned and everyone will be spared punishment, appointed to an office, promoted in rank, and richly rewarded. But if you do not surrender, you all will be massacred together." When Zhang Bao heard this he was enraged and immediately wanted to open the gate and engage him in battle.

But Zhang Biao said, "No way! When I was at Apricot-Forest Village, this guy rode right into my camp on a single horse; none of my troops could stop him. That's why Apricot-Forest Village was lost." When Zhang Bao asked, "What should we do in this case?" "Seal the gates tight," answered Zhang Biao, "And don't go outside, lest Zhang Fei have some trick up his sleeve. Let's send a written report to Yangzhou to ask for relief." Zhang Fei yelled out at the foot of the wall, but the people on top kept silent. A furious Zhang Fei circled the city cursing them loudly, but nobody reacted. He made another circuit and reached the south gate, where he shouted from the foot of the wall, "Who is guarding the gate?" But again nobody reacted.

When Zhang Fei saw no response, he said to his troops, [9b] "From the time we became soldiers of the Han, our saddles have never left our horses, and our armor has never left our bodies; pillowing on our bows, the sand was imprinted with moons, sleeping in our armor, the earth grew scales. On bitter campaigns in fierce battles, grappling with the enemy to see who lives or dies, we have really suffered! But today, we reach these willow trees here by the moat.

---

29. These are forked and sharpened branches that are set in the earth as a defense against cavalry.

30. Raised and lowered along the outside of the wall to crush attackers.

Let us shed our armor in the willows' shade, and bathe in the city moat while our horses rest under the trees." While doing so, Zhang Fei pointed to those on the city wall and cursed them once again.

Zhang Biao became enraged and, seeing that Zhang Fei was bathing in the city moat leaving man and horse unprepared, said to his elder brother, "If I do not kill this lout now, would I be capable of dying without shame?" His elder brother Bao said, "We have roughly five hundred thousand troops and a thousand officers. With a hundred thousand troops at its head, our army has rampaged throughout the world and no one dared oppose us. We have occupied two-thirds of the world of the Han. Look, soon all the land will belong to us. Today Zhang Fei appears on the scene. Just because you lost that little camp at Apricot-Forest Village, you are suddenly filled with fear and trepidation. Whether it be the highest general or the lowest of disbanded soldiers, if any among them dare to fight that Zhang Fei, I will give him rich rewards, and to hell with you." Zhang Biao said, "It was dark in the evening that day, my troops were not dressed in armor, and the horses were not saddled. And there was a ⚹ great force behind him. That's why I lost the camp at Apricot-Forest Village. But today that Zhang Fei is one of only thirteen men. After I lead a company of five thousand soldiers, I will surely capture Zhang Fei!" Zhang Bao said, "Younger brother, what you say is absolutely right."

He immediately took command of five thousand troops, lowered the drawbridge, and came out of the city. When Zhang Fei saw these troops leaving the city, they quickly mounted their horses and while on horseback put on their armor. Each held a weapon as they fled toward the south. They reached Yao Family Village, just forty *li* short of Yanzhou. Zhang Biao pursued them all the way to Apricot-Forest Village, where he saw a company of soldiers of over a thousand men, and the head general was none other than the vanguard commander Liu Bei. Holding his paired swords and dressed in a brocade battle gown, he halted his horse below his battle flag and shouted, "Who is the captain of these bandit troops?" "I am Zhang Biao!" When Xuande heard this he wheeled his horse and the two men began to fight. After some twenty rounds, five hundred troops launched a surprise attack from the rear. Their leader was Jian Xianhe. In the melee [10a] they inflicted a heavy defeat on Zhang Biao.

Zhang Biao turned his army toward Yanzhou and fled. Behind him, Liu Bei pressed the attack. At his front was a large forest from which another company of soldiers dashed out; there were over a thousand men. Their leader halted his horse and rested his sword across his saddle. Zhang Biao asked in a panic, "Who are you?" "I am just a soldier under the command of the vanguard of the ⚹ Han, a certain Guan Yunchang." He went on, "Bandit general, why don't you dismount from your horse and surrender?" Zhang Biao was alarmed. Yunchang came forward with his sword out, and Zhang Biao was even less inclined to meet such an enemy, so he fled by the backroads.

Liu Bei's troop caught up, and with Lord Guan they quickly dispatched nine-tenths of Zhang Biao's command leaving behind only a mere hundred or so. The battle continued until evening, moving forward to the walls of Yan-zhou. In a panic Zhang Biao shouted, "Open the gate! Behind is an ambush army that is about to overtake us." On top of the wall, Zhang Bao had the gate opened as fast as fire, and Zhang Biao and his troops, merely fifty or seventy men, entered the city. Outside the moat in the willow grove, Zhang Fei and his troops were lying in ambush and quickly rushed the city. Of Zhang Biao's troops who were killed, many fell into the water. Leading a hundred men or so, Zhang Fei shouted out, "Cut the cables of the drawbridge!" The whole pursuing army entered the city walls. Zhang Bao and Zhang Biao had no clue how many Han troops there might be, so in their panic they fled in the dark of night, out through the north gate. Yanzhou had been recaptured.

The next day, when the grand marshal had arranged a banquet and while they were deliberating what to do, a spy returned to report that the defeated army had entered Guangning Commandery. The grand marshal said, "Van-guard, tomorrow you lead your troops and go on ahead, then the main body of troops will break camp and we will all go to Yangzhou." He took the road to Shengzhou, passed by Haizhou, followed the Lian River and forded the Huai, passed Taizhou, and turned west to Yangzhou. The vanguard of Liu Bei arrived together at a place no more than a bowshot from the city, and there they made camp.

Let us speak now of Zhang Biao who did a roll call of his army. When Zhang Bao could not be accounted for since he had died in the melee, Zhang Jue was furious. On top of that a spy arrived to report, "We have discovered that the army of the Han is quite close and the vanguard Liu Bei has made camp a bow-shot away from the city wall." Zhang Jue summoned his officers and gave them explicit instructions, "Tomorrow the whole army has to empty out the city to go out to confront Liu Bei."

At daybreak the next day Zhang Jue led his army out. Liu Bei had divided his troops in three companies, and Guan Yu and Zhang Fei each led [10b] one. As soon as first forces arrived, the two armies engaged in battle. Guan Yu sud-denly attacked them from the rear and Zhang Fei pressured them from the sides. Liu Bei told his corporals to shout out, "If you bandit troops take off your yellow scarves and throw down your weapons, you will be covered by a pardon. If one of you captures Zhang Jue you will be ennobled as a Five-Hegemon Liege Lord!" As he finished speaking, the army of the grand marshal arrived. When the bandits saw this, they threw down their spears and discarded their armor. Countless numbers took off their yellow scarves and bowed down to submit. Zhang Jue and Zhang Biao died in the melee.

Once Liu Bei had captured Yangzhou, the grand marshal led his army into the city and issued an order to comfort the common people so they would not suffer in the slightest. Anyone who disobeyed would be punished according to military law. So the common people were all happy. The grand marshal also issued this order: that from the vanguard down, all officers and troops should join him for a banquet the next day.

Humiliation at Court and in the Province

The following day all attended the banquet, and the grand marshal said, "My officers, many thanks for all your efforts in defeating the Yellow Scarves." After giving each man a reward, he wrote a memorial to the court and selected an auspicious date to return with the army. When they arrived at Chang'an, the grand marshal ordered them all to make camp outside the eastern gate. He told Liu Bei, "All of the merit from defeating the Yellow Scarves is yours. After I have had an audience with the emperor, and I will tell him everything about this defeat of the Yellow Scarves, and our lord and king will clearly understand." "Make camp outside the eastern gate," he told Liu Bei, "and wait for two or three days."

One day when Liu Bei was seated with some liege lords, a corporal came to report that an emissary of the Han wanted to see the vanguard. As soon as Liu Bei heard this, he hurried out of the palace gate to welcome him. After this emissary had taken his seat in the central commander's tent and, when Liu Bei was done with his formal greetings, Liu asked, "Constant Attendant, why are you here?" "Don't you know who I am? I am one of the Ten Constant Attendants!"[31] This person, Duan Gui, went on to berate him, saying, "All of us have discussed this. Lord Xuande, you must have collected a countless number of gold, pearls, and other precious goods when you defeated those Yellow Scarves. If you are willing to offer us three hundred thousand strings' worth of gold and pearls, we will have you enfeoffed as a marquis with full regalia—your belt will be gold and your gown will be purple." Liu Bei replied, "I have taken no more than cities and military camps. All the gold and pearls and woven goods were collected by the grand marshal. I never received the slightest portion." Upon hearing this, Duan Gui abruptly rose to his feet and, after he had taken a few steps, turned his head to glare at Liu Bei, "You starving beggar from Upper-

---

31. These were a group of twelve eunuchs who held considerable power under Emperor Ling, who actually called two of them his father and mother. Duan Gui was one of the twelve.

Mulberry Village! [11a] You have plenty of gold and pearls, but are unwilling to give them to anyone else." Zhang Fei was enraged, and with flailing fists he stepped right up to Duan Gui, and before Liu Bei and Lord Guan could pull him back by his clothes, his fist hit Duan full on his lips. His back teeth fell out of his mouth and two front teeth were also knocked out. His mouth was filled with blood. Duan Gui went back with his hand covering his mouth. And Liu Bei said to Zhang Fei, "You've caused trouble for our men!"

At daybreak the next day, the grand marshal came and invited Liu Bei, "My report has already been submitted to the emperor. The merit is all yours." He instructed him to wait the next morning in a green robe and with a sophora tablet outside the palace gate for the sagely edict.

Liu Bei went to the palace gate but even after about half a month he still had not been summoned, "I see that all of the generals under the command of the grand marshal have been summoned, have all received an official title, have been rewarded, and have gone to their place of appointment." But outside lingered Liu Bei, who waited for over a month and still was never summoned. When the three of them were in their own camp, Liu Bei was depressed and eyed Zhang Fei, "That one blow you landed on Duan Gui has implicated the whole troop and brought them suffering." When he was pondering this, the troops of the Mixed Tiger banner all came to complain to Liu Bei and to say goodbye to Zhang Fei, "We officers all see that those who have merit are never called while those without merit receive rewards. We can wait no longer and each of us will now head back home." Liu Bei told them, "Every iota of the merit belongs to our army. If troops without merit receive a reward, how much more do we deserve it? The Han emperor will make no mistake in this; he must be computing the greatness of our merit. You should all wait for a few more days."

The next day, Liu Bei once again went to the palace gate to wait for the sagely edict. When the morning audience was finished and the civil officials and military officers all left through the inner gate, he saw a four-horse carriage with silver bells, gold stupas, and a brown canopy. After Liu Bei shouted "Injustice" three times, the official in that carriage asked, "Who are you, you who are crying that you have suffered an injustice?" Liu Bei stood in front of the carriage and said, "I am the vanguard Liu Bei who defeated the Yellow Scarves." "And why do you claim that you have suffered an injustice?" Liu Bei replied, "All of the other officers under the command of the grand marshal have received rewards and, after promotion, have gone to their place of appointment. Only I, Liu Bei, and my troops have attended the court for over a month without ever being summoned. Now my soldiers are all starving and are leaving me." The man in the carriage was Dong Cheng, an imperial relative, the father-in-law of the emperor, and he said, "That's yet another case of the Ten Constant Attendants creating disorder. Vanguard, please wait outside the inner gate and let me go back to report this to the emperor."

After some two hours he came back out of the palace and said, "Vanguard, come along with me." [11b] When they arrived at his house, the emperor's father-in-law invited Liu Bei to a simple meal. Liu Bei bowed and showed his respects with folded hands as he asked, "Father-in-law of the emperor, may I be allowed to ask what kind of memorial was submitted by the grand marshal?" "Today it was already too late to ask. But tomorrow during the morning audience the high ministers will discuss your case and determine your office and rewards. Tomorrow you will hear the sagely edict."

The following day when he went again to the palace gate to hear the sagely edict, the Ten Constant Attendants summoned him inside, "The vanguard Liu Bei is called to hear the Sagely Edict!" When Liu Bei had made his bows and had prostrated himself on the ground, he was asked, "How many days have you been without provisions since you arrived here, in Chang'an?" Liu Bei replied, "Thirty-seven days." "From Chang'an to Dingzhou is only a few days of travel. When you get to Dingzhou, you calculate the total number of days and then ask for provisions. The grain and straw that was earlier not paid out[32] will all have to be made up then. Liu Bei will take up the position of defender of Anxi District at Dingzhou. Because the bandits and robbers in the Taihang Mountains are so numerous, you will suppress them with the troops under your own command."

Liu Bei set out and when he arrived in Dingzhou, he paid his respects to the magistrate of Anxi district; when he visited the county office, a clerk read out his visiting card addressed to the officials of Dingzhou, "The district defender of Anxi district presents himself!" When he arrived before the hall and had barely begun to make his bows, the enraged prefect shouted, "Liu Bei, stop bowing!" He ordered his underlings to grab Liu Bei and said, "Those Yellow Scarves that you failed to defeat are now hiding away in our mountains and fields, terrorizing the common people!" And the prefect also asked, "From here, Chang'an is quite close. How come you have surpassed the set number of days for travel by more than half a month? Soused with wine and proud of your merit you must have thought your office too small and so on purpose have delayed your arrival." Liu Bei replied, "Prefect, with your permission, three thousand five hundred men with their dependents are roughly twelve thousand people, all pushing carts or carrying loads and carrying their children in their arms. The old and weak also cannot proceed so quickly. So I beg Your Excellency to be merciful, and I will ask for no additional rations at all." The furious prefect interrogated him again, "One way or another you should have sent the soldiers on ahead first and let the old and young follow behind. Don't try to worm yourself out of this!" He ordered his underlings to lock him up and

---

32. The Chinese text says "discarded" or "abandoned."

obtain a confession for "dilatory obstruction." But the moment he was about to put his brush to paper to formalize his decision, his underlings suggested to Yuan Qiao, "In view of his merit in defeating the Yellow Scarves spare him for the moment from caning!" So he ordered his underlings to drag Liu Bei [12a] around the hall three times, but after the subordinate officials to his left and right had once again pleaded with him, the prefect shouted, "District defender, go back to your own office and be very careful in what you do!"

When Liu Bei arrived at his office and greeted Guan, Zhang, and the other officers, he invited them to the front hall. While they were having their meal and sitting there, Zhang Fei asked Xuande, "Brother, how come you are so distraught? Liu Bei replied, "I have now become a district defender, but it's only an appointment of the ninth rank. You, Guan, Zhang, and the other officers while in the army defeated over five hundred thousand Yellow Scarves, but whereas I became an official, you, my two brothers, received no office. That's why I am so distraught." "Brother, that can't be the case!" Zhang Fei said, "You were not distraught during the ten days on the road from Chang'an to Dingzhou. So why are you so distraught after coming back from paying your respect at the county? It must be that the prefect treated you badly in some way. Elder brother, you should tell us." But Xuande didn't say a word.

After Zhang Fei had left Xuande, he thought, "If I want to know the truth, I will have to make some inquiries." He went to the back stables where he saw Liu Bei's two personal attendants, but when he asked them, they refused to tell him anything. After Zhang Fei had questioned them, he flew into a rage. When the second watch came that night, he left the office of the defender with a sharp sabre in his hands. He reached the rear of the county compound, jumped over the wall, and went on. As he reached a flower garden in the back, he saw a woman and asked her, "Where are the sleeping quarters of the prefect? If you don't tell me I will kill you!" Her body quaking and filled with fear, she said, "The prefect is sleeping in the back room." "And what are you to the prefect?" "I am the woman who makes his bed." Zhang Fei said, "Then take me to the back room."

The woman led Zhang Fei to the back room, where he killed her, and then he also killed the Prefect Yuan Qiao. There was a concubine in the lamplight who cried out, "Murderer!" So he also killed the concubine. But, because of this the yamen night guard was aroused, and about thirty men rushed in to seize Zhang Fei. He slew more than twenty archers, leapt over the rear wall, and escaped, returning to his own compound.

At dawn the next day all of the officials, high and low, called on the District Defender, Liu Bei, to discuss the situation. Liu Bei was determined to pursue the killer and immediately notified the court of his intention. But, the Ten Constant Companions declared, "The murderer who killed the prefect had [12b] to have been someone from the District Defender's group."

The court dispatched the Inspector General Cui Lian to go, in the capacity of Censor, to settle in at Dingzhou Posthouse. All officials high and low paid a visit to the envoy and asked him, "Sir, what assignment do you have?" The Inspector General replied, "They have sent me here to question you because of the murder of the magistrate. Is the District Defender here?"

"The District Defender is outside but dares not pay his respects." The envoy then summoned the District Defender, who entered to make a formal visit with three hundred soldiers, among whom were Guan, Zhang, and twenty or thirty of the defender's entourage. The envoy said, "Are you the District Defender?" "I am," replied Liu Bei. "Did you kill the magistrate?" asked the envoy. Liu Bei replied, "The magistrate was in his rear apartments; they were lit by lamps and candles, and there was a night guard of thirty or so men. If you insist that the man who killed twenty or so of the magistrate's men and then escaped from such a well-lit place must have been Liu Bei, then of course it must have been Liu Bei."

The Inspector General spoke angrily, "In the past you were the reason that your sworn brother Zhang Fei knocked out Duan Gui's two front teeth. Today the sage's directive has sent me here to question you about the magistrate's killer. Earlier, when you paid your respects at the county, you had failed to arrive within the prescribed number of days allowed for travel. You should have been sentenced for that crime, but out of respect for all of the officers, you were not. Because of this incident you bore resentment and killed the magistrate. So don't try to wriggle your way out of it!" He shouted to his attendants, "Take him!"

On either side, Guan Yu and Zhang Fei were enraged, and each ran up into the hall carrying a blade and frightened the host of officials, who all fled. They captured the envoy and stripped him. Zhang Fei helped Liu Bei sit on a chair, and then he bound the envoy to a hitching post at the front of the hall, where he was soon dead after being bastinadoed more than a hundred times. The corpse was split into six sections, the head was hung outside the north gate, and the feet and hands strung from the four corners. Then Liu Bei, Guan Yunchang, Zhang Fei, and all of the generals and troops went to ground in the Taihang Mountains.

The court was informed of this. One day the emperor received his ministers in audience, and asked the civil officials and military officers, "At present there are still very many Yellow Scarves who have not yet been defeated, and now Liu Bei has rebelled too. What should we do if these two join forces?" The Imperial Father-in-law [13a] Dong Cheng stepped forward from the ranks and said, "May Your Majesty live a myriad years. At present Liu Bei has not rebelled. It is all because of the Ten Constant Attendants who measure out on their scales the value of official posts in order to sell them: those who have money and goods become officials, and those who have merit are not rewarded. Your Majesty, if you follow my advice, Liu Bei will not rebel." The emperor said, "How can we invite Liu Bei to surrender?" "Now kill the Ten Constant Attendants and take the heads of seven of them to the Taihang Mountains, then you can invite those three brothers to surrender." The emperor said, "We will follow your advice." And he asked, "Who can go?" Dong Cheng replied, "I will go."

While Dong Cheng was going to the Taihang Mountains with the heads of these seven men, he ran into a band of soldiers. Dong Cheng engaged in conversation with these troops, and said, "I bring a sagely edict inviting you to surrender. Because the Ten Constant Attendants squeezed the court and the provinces for money and bribes, carefully calculating profit in order to sell offices, they have been executed and killed. I now bring their heads to show to you brothers, and you are also pardoned for the crimes of killing the prefect and whipping the inspector to death—it's all covered by the pardon." Liu Bei prostrated himself on the ground as he listened to the proclamation of pardon. After Liu Bei had expressed his gratitude for the imperial favor, he followed the Imperial Father-in-law back to Chang'an, where he was received in audience by the emperor. The happy emperor gave him rewards and promoted him to office, sending him to be the assistant magistrate of Pingyuan district in Dezhou. The subordinate officials to his left and right also received rewards.

Dong Zhuo and Lü Bu

Because Emperor Ling had passed away, Emperor Xian was immediately elevated as lord. He left Chang'an and established his capital at the Eastern Capital Luoyang. The prime ministers were Wang Yun, Cao Yong, and Ding Jianyang. One day the emperor received his ministers in audience. Wang Yun stepped forward from the ranks and reported to the emperor, "We have received a written report from Xiliang Prefecture that the two Yellow Scarves, Zhang and Li, and two other major miscreants have occupied Xiliang Prefecture with over three hundred thousand troops." The emperor said, "What should we do now?" And the emperor also asked Wang Yun, "Who dares go?" Wang Yun proposed, "You should summon Dong Zhuo as grand marshal. Dong Zhuo has a courage to which ten thousand men cannot stand up. He is eight feet, five inches tall; he is fat and well muscled and has a huge belly, and can be recommended to capture those bandits.[33] When he joins the fray he wears heavy armor, runs as fast as a runaway colt, and sitting, he can snatch a flying swallow right out of the air. He can do the job as grand marshal. Under his command he has a thousand battle-tested officers and he leads over five hundred thousand troops."

---

33. The Chinese texts here write "*ju tao wang zhi zuo* 舉討王之作," which makes no sense. One possibility is that the word "king" (*wang*) is a mistake for *zei* 賊, "bandit," although the mistake would neither be a scribal miscopy nor a phonological replacement.

The emperor followed his advice and summoned Dong Zhuo to court, where he promoted him in rank and nobility and appointed him as grand master and grand marshal of the empire. The emperor asked Dong Zhuo, "Now [13b] we have received a written notification from Xiliang that over three hundred thousand Yellow Scarves are causing havoc there. Who can defeat them?" Dong Zhuo replied, "I want to go!"

As he was about to set out with his army, they suddenly heard a great commotion inside the city walls. The city gates were closed as, immediately, thousands of soldiers were given their orders. All of the streets in the front and alleys behind were guarded by soldiers who had covered everything like a net-weave that was tied tight at the corners. They saw a man on horseback who looked like a fierce tiger. He set the government troops aflight—who knows how many he killed. The number of troops and officers was increased and increased again, until there were enough to finally subdue this man. The Grand Preceptor Dong Zhuo loudly shouted, "Who are you?" But the man did not answer. The common folk all shouted out at the top of their voices, "This guy is a slave of Ding Jianyang. He just killed Minister Ding and the army subdued him just as he was fleeing on the minister's horse!" The Grand Preceptor was blessed with more troops and officers and therefore could nab this man; after tying him up they took him to the commander's headquarters.

Dong Zhuo settled into his seat and then interrogated him, "Just who is the one we just caught? What is your name?" As soon as he had finished speaking came the reply, "I am Lü Bu, also known as Fengxian." "Why did you kill all the people on the street with your dagger-axe?" He was just about to get into the details when someone from Minister Ding's household said, "He killed Prime Minister Ding for no other reason than this horse!" When Dong Zhuo asked him what was so special about this horse, this servant of Ding's replied again, "This horse is out of the ordinary. The spots of blood that appear all over it are bright red, and its manes and tail are like fire, so it is called Red Harrier. The prime minister said that it was not called a red harrier because it was bright red, but it was called a harrier horse because it was used for hunting hares with a bow: when you were riding on dry land and if it sees a hare, it will not start, so there is no need to rein it in or to make it hold firm for the bowshot. That's why it is called Red Harrier.[34] He also said that when this horse came to a river, it would ford the water just as if it were on level land. When it reached the middle of the river, it didn't eat grass or straw but swallowed fish and turtles. This horse can go a thousand *li* in a single day and can carry over eight hundred pounds. This is no ordinary horse!" When he finished speaking, Lü Bu said, "I did not

---

34. Following the reading of Nikaidō and Nakagawa (1999, 68). "Harrier," while usually referring only to foxhounds, is used here to avoid the mistake of thinking the steed resembles a large red hare, rather than being an excellent mount for chasing hares.

kill my master because of the horse." Bu went on, "Over a long period of time my master constantly shamed me. That's why I killed Prime Minister Ding."

Dong Zhuo saw that this Lü Bu was ten feet tall and had a waist of seven double handspans. Alone he had slain over a hundred people: such a hero was rare in the world! [14a] "Right now is the time that such people as you are needed. What if I pardon your crime?" "Grand Preceptor," replied Lü Bu, "I will be happy to present you your whip and hold up your stirrups.[35] Allow me to honor you as my father." A very pleased Grand Preceptor thereupon released Lü Bu.

That day the Grand Preceptor took command of his troops of five hundred thousand and a thousand battle-tested officers. To his left rode his adoptive son Lü Bu, astride Red Harrier, dressed in golden armor and wearing a *xiezhi* cap.[36] He used a twelve-foot-long square-heaven dagger axe;[37] from its top dangled a yellow pennant and leopard tail. He could run faster on foot than any cavalry mount. He served as General of the Left. To Dong Zhuo's right rode Li Su, a descendant of Li Guang[38] of the Han. This man wore a silver helmet and an armor of silver chainmail over a white battle dress. He used a fifteen-foot spear with a sickle-shaped Wu hook with a gathering of strings hanging from the base of its blade. He also carried a bow and arrow. For those who excelled in the civil arts, he had the grandee Li Ru, and for those who excelled in the martial arts, he had Lü Bu and Li Su—these three people supported Dong Zhuo.

When Dong Zhuo had led his army to Xiliang Prefecture, he conquered it at the first roll of the drum. He accepted the surrender of Zhang and Li and those two other miscreants together with their three hundred thousand troops. He then proceeded to the Eastern Capital Luoyang, and some twenty *li* to the northwest of Luoyang he had corvée laborers construct a walled city, which he called Meiyang.[39] He ordered Zhang and Li to station their troops there and

---

35. A humility, "to serve you in the meanest position."

36. This was a cap worn by censors and judicial officials, which was usually square with a long horizontal nail through it. Its name comes from that of a mythical beast, the *xiezhi*, that could root out evil with its single horn.

37. The "square heaven" dagger axe had two crescent-shaped blades set opposite each other on the staff, below the point. The tips of the crescents are at the right angles of a perfect square.

38. A famous general of the Han dynasty.

39. Zhong Zhaohua (1990, 409 note 178) suggests that Meiyang (梅陽) may stand for 美陽, which is the name given to a site west of Chang'an in Dong Zhuo's biography in the *Documents of the Later Han* (see Fan Ye 1965, 2320). On his return from Xiliang, Dong Zhuo made a walled encampment here to "guard the imperial mausoleum." While this may be true, it is more likely that it is a loan for the homophone 郿, a walled and fortified site that Dong Zhuo created for himself and his family just east of Chang'an, known as Meiwu 郿塢. See Fan Ye (1965, 2029). None of these historical sites are near Luoyang.

to request government provisioning. Dong Zhuo was going to stage an armed rebellion and he was constantly plotting for the empire of Han.

Dong Zhuo asked Li Ru, "Who can hold Xiliang Prefecture now that those four major bandits have left Xiliang?" "Grand Master," replied Li Ru, "your son-in-law Niu Xin is suitable." The Grand Master summoned Niu Xin to lead one hundred thousand troops to Xiliang and garrison the place.

Let us return now to Emperor Xian, who secretly summoned the Imperial Father-in-law Dong Cheng to the inner apartments. When the latter arrived there, the emperor stated his sagely command, "At present Dong Zhuo usurps my power. What can be done about it?" Dong Cheng replied, "My king, summon the liege lords of the empire and let them take you to Chang'an to establish your capital there. Then order the liege lords of the empire to combine their forces to kill Dong Zhuo. In that way peace will return to the empire." The emperor asked, "Who is suitable to undertake this mission?" "I have under my command a colonel in charge of storerooms.[40] He is right for the mission for he has the right bold mettle. If he carries off this important affair then he can be made grand marshal. Summon the Prince of Ji, Yuan Shao, and the Prince of Zhenhuai, Yuan Shu, and as army supervisor employ the Prince of Changsha, Prefect Sun Jian." [14b]

A man came before the steps and, after he had loudly shouted out "Ten thousand years," the emperor asked him, "Your name, sir?" "I am Cao Cao, also known as Mengde." When Emperor Xian observed this man closely, he was a match for twenty Dong Zhuos. At this moment the empire of the Han was at a loss what to do, so it had to employ this man! Emperor Xian gifted Cao Cao with rewards and sent him off, but with fear in his eyes, "If you succeed in this great mission, I will promote you to grand marshal of the empire. Be very circumspect in what you do. If you achieve success, I will promote you to Prime Minister of the Left."

After Cao Cao had taken his leave from the emperor and left the city to unite all of the liege lords, he then proceeded to Dingzhou to meet with its prefect Gongsun Zan. As he was traveling, he noticed that the *li* markers were properly arranged and that bridges and roads were in good repair; the communities were populous and cattle and horses in good supply; no fields were left fallow and the harvests were plentiful. Cao Cao called a farmer over and asked him, "What is this place?" The farmer answered, "Let me inform you, your honor: this is Pingyuan District in Dezhou." A surprised Cao Cao asked the farmer, "Who is the district magistrate here?" The farmer replied, "The district magistrate pays

---

40. While the text clearly writes *dianku* 典庫, it is likely that this is a scribal error for one of the "Eight Colonels of the Western Garden" (西園八校尉), known as "The Colonel of the Rear Guard" (*dianjun xiaowei* 殿軍校尉).

no attention to anything, only the assistant magistrate does." When he asked who the assistant magistrate might be, the farmer answered, "It's that Liu Bei who defeated the Yellow Scarves a while back." Cao Cao was greatly surprised and said, "If I can unite the liege lords, this place will provide the executioner who will behead Dong Zhuo!"

With thirty riders, Cao Cao waited outside the gates of the district yamen, and had his servants report to Liu Xuande that he was there. The gate guard told Liu Bei, "There is an imperial envoy of the Han outside of the yamen gate. You, sir, should hurry out to receive him." The various officers greeted Cao Cao, led him into the yamen, and had him sit at the head of the hall. When the ritual greetings were finished, each took their place at the feast mat. After they had gone through several courses, each accompanied by wine, Cao said, "I bear the Sage's directive to summon the liege lords of the twenty-eight garrisons. Now Dong Zhuo wields the power of the throne and has long plotted to seize the world of Han. I am to direct all the liege lords to protect His Majesty, pacify the empire, and smash Dong Zhuo. But there are Lü Bu and Li Su, each of whom has unmatched courage—no one can match them. Because I was on my way to inform Han Fu in the Henghai Command in Cangzhou, I passed by Pingyuan District, and heard that Xuande was here. So I came particularly to pay you my respects. Please don't throw up any barriers to this, Lord Xuande. For the sake of the world of Han, if you go to Tigerkeep Pass and smash Dong Zhuo and Lü Bu, [15a] I will recommend you, sir, to be invested as a myriarch liege lord and be placed into the ministerial offices."

Cao Cao took up his cup and toasted Liu Bei, who said, "I, this humble officer, have no skill in the martial arts and am unfamiliar with bow and horse; I fear I will ruin this affair of state." At his side Zhang Fei spoke up, "Brother! From the time we bound ourselves in righteousness at the Peach Orchard, together we have smashed the Yellow Scarves and made a name for ourselves in history. Now, for the state, this is precisely the juncture to utilize men. Let us follow all of the liege lords to Tigerkeep Pass and do battle with Dong Zhuo and Lü Bu. Relying on the emperor's great beneficence, after we kill Dong Zhuo and Lü Bu we will have our names inscribed in the Lingyan Gallery.[41] And that is so much better than being just a magistrate in Pingyuan District. We will be able to wear golden belts and robes of purple, to offer protected privilege to our sons, and to have our wives invested with noble title. If you don't want to go, brother, I do." Cao Cao thanked him as soon as he heard this utterance. When the feast was done, Cao Cao reminded them twice and then once again,

---

41. An anachronistic reference to the palace of the founding emperor of the Tang, where he had portraits painted of twenty-four people who aided him in establishing the dynasty. Here it simply means "we will become noted men who have aided the continuation of the Han."

"General Zhang has promised to go. But if he arrives late, I will send an envoy to request the three of you." Cao Cao withdrew and started down the road.

Xuande returned to his lodgings where he discussed it all thoroughly with his brothers. He explained, "If we go and we wind up unused after we get there, where can we return?" "Relax, brother," said Zhang Fei, "I'll go alone to smash Dong Zhuo and execute Lü Bu." Xuande said, "Wait until the envoy comes before you leave."

The Battles at Tigerkeep Pass

Let us go back now to speak about Emperor Xian in Luoyang, who was weak and incompetent as a ruler. The Grand Preceptor Dong Zhuo wielded all power. Dong weighed three hundred pounds and was set on usurping the state. He carried his sword when he entered the palace[42] and everyone—civil and military—was terrified of him. He constantly bullied and suppressed the liege lords of the empire, and he relied on these subordinates: his adopted son Lü Bu, the civilian Li Su, the four bandits, and the eight strong generals.

Let us now speak instead of the prefect of Qiao Commandery, Cao Cao, who had gone to court a second time to have an audience with the emperor. Seeing how Dong Zhuo used his power to bully others, he found the situation even more unbearable. When court was finished, he again sent up a memorial to the emperor to discuss how he might, in a hidden way, put a secret edict into effect to assemble all of the liege lords in the empire in front of Tigerkeep Pass, there to join together to smash Dong Zhuo. The emperor decreed that on the third day of the third month of the fifth year of Zhongping[43] the multitude would assemble before Tigerkeep Pass. Immediately he ordered him to summon all liege lords across the empire and to arrive as soon as possible before the pass.

The soldiers of Changsha were the earliest and the prefect of Changsha, Sun Jian, was the first to reach the pass. Yuan Tan of Qingzhou did not go. When all the armies and horses of the empire were in front of the pass, they lacked [15b] fodder and provisions. In order to press for grain, Cao Cao went to pressure Yuan Tan to go. In a few days, Cao had gone as far as Pingyuan District where he, when he finished greeting Xuande, said, "All of the liege lords are at Tigerkeep Pass, what about you three generals?" Xuande said nothing, but Zhang Fei spoke, "I see that the world of Han is now without a proper ruler, and that we should slay that traitorous official, the Grand Preceptor, to reestablish the

---

42. Forbidden to any, except the imperial guard.

43. April 15, 188.

house of Han." The First Ruler Liu Bei[44] finally relented. Cao said, "The Prince of Ji, Yuan Shao, is now the generalissimo, and you can take a letter to him." The prime minister then wrote a letter and turned it over to the First Ruler. After Lord Cao departed, he went straight to Qingzhou.

But let us now speak of Guan, Zhang, and Liu, who mobilized three thousand brave cavalry from their subordinates and selected a day on which to begin their journey to the southwest. They had been on the road for several days when they set up their tents about five or six *li* from the main camp at Tigerkeep Pass. On the next day the three put their battle raiment in order and went first to see the generalissimo, arriving at the gate of the camp.

Let us return now to Yuan Shao, Prince of Ji, who had assembled the liege lords in his tent, and asked them, "The house of Han is now without a ruler and a traitorous official is wielding power. Emperor Xian is in Luoyang but is incompetent and weak. Dong Zhuo is at Tigerkeep Pass, where he has a hundred noted generals. The best of those is the unmatchable Marquis of Wen, Lü Bu, who is nine feet, two inches tall and employs a 'square-heaven halberd.' You many liege lords: how can you set a plan to execute the traitorous minister to repay the court and leave a name for those who follow?" The whole group of officers was silent.

Suddenly they heard the sound of a commotion outside the camp gates. The gate guard reported, "There are three generals outside the camp gate to see you." The Prince of Ji quickly ordered them to be brought before him. The host of officers all looked at the general who was the leader. His face was like a full moon, his earlobes hung past his shoulders, his arms drooped below his kneecaps, and he had an aquiline nose and dragon face. He truly had the features of an emperor and king. The general below and to his left was nine feet, two inches tall, a man of Xieliang in Puzhou, called Guan Yu, also known as Yunchang. Below and on his left was a man of Zhuojun in Youzhou, Zhang Fei, also known as Yide, who had a leopard head and round eyes, the neck of a sparrow, and the whiskers of a tiger. The Prince of Ji asked, "Who are you three generals?" The First Ruler replied, "This useless one is a man of Dasang Village in Zhuo Commandery, in Youzhou. I am Liu Bei, currently District Magistrate in Pingyuan." "Are you the 'green robed one with [16a] sophora screed?'"[45]

44. Liu Bei is often referred to as the First Ruler, as eventually he would become the first ruler of Shu-Han. He is distinguished in this way from his son, the second and last ruler of Shu-Han, who is often called the Young Ruler or Later Ruler.

45. A lower-level official; so named because of the green robe and official plaque made of sophora wood. Here the use is a denigrating designation for Liu Bei, who stood outside the palace gates in such attire for weeks awaiting an audience.

"Yes," replied the First Ruler. "Because the prefect of Qiao Commandery passed by and left a letter for me, I've now come to the pass to smash Dong Zhuo together with you." The Prince of Ji was elated.

The First Ruler took out the letter and turned it over to Yuan Shao. After Yuan Shao finished reading it, he asked the host of liege lords, "What about this?" In a thundering voice one of the generals in the tent shouted out, "The liege lords have assembled here at Tigerkeep Pass and will cut off the heads of that traitorous minister Dong Zhuo and Lü Bu within days." The officers looked and it turned out to be the Grand Protector of Changsha, Sun Jian. Song Wenju said, "We don't need any 'green-robed esquire' to help us kill Dong Zhuo at the pass." When the host of officers heard this, they were all happy. The Prince of Ji asked again, but none of the officers spoke.

The three generals bade goodbye to the Prince of Ji and went out of the camp to their own bivouac about five or six *li* to the northeast. "If we had been in Pingyuan," said Zhang Fei, "we would never have suffered such shame because of another." They had an audience with Yuan Shao at dawn on the following day, but the host of officers expressed their displeasure again. The three generals went back out again, and the next day they hit the road directly back to Pingyuan. They had gone but a few *li* when they encountered Cao Cao, and they told him truthfully everything that happened. Cao Cao laughed and said, "Follow me back again. If you smash this traitorous official and establish great merit, no office is out of your reach." The next day they returned with their army and reached the grand camp of Yuan Shao.

Two days later, Cao Cao spoke in the camp, "Xiao He recommended Han Xin three times, and this gave rise to the Han, which has lasted for four hundred years." The Prince of Ji was setting out a grand feast and invited Prime Minister Cao and the liege lords. Just as the main banquet was progressing, someone reported that the Marquis of Wen, Lü Bu, was challenging them to battle at Tigerkeep Pass. The Prince of Ji asked, "Who dares battle to death with Lü Bu?" He hadn't finished speaking when everyone saw a general come forth, and they recognized him as the Infantry General Cao Bao, who was in the employ of Tao Qian, the prefect of Xuzhou. He spoke of his own volition, "I will battle to death with Lü Bu, and I want to capture him." The assembled officers were all delighted. He got on his horse and arrayed his troops against Lü Bu, but he was quickly taken by Lü. In less than two hours his defeated troops had returned, explaining that the Marquis of Wen had seized Cao Bao after a single round. The Prince of Ji was alarmed. Someone then said, "But they have released Cao Bao to return!" When Cao Bao entered the camp, the host of officers all said, "Lü Bu is undefeatable and wants only to capture us, we liege lords of the eighteen garrisons." Every one of the officers was filled with fear.

At dawn of the next day, a spy reported, "Lü Bu has left Tigerkeep Pass with an army of thirty thousand [16b] and challenges us to battle." The Prince of

Ji asked the host of officers, "Who will do battle with the Marquis of Wen?" Before he had finished speaking, Sun Jian, prefect of Changsha, had led out his army and horse to face off with Lü Bu. He and Lü Bu had only fought for three rounds before Sun Jian was mightily defeated. Lü Bu chased him into a great forest and launched an arrow that struck Sun Jian. Sun Jian then employed "the golden cicada husks off its shell" stratagem—that is, he hung his armor and clothes on a tree and fled. Lü Bu sent the strong general Yang Feng off to Tigerkeep Pass with Sun Jian's helmet and battle garb to turn over to Dong Zhuo. But on his way, he ran smack into Zhang Fei, who wrestled the helmet and battle garb away from him.

At day's light, Zhang Fei reached Yuan Shao's great camp and got off his horse. He went to see the First Ruler and Lord Guan. Xuande explained, "Sun Jian said that we were nothing but cats and dogs, just sacks to stuff with food and bone racks on which to hang clothes." The First Ruler said, "He is the prefect of Changsha, and I am just a green-robed esquire. How can I even hope to get the best of him?" Zhang Fei laughed and shouted, "A real man doesn't worry about life or death, but plans a name for later generations!" Neither the First Ruler nor Lord Guan could stop him, and Zhang Fei took off straight for the Prince of Ji's tent, where he presented the helmet and battle garb to the prince. The Grand Protector Sun Jian and the other officers were silent. In a voice like a huge bell, Zhang Fei said, "Earlier the prefect called us the likes of cats and dogs. But when Lü Bu came out of the pass, the prefect got to escape by husking off his battle garb." Sun Jian was outraged when he heard this, and pushed Zhang Fei out with the intent of cutting off his head. All of the liege lords stood up, but Yuan Shao, Prince of Ji, Liu Biao, Prince of Jing, and Cao Cao of Qiao Commandery said, "Lü Bu's might cannot be matched. If we decapitate Zhang Fei, who will smash Dong Zhuo?" Sun Jian was silent, and Zhang Fei offered, "When Lü Bu comes out of the pass, we three brothers will cut the head off that slave." The host of officers was delighted and Zhang Fei managed to get out of it.

On the third day, Lü Bu came out to battle again, and all the liege lords went out of the encampment to face off with Lü Bu. Zhang Fei rode out holding his spear

The Three Battle Lü Bu

and battled with Lü for more than twenty rounds, but there was no clear winner. Lord Guan flew into a rage, let his horse run free, and twirling his blade battled twice with Lü Bu. The First Ruler couldn't stand it anymore and employed his double blades, riding three times against Lü Bu, who was greatly defeated and fled, returning back up Tigerkeep Pass to the northwest.

The next day Lü Bu came down out of the pass and shouted, "Send out the big-eyed fellow!" [17a] Zhang Fei, greatly enraged, came out on his horse, holding his divine eighteen-foot spear, and with round eyes glaring went straight away to seize Lü Bu. The two horses met for more than thirty rounds, but there was no clear winner.

Zhang Fei Battles Lü Bu Alone

Zhang Fei had always loved battle and he smashed into his opponent and battled him for thirty more rounds, and in that fight one of Lü Bu's battle flags wrapped around his face. Zhang Fei was like a god and Lü Bu quailed in his heart, and spurred his horse back up into the pass, closed it tightly, and did not come out again. Lü Bu had the four miscreants tightly guard the pass. These four miscreants were Li Jue, Guo Si, Zhang Ji, and Chu Chou.

Diaochan

Let us go back now to speak of Grand Preceptor Dong, who had intercepted the royal chariot in Luoyang and taken the emperor west into Chang'an. The emperor took a seat in the Palace of Eternal Peace and ordered the Grand Preceptor to lay a banquet. When it got late, the emperor, feeling the effects of the liquor, returned to his rear chambers. Dong Zhuo spied Consort Four,[46] and began to flirt with her in suggestive language. There was a prime minister there, Wang Yun, who in pique said to himself, "There is no ruler in the empire!"

Wang Yun went back to his residence and dismounted, and sat glumly in a small courtyard. He told himself that Emperor Xian was weak and powerless; now that Dong Zhuo had grasped power, the empire was in deep peril. Suddenly he saw a woman burning incense, remarking that she would not be able to return home and see her master again. She burned incense and made two bows. Wang Yun said to himself, "I am troubled by state affairs, but what's this woman praying for?" He had no other recourse but to go and ask her, "Why are you burning incense? Tell me the truth." He scared Diaochan so much that she fell quickly to her knees, daring not to hide anything. She truthfully revealed her feelings, "This humble concubine was originally surnamed Ren, and my child name was Diaochan. My master was Lü Bu, but we were separated at Lintao and haven't seen each other since. This is why I'm burning incense." The prime minister was overjoyed, "This woman is the one who will bring peace to

---

46. Emperor Xian's consort.

the Han empire." He returned to a hall and summoned Diaochan, "I will look upon you and treat you as my own child." He then gave her gold, pearls, and bolts of silk and sent her on her way.

Several days later, the prime minister invited Grand Preceptor Dong Zhuo to a banquet. As the day drew late, the Grand Preceptor was feeling the effects of the wine and the candles and lamps appeared to be flickering and shimmering. Wang Yun gathered dozens of beautiful women in a cluster, and placed Diaochan in the middle with the others around her. In her chignon were stuck short golden pins with green-tinted white jade; on her body she wore a chemise of crimson silk woven with golden threads. She was a veritable state-toppling, city-toppling beauty! Dong Zhuo [17b] was greatly taken aback, and his gaze moved over her awhile before he said to himself, "My rear chambers simply lack a woman like this!" Wang Yun had her sing, and the Grand Preceptor was delighted. Wang Yun said, "She's a person from Lintao, west of the pass;[47] her surname is Ren, and her child name is Diaochan." The Grand Preceptor became infatuated with her, and the prime minister assented to the match. When the feast ended, the Grand Preceptor also arose.

At dawn the next day, the prime minister thought to himself, "I have eaten my lord's salary as a minister, but now I have come up with a plan to make the house of Han secure once again. If I am not successful, I will at least earn a reputation through my death." Immediately he invited Lü Bu to a meeting and fêted him until late in the day, when the minister once again had Diaochan come out and sing at the banquet. Lü Bu looked at her and thought to himself, "Ding Jianyang rebelled at Lintao in those days past, and I didn't know where my wife Diaochan ended up. But here she is today!" Wang Yun took up a cup and spoke, "Marquis of Wen, your face has taken on a look of anxiety, but why?" Lü Bu rose from his seat and told everything in precise detail. The prime minister was overjoyed, "Now there is a ruler in the empire of Han!" The prime minister spoke again, "I didn't know she was your wife. There's nothing happier in the world than the reunion of husband and wife." And then he went on, "I have treated her as if she were my own daughter. Let's select an auspicious date and propitious hour, and I will send Diaochan to the residence of the Grand Preceptor, where she can become your wife again." Lü Bu was extremely happy, and as it drew late, he announced he was going home.

Within a few days Wang Yun dispatched Diaochan, accompanied by a young serving girl, in a four-in-hand, bearing rich gifts to the Grand Preceptor's residence. That day, the third day of the third month of the seventh year of the Zhongping reign,[48] the Grand Preceptor was sitting silently when someone

---

47. In modern Gansu.

48. This date does not in fact exist. The Zhongping reign ended in the sixth year. If this is the first year of the subsequent reign, it would be April 25, 190 CE.

reported, "Prime Minister Wang Yun has sent someone here in his four-in-hand and with rich gifts." The Grand Preceptor scurried out and welcomed him in the reception hall, remarking, "Is it Diaochan?" "Yes, it is," said Yun. The Grand Preceptor had wine put out. Wang Yun spoke, "I am feeling a little ill, so I won't tarry here." He bade the Grand Preceptor goodbye and left.

Late that night, Dong Zhuo and Diaochan drank together. Now Dong Zhuo was a lecher and a drunk. About two days later, when Lü Bu returned from the Serpentine,[49] he dismounted at the front of the residence, and his eight strong generals all scattered. Late that night the Marquis of Wen heard the sound of music tinkling and ringing in the residence, and he asked his attendants why it was happening. All of them explained, "He's got a woman from the prime minister; it's that Diaochan!" Lü Bu was greatly shaken and walked to a place underneath the gallery corridor, [18a] but there was no way he could see inside. Suddenly he saw Diaochan push aside the curtain and come out. Lü Bu was incensed and asked, "Where is that miscreant?" "He's already drunk," replied Diaochan. Lü Bu raised his sword and went into the hall, where he saw Dong Zhuo snoring like thunder, lying there like a mountain of flesh, and cursed him, "You, miscreant, you have no morals!" A single swipe of the sword cut his neck, and the fresh blood spurted out. He stabbed Dong Zhuo, who then died.

Lü Bu went quickly out of the house and fled to the prime minister's residence. Wang Yun quickly asked him what was happening. Lü Bu told him the whole story from the start. The prime minister, overjoyed, said, "You will be the most famous man of this age! If you had not slain Dong Zhuo, the Han empire would be in as much danger as a stack of piled-up eggs!" As they were speaking, a gate guard reported, "Li Su is outside, sword raised, looking for Lü Bu." The prime minister went outside with the speed of fire and saw Li Su approach, who said, "Lü Bu has killed the Grand Preceptor. If I see Lü Bu, a thousand slices will cut his body to shreds." Wang Yun said, "You are mistaken, general. The house of Han has lasted for four hundred years. Your ancestor Li Guang supported the house of Han. Dong Zhuo has recently monopolized all the power and Lü Bu has extirpated him. You say you 'will slay Lü Bu,' but if you do your name will be cursed throughout the world—unlike your ancestors. One who can dismiss the dark to let the light shine is truly a great man." Li Su threw his sword on the ground, clasped his hands, and bowed, saying, "You are right, Prime Minister. I request to speak with the Marquis of Wen." When the two met, Lü Bu told him all about Dong Zhuo's immorality. Li Su said in a rage, "I never knew the truth of the matter!"

---

49. This was a park with a twisting waterway that was called the Plain of Happy Wandering during the Han (formally named the Serpentine later, in the Tang), and was the site of outings for the *Shangsi* festival; see note 3.

Lü Bu had taken his leave of Wang Yun and returned to his house when the gate guard reported, "Defender-in-Chief Wu Zilan has surrounded the residence with ten thousand soldiers." Lü Bu thought to himself, "I cannot stay in Chang'an any longer." He summoned the eight strong generals, and with three thousand men, he took the eastern gate and then departed. Defender-in-Chief Wu Zilan was catching up behind him and another ten thousand men blocked the way ahead. But when the dead Dong Zhuo's four grand marshals—Li Jue, Guo Si, Fan Chou, and Zhang Ji—cursed him as a "slave," the Marquis of Wen gave no response and smashed through their formation.

Lü Bu and Liu Bei

Ahead, he reached Tong Pass, where the prefect of Qiaojun, Cao Cao, blocked his way and this set the two armies against each other. Lü Bu took the pass and went out. After he had gone eastward for many *li*, he came across the prefect of Suiyang [18b] Guo Qian, who said, "Marquis of Wen, don't enter my city, I will give you gold and pearls." Lü Bu went on in a northeastern direction. After a few days he came to a place that was very rich in mulberry and hemp. When he asked which place this was, people told him, "This is the area of Xuzhou." And when he asked who the prefect of Xuzhou might be, they told him, "That was the old general Tao Qian. But on his deathbed he thrice ceded Xuzhou to Xuande." Lü Bu thought to himself, "In front of Tigerkeep Pass we became enemies for life." But he also thought, "I have not even a square inch of land to call my own." At his side Cheng Gong said, "Guan, Zhang, and Liu Bei are all tigerlike generals." When the marquis of Wen kept silent, Chen Gong continued, "Liu Bei is a man of humanity and virtue. You should write him a letter."

Lü Bu immediately wrote a letter for Chen to take into Xuzhou to show Xuande. Xuande invited Chen Gong to sit down. Chen Gong presented the letter to Xuande, and he read its contents.

> Filled with shame, your younger brother Lü Bu kowtows and addresses the general's banner of Lord Xuande, warden of Xuzhou.
>
> At present the weather of the first month of summer is clear and pleasant, now that the plum rains have just cleared away. Humbly I consider that Your Honor is advancing in rank with each action and from his tiger tent conducts his administration with ease, and I therefore have the temerity to implore your divine intelligence to rescue and protect me.
>
> The battles at Tigerkeep Pass were not my crimes, but all the fault of Dong Zhuo. But I am only too well aware of my own crimes and am filled with worry on that account. I should have visited your abode earlier to pay

my respects and offer my apologies for transgressions of former days. Since I have left Chang'an, my men are worn out and my horses lack fodder, so we cannot proceed any further. If you would be so kind as to forgive me, I would be unable to contain my joy. Take good care of yourself until the day we may meet.

In haste.

Lü Bu Submits to Xuande

When Xuande had read the letter, he was very pleased, and after he had treated Chen Gong to wine and a meal, the latter took his leave and left. One general stepped forward and said to Xuande (this general was Jian Xianhe), "My lord, haven't you heard about Prefect Ding Jianyang from Lintao? Lü Bu addressed him as father but killed him because of that Red Harrier. Just recently in Chang'an he killed Dong Zhuo because of Diaochan. What to do if this Lü Bu, while the two generals Zhang and Guan are not in this city, would betray us and rob us of Xuzhou?" The First Ruler said, "Lü Bu may lack humanity, but he is now without fangs and claws, and he also begs us piteously in this letter, so he can rest for a while in this city." Liu's officials could not change his mind.

The next day at break of dawn, the First [19a] Ruler invited Lü Bu into the city to the music of drums, and banqueted him in the big hall for a few days. To the consternation of his officers, Xuande addressed Lü Bu as elder brother. A flustered Jian Xianhe immediately secretly dispatched a trusted follower to get Guan and Zhang and bring them back into the city.

The next day, at break of dawn, Xuande and his two younger brothers met with Lü Bu. A few days later, Lü Bu raised a question with his officers, saying, "From the time we crossed Tong Pass we have not found a single square inch of land to call our own." Chen Gong said to the Marquis of Wen, "You must have heard that the world consists of nine regions and that Xuzhou is the top commandery. It is a place from which kings rise. Once you obtain Xuzhou, you can consider the rest of the empire as nothing." Lü Bu replied with a smile, "Of course I want to take Xuzhou, but Xuande has treated me extremely well. On top of that, Guan and Zhang are generals who are as fierce as tigers and wolves. What would we do if we fail?"

A few days later, when Lü Bu and Xuande were sitting together, the First Ruler said, "Fengxian, you have no place to stay. It is only my humble opinion, but eighty *li* to the northwest is Xiaopei. What about stationing your troops there to build up your strength?" Lü Bu was very pleased and the next day he took his leave of the First Ruler and led the troops under his command to Xiaopei.

Half a year later, more or less, someone reported to the First Ruler, "Yuan Shu in Shouchun, four hundred *li* south, has sent out his Crown Prince Yuan Xiang at the head of an army that is on its way to take Xuzhou." The First Ruler immediately appointed Zhang Fei as a reception envoy to welcome Yuan Xiang in the south. Some thirty *li* of travel brought Zhang to a pavilion called Stone Pavilion Posthouse, where he received Yuan Xiang. When the two had exchanged ritual greetings, Zhang Fei set out three rounds of wine, and when this was finished, Yuan Xiang discussed the matter of Xuzhou. Zhang Fei did not accede to his demands, so Yuan Xiang rudely swore, "Xuande is a hick who weaves mats and plaits sandals!" Enraged, Zhang Fei cursed, "My brother is the son of a whole line of emperors and kings, the seventeenth-generation grandson of Emperor Jing of the Han, and a descendant of the Quiet Prince of Zhong-shan. When you curse him as 'a hick who weaves mats and plaits sandals!' you insult my brother. Truly, it's your ancestors who are nothing but farm boys." Zhang Fei was about to leave abruptly when Yuan Xiang began to strike him.

Zhang Fei Hurls Yuan Xiang to the Ground

Zhang Fei grabbed him tight, lifted him up with his hands, and hurled him down to the ground at the Stone Pavilion. None of the officers exhorted him not to, so he killed Yuan Xiang by smashing him on the ground.

Those who accompanied Yuan Xiang went back and saw Yuan Shu. Yuan Shu wept, [19b] "That damned Zhang Fei!" He immediately ordered his major general Ji Ling to take Xuzhou with three hundred thousand troops. The First Ruler left Zhang Fei in charge of Xuzhou, while he and Lord Guan and the other officers went south to confront Ji Ling and they stayed away for a month.

But let's now tell how Zhang Fei was drunk every day and never once sobered up. He did not attend to business. Cao Bao, one of two officials who served Zhang Fei, vilified the deceased Tao Qian, "Couldn't you entrust Xuzhou to me? No, you had to cede it to Liu Bei! Liu Bei has gone south to confront Ji Ling; no one is sure how the battle will turn and Liu Bei has placed this nobody in charge of the prefecture! All the common people are filled with resentment." Cao Bao tried to coax Zhang Fei through rhetorical persuasion, and when the latter did not heed him, he vilified Zhang Fei. Zhang Fei flew into a rage and said, "I have been the first in giving my all for the state. Since my brother has taken Xuzhou, it's right that he puts me in charge in the interim." Then he whipped Cao Bao. When Cao Bao went to his eastern residence, he came up with a plan that would pay back the injustice he had just suffered. He had his son-in-law Zhang Ben secretly write a letter and go to Xiaopei to see Lü Bu, who not only wined and dined him, but also gave him gold and pearls. After

Zhang Ben went back, Lü Bu asked his officers, "What shall we do now?" Chen Gong replied, "Xuande went south to confront Ji Ling, and Zhang Fei is totally drunk every day."

Cao Bao Offers Up Xuzhou

The Marquis of Wen led his troops to Xuzhou where Cao Bao immediately offered up the west gate, and Lü Bu entered the city. Zhang Fei was drunk as a skunk when someone advised him, "Her Ladyship is coming." This was Xuande's wife. Her Ladyship said, "Uncle, your elder brother has gone south to defeat Ji Ling and the outcome of that battle is still unclear. But you are 'under the weather' every day. What will happen to us if Xuzhou is lost?" But Zhang Fei replied, "Who would even dare glance at Xuzhou?" Before he had finished speaking they suddenly heard war cries shaking the earth and someone explained to Zhang Fei, "Cao Bao has seduced Lü Bu into action and led him into the city." Zhang Fei was flabbergasted and Her Ladyship looked up to heaven and wept. Zhang Fei mounted his horse and engaged Lü Bu in battle, and the confused struggle lasted until evening, when Zhang Fei took the gate and made his escape. Two hundred *li* down south he met up with the First Ruler and explained the incident in detail. Lord Guan was furious with Zhang Fei.

The next day the First Ruler marched his army back and at some twenty *li* from Xuzhou he made camp. Xuande also thought, "Lü Bu is bound to kill [20a] my wife and son, so let me write a letter to him in order to save my family." He immediately wrote a letter and had Jian Xianhe take that missive into the city and deliver it to Lü Bu. When Lü Bu read it, it turned out to reveal that Liu Bei was willing to abandon Xuzhou and retire to Xiaopei. Very pleased, Lü Bu sent Her Ladyship Mi and the Crown Prince Aji[50] out of the city to meet with Xuande. Xuande promptly started to lead his troops to Xiaopei to live in retirement.

But someone then reported, "Ji Ling had brought thirty thousand troops and demands Xuzhou." Now Ji Ling was a famous general of Yuan Shu. The First Ruler immediately led his troops and made camp on the western side, while Ji Ling made camp on the southern side, since their plan was to starve Xuzhou into submission. Lü Bu then also led his troops out of the city and made camp on the eastern side. Lü Bu wrote a letter to Ji Ling and Liu Xuande, in which he set a day for a banquet, "To which I invite the two of you."

---

50. The text constantly miswrites the name of the Crown Prince, Aji (阿計), as Adou (阿斗); this could be a simple scribal error of mistranscribing the simplified form of *ji* 计 as *dou* 斗.

Lü Bu was seated in the tent that he had set up on a high hill. When the banquet was over, he said, "The emperor of the Han is a coward and a weakling, and the empire is still in turmoil. Yuan Shu in Shouchun should stick to his eastern garrison. As for Xuzhou, when Tao Qian was still alive he originally ceded it to Lord Xuande. But recently Yuan Shu has demanded Xuzhou. Let me now solve both of your problems." At a distance of one hundred and fifty paces he had his men plant a square-heaven dagger axe in the earth, and he said, "I will shoot one arrow to hit the hole in the coin on top of the dagger axe. If I hit it, you two end your campaign. If I don't hit it, Ji Ling still will march his army back, and if he doesn't do so, I will help Xuande attack Ji Ling. And if Xuande doesn't send his armies back, I will assist Ji Ling in attacking Liu Bei." The two generals agreed to the proposals, and Lü Bu released his arrow. A poem reads,

> The merit of a single arrow achieved the establishment of great peace:
> Thirty thousand heroic soldiers threw down their lances and spears.
> In those days his daring and courage were without equal among men,
> And so we in later generations still praise his pure name.

Lü Bu's single arrow hit the hole in the golden coin, so Ji Ling marched his army back. The First Ruler treated Lü Bu to a banquet. After three days he returned to Xiaopei, while Lü Bu returned to Xuzhou.

About a half-year later when Liu Bei one day was seated in his office the gate-keeper reported, "Some elders have reported to me that the countryside is swarming with bandits." The First Ruler ordered the two generals Guan and Zhang to go and arrest these bandits. Zhang Fei led a mixed group of one thousand brave horsemen twenty *li* directly east of Xiaopei. When he arrived at the edge of a forest, [20b] he dismounted and sat down. His underlings brought wine and offered a cup to Zhang Fei, who said with a smile, "What I love is this good brew!" He finished it in one gulp and then fell asleep, leaning against a tree. When it came to the second watch, straight east the sound of bells could be heard. His aide alerted Zhang Fei, who mounted his horse and went due east. After a few *li* he came across a thousand soldiers, including their leader, who were escorting who knows how many boxes and bags, crates and baskets. Zhang Fei thought, "This must be those bandits." With one single loud shout he scared those people away and stole their money and goods. But their leader Hou Cheng[51] said, "The Marquis of Wen has sent me to Yanjing to buy horses." Zhang Fei didn't believe him and had his soldiers take the booty to Xiaopei and present it to the First Ruler. Hou Cheng told Liu Bei, "Those are the money and goods for buying horses and belong to the Marquis of Wen."

---

51. One of Lü Bu's "eight stalwart generals."

When the First Ruler looked at them more carefully, he was frightened and cursed Zhang Fei—all those goods did belong to Lü Bu. The First Ruler and Lord Guan wanted to send Zhang Fei to Xuzhou and offer him up to Lü Bu, but then they thought of their oath in the Peach Garden.

A few days later Lü Bu led thirty thousand troops and his eight stalwart generals and made camp twenty *li* from Xiaopei. The next day he led his troops to the city walls and engaged in a conversation with Xuande, and said he only wanted Zhang Fei, but the First Ruler refused. Lord Guan said, "Zhang Fei, you whipped that inspector general in Anxi and we lost half our troops and had to live as bandits for three years. Just now Xuzhou was lost. That was all your fault. And now you have seized Lü Bu's money and goods, and that is your fault too!" Enraged, Zhang Fei mounted his horse, saying, "Those who dare die follow me!" Thirty-eight horsemen lined up for battle.

Zhang Fei Thrice Leaves Xiaopei

After they had gone for some twenty *li* they arrived at a large forest where they dismounted. Yide said, "I lost Xuzhou and now Xiaopei is endangered; it is all my fault. If I don't achieve merit, I will be too ashamed to face my brothers." And Zhang Fei also explained, "Lü Bu committed a crime in Chang'an and then fled east through Sword Pass to Xuzhou. Recently it's come to light that Cao Cao, under imperial orders, is encamped at Suishui in command of an army of a hundred thousand with a thousand famed officers, solely to track down and arrest Lü Bu. With my eighteen horsemen I will go to Suishui, see Lord Cao, and borrow troops to defeat Lü Bu."

After a few days on the road they arrived in Suishui, where he paid court to Cao Cao and told him the whole story, asking for troops to save his brothers. [21a] But Cao Cao said, "I haven't seen Xuande from the time he left Tiger-keep Pass, so I cannot know whether you speak the truth when you want to borrow troops."

"Prime minister, you are right," said Zhang Fei, "I will return to my brother and get a letter." Too hurried to take proper leave of Cao Cao, he immediately mounted his horse and returned with his eighteen horsemen to Xiaopei. When Zhang Fei saw that Lü Bu had encircled the city as tightly as an iron bucket, he had to really make an effort before he could open up a bloody passage into the city. His two brothers asked him, "Where have you been these last few days?" And Yide explained, "I fought my way through the battle line and was able to reach Cao Cao in Suishui to ask for relief." The First Ruler was greatly surprised and asked, "And didn't you get any troops?" Zhang Fei replied, "The prime minister said that I wasn't carrying any proof, so I've come back to get a letter." The First Ruler immediately wrote a letter, which he entrusted to Zhang Fei.

The next day Zhang Fei once again left the city with his eighteen horsemen and fought Lü Bu. The latter thought, "That bandit general has been coming and going a number of times, so he must be seeking a relief force." But the Marquis of Wen was unable to block his way and Zhang Fei and his eighteen men smashed through the battle lines. After a few days he reached Cao Cao's major camp. When the prime minister heard this, his pleasure was boundless. Zhang Fei delivered the letter to Cao Cao, and the letter read,

> Filled with shame, your friend Liu Bei kowtows and addresses the banner of the prime minister.
>
> At present it is the middle month of autumn. Humbly I consider that Your Excellency with each action he takes rises in rank. But not shying away from your power and authority I have the temerity to inform you of my distress.
>
> Presently there is that bandit Lü Bu, who executed Dong Zhuo and then fled from Chang'an. Once he obtained Xuzhou through surprise attack, he is now besieging Xiaopei. Alas, my army is small and my officers are few, the moat is shallow and the walls are low. Our situation is as urgent as if we were hanging upside down, and as perilous as that of piled-up eggs. I have therefore ordered Zhang Fei to take a letter and visit you despite the distance. If you would show us the kindness of your great grace, and especially if you would end the siege for us, not only would I, Liu Bei, receive your favor but the common people would benefit from your grace as well. If we can capture Lü Bu alive, the emperor will see Great Peace. Humbly I beg you to consider this request.

In haste

When Cao Cao had finished reading this letter, he was overwhelmed by joy. And he also said, "Zhang Fei's bravery caps the world. None of the officers under my command are his like!" He also explained, "Zhang Fei, you are non-officially appointed General of Chariot and Horse! If I return to court after this campaign in the east against Lü Bu, I will have you formally appointed!" He ordered that Zhang Fei and his eighteen riders be given wine and meat. [21b] He ordered people to carry the wine out of the camp. From a tent to the southeast two officers appeared, and one of them called Zhang Fei to dismount so they could meet, and when these two met each other, they were very happy. Lord Cao said, "This is Xiahou Dun." Xiaohou said, "I see that the prime minister intends to go north and save Xiaopei, so who will be vanguard?" So he immediately appointed Xiahou Dun vanguard.

Within a day or so the prime minister broke camp and set out with all his men and after a few days they reached Xiaopei. Lü Bu and his troops came out to confront them and Xiahou Dun rode out to do battle with Lü Bu. After only a few rounds Lü Bu feigned defeat, and when Xiahou Dun hotly pursued him, Lü Bu released an arrow that struck Xiahou Dun right in his left eye. Xiahou Dun dropped from his horse and pulled out the arrow. Xiahou said, "This eye is the seed of my father and the blood of my mother: it cannot be discarded!" Holding his eye in his mouth he mounted up and continued the fight. Lü Bu said, "This is no ordinary man!" Lü Bu was utterly defeated. Seven *li* from camp on his return, Xiahou Dun saw Zhang Fei who had also employed his troops. The latter hastily joined Xiahou Dun and they returned to see Cao Cao. Cao Cao treated Xiahou Dun's wound with 'metal arrowhead medicine.'

Three days later Lü Bu once again issued a challenge to battle. Zhang Fei fought more than three hundred rounds with him but the outcome remained undecided. But when the First Ruler of Xiaopei, Lord Guan, and the other officers together with the thousand of mixed brave horsemen inflicted a huge defeat on Lü Bu, he fled in an easterly direction toward Xuzhou. Ten *li* from the city, he heard a great commotion in front of him. Someone told the Marquis of Wen that there were defeated troops ahead.

Among them was Diaochan, who came to see him awash with tears, and who told him that Cao Cao had ordered Xu Chu to occupy Xuzhou. Lü Bu thought to himself, "Xuzhou is already lost; there is also Cao Cao who will have an overwhelming force when he unites with Liu Bei, Lord Guan, and Zhang Fei." So he fled eastwards toward Xiapi. When he had arrived in that city, he did not leave its walls for several days. Someone told Lü Bu, "They are coming again." When he had asked about their numbers, Chen Gong spoke up and said, "Marquis, you should divide your troops in two companies. Eighty *li* to the northwest from here is Ram's Head Mountain, a place that can be easily defended. While you stay here at Xiapi, I will go to Ram's Head Mountain. In case Cao's troops attack Xiapi, I can protect you, and in case Lord Cao attacks Ram's Head Mountain, you can protect me." Chen Gong added, "Master Sun Wu has said. . . .[52] Even I cannot oppose the power of Zhang Fei!" Lü Bu replied, "Chen Gong, what you propose is right on the mark!"

Lü Bu met with Diaochan in the back room. When he explained it to her, [22a] she wept and said, "Fengxian, don't you remember how we were separated when Ding Jianyang rebelled in Lintao and the troops of Ma Teng arrived on the scene? We were separated and for three years could not see each other. After you killed Dong Zhuo you had no place to turn and fled east of the Pass. But now Xuzhou is lost. If you divide your army into two companies, the two forces will be separated. If we are separated, when will I see your face again?" Diaochan added, "'In life we share a room, in death we share a grave.'

---

52. Zhong Zhaohua (1990, 397) suggests that some words have dropped out of the text following this line.

I will never leave you 'til the day I die." "You are right," a happy Lü Bu replied. The Marquis of Wen enjoyed his happiness with Diaochan every day. When someone came to tell him, "Lord Cao's army has arrived, and the city is in imminent danger," he seemed not to care at all, and none of his officers could talk sense into him. A few days later someone knocked on his window in the fourth watch of the night, shouting, "Xiapi is on the verge of being lost!" When the Marquis of Wen put on his clothes and came out, he saw his stalwart general Chen Gong, who said, "Cao Cao has opened the dikes of the Yi and the Si Rivers, inundating the area all around Xiapi." At daybreak all the officers followed Lü Bu as he climbed the wall, and Chen Gong also said, "Marquis, when I earlier suggested that you divide your army into two companies in order to protect Xiapi, you didn't listen to me. Now Minister Cao has inundated the fields outside Xiapi, and there are no plans left to consider." The Marquis of Wen did not say a word, but descended from the wall and went to his compound, and again enjoyed his happiness with Diaochan every day, leaving his officers fuming with rage.

About half a month later he suddenly saw several men pull aside the curtain and enter. Among them Lü Bu recognized Chen Gong, Hou Cheng, and Zhang Liao. Hou Cheng was the one who addressed him, saying, "Marquis, we have followed you all the way from Lintao, but now after several years we still have not a square inch of land to call our own. Now Cao Cao and Liu Bei are camped outside the city with their two huge armies, the waters of the Yi and the Si are seeping into Xiapi, and our provisions are almost gone. Any day now Xiapi will be forced to surrender and then we all will die, but you are just enjoying each day with Diaochan." Lü Bu laughed and said, "Those outside are Cao Cao and Liu Bei, they know me well! If the city is flooded by the water of the Yi and the Si, I have a horse called Red Harrier and Diaochan and I will flee on the back of that horse. That horse can cross moats, so what should I fear as I float away with Diaochan?" One of those men loudly cursed him out, "Lü Bu, you are a lowly born cur! You may say you will get away with Diaochan afloat on the water, but what about our troops and officers who number thirty thousand and the thirty thousand families of the common people inside the city?" He had barely finished speaking when he cursed him again. Lü Bu saw that it was Hou Cheng and ordered him shoved outside and beheaded. The other officers pled on his behalf and were able to save his life but he received thirty strokes with the cudgel. Lü Bu went back to his room, and the officers dispersed.

Three days later the officers still couldn't let go and a drunk Hou Cheng cursed Lü Bu. That night he went straight to the back courtyard,

Hou Cheng Steals the Horse

and when he saw that the grooms were drunk as skunks, he stole the horse. When he arrived at the west gate he ran into the stalwart general Yang Feng who said, "Hou Cheng, you are stealing the horse." After he was killed by Hou Cheng, the latter breached the west gate and crossed the flood floating on the horse. At the fourth watch Guan Yu was on his rounds and captured Hou Cheng, and he obtained the horse. At daybreak he visited Cao Cao and told him the whole story. Minister Cao was very pleased.

Let us now go back to speak about Lü Bu who was sitting across from Diao-chan. When someone told him that Hou Cheng had stolen his horse, Lü Bu was greatly surprised. The person went on, "He has killed Yang Feng and joined Cao Cao. What shall we do now?" None of his officers said a word.

In just a few days Cao Cao gave orders to block the upstream part of the river with boards, and he opened a riverway downstream. He released all of the water, and had the moat filled with sand and stone, and bushes and trees. He erected catapults to bombard the city walls. Cao Cao brought his army forth and issued a challenge. Lü Bu came out of the city gate on a different horse to confront the enemy. Engaging in battle with Xiahou Dun he feigned defeat. But when Lü Bu took flight, Cao Cao led his troops in a massive attack as soldiers lying in ambush rose on all sides. Lü Bu fled west in a panic but ran smack into Lord Guan. Then Lü Bu had an idea to go east to Xiapi but he ran straight into Zhang Fei.

Zhang Fei Captures Lü Bu

Together the generals captured Lü Bu and made him prisoner. Cao Cao sent someone to shout out loudly to the eight generals and other officers, and they all came to surrender. Cao Cao marched his troops back. Upon entering his camp, he took his seat in his tent and questioned these officers. Then, he ordered that the shackled Lü Bu and Chen Gong be brought before him. He asked Chen Gong, "You first served me, later joined Gongsun Zan, and then secretly fled to cast your lot with Lü Bu. What to do now this enterprise has failed?" Chen Gong replied with a smile, "It's not my fault. I first joined you, Prime Minister, but you harbored the intention to usurp the throne. I later saw that Gongsun Zan messed up [23a] completely, so I joined Lü Bu. But who could have known that this bandit would rebel? Now that I have been captured, only death will be appropriate." Cao Cao said, "What if I would spare your life?" But Chen Gong said on his own initiative, "That won't do. Prime Minister, if I first joined Gongsun Zan and then served Lü Bu and if I cast my lot with you a second time, people of later times would consider me a man without principle, so I prefer to accept death."

Cao Cao Beheads Chen Gong

The prime minister said, "It is fitting to behead Chen Gong, but we should free his dependents." Chen Gong loudly shouted, "Prime Minister, you make a mistake! As long as you allow my son to live, you are bound to cause yourself trouble in the future. But please pardon my mother and my wife." After Cao Cao had given the order for their beheading, he allowed his mother and wife to live.

Next he ordered that Lü Bu be led before him and said, "He who stares a tiger in the eye does not speak of 'danger.'" When Lü Bu saw that Cao Cao and Xuande were both seated in the tent, he said, "Prime Minister, if you will spare my life, I will pay you back with my death. I hear that you are good at commanding infantry and I am good at commanding cavalry. Now if cavalry and infantry would work in tandem, conquering the empire will be as easy as turning over one's hand." Cao Cao didn't say a word, but looked at Xuande, and the First Ruler said, "You must have heard about Ding Jianyang and Dong Zhuo."

Beheading Lü Bu at the White Gate

So when Cao Cao said, "Have him beheaded!" Lü Bu vilified Xuande, "You big-eared bandit! You really want to do me in!" Cao Cao had Lü Bu beheaded.

Alas, the day he ate the blade below the city wall
Was quite unlike that time he shot at the battle-axe in his camp.

After he had beheaded Lü Bu he consoled Xiapi. Of the generals who had surrendered, Cao Cao especially appreciated Zhang Liao as the equal of Liu Bei, Guan Yu, and Zhang Fei. Holding hands, the prime minister each day drank wine with Xuande, as he hoped to make use of the First Ruler's support. What did it look like? There is a poem that offers a description. The poem reads,

Liu Bei's two eyes could see the lobes of his ears:
Arms so long they fell below his knees—he was an extraordinary man.
He was in origin a descendant of the Prince of Zhongshan—
Would he be willing to be a minister under the ministers of Lord Cao?

Newly Printed in the Zhizhi Period: The Completely Illustrated Plain Tales —Records of the Three Kingdoms, Part I. Twenty three pages, the end.

諸葛亮馬見曹操正率大軍望江陵而來諸葛亮知荊州劉琮又投
了劉備諸葛亮後追尋不見且說曹操領兵百万雄至荊州劉琮
降了曹操諸軍有兵在荊壁處劉琮不肯暗與他南趙江
入衛伏諸葛亮諸說曹公一里各下家有
樊城事失遠趙淪是其有意授劉琮玄德見
諸葛孔明看書中云行橋頭自狀申報
權言諸葛孔明請了孫權食開看書中云
過江東船趙金陵館內了諸葛亮至來見孫權見
玄德乘舩趙金陵館內了諸葛亮至來見建安當地
全來用上諸軍托曹將軍先王張慕官在夏口城內皇
趙雲常瞞日眾官曹慕中皇帝軍重孫
博書得皇軍師諸葛孔明又托曹將軍使至
一城各曰復口水運三面住歌乱門曹慕曰使至大
皇上取諸葛當按我上公曹操從捌尚下里名下家有
只見家見劉琮懼翻不肯暗與劉琮與弓相知有
了劉備諸葛亮後追尋不見且說曹操領兵百万雄至荊州劉琮

Newly Printed in the Zhizhi Period:
The Completely Illustrated Plain Tales—
Records of the Three Kingdoms, Part II

Dashed Hopes and New Friends

[1a] Cao Cao led the troops of Lord Guan, Zhang Fei, and Liu Bei back, marching due west for several days until they reached Chang'an. Within three days he was received in audience by the emperor where he reported that he had beheaded Lü Bu. Pleased, the emperor wanted to promote him in office, but Cao Cao reported, "This was not my merit."

"Whose was it?"

"The three from Zhuojun: Liu Bei, Guan, and Zhang."

When the emperor summoned the three, they borrowed court gowns so they could be received at imperial audience. Emperor Xian saw that the First Ruler's face was like a full moon, that his earlobes hung down on his shoulders, and that he bore a distinct resemblance to Emperor Jing. So he asked Xuande, "How are you related to our ancestral clan?"

"I am a seventeenth-generation grandson," replied the First Ruler, "a descendant of the Quiet Prince of Zhongshan. Because the Ten Constant Attendants monopolized power under the former emperor, Emperor Ling, our status was reduced to that of commoners."

The emperor was taken aback and summoned the prime minister in charge of the Office of the Imperial Genealogy to check the imperial line of descent. The Imperial Father-in-law, Dong Cheng, informed the emperor, "Liu Bei belongs to the imperial clan of the Han." The emperor was very pleased and immediately promoted Xuande to Warden of Yuzhou, General of the Left, and Imperial Uncle. He also summoned the two generals Guan and Zhang; he gifted them each with his grace and rewards and entertained them at an imperial banquet. After several days, the emperor grew greatly pleased and thought to himself, "There is the Imperial Uncle, the Prince of Jing, Liu Biao, and there is Liu Bi of Cangzhou.[53] But they have long been absent from my presence. Now I have this Imperial Uncle Xuande; the empire of Han has its ruler!"

---

53. The imperial relative Liu Bi 劉璧 remains a shadowy character in the *Plain Tales*. He is here said to reside in Cangzhou 滄州 (southeastern Hebei), but later (probably more correctly) associated with Cangwu 蒼梧 (written in the text as 滄梧), which refers to the region of modern Guangxi. As governor of Cangwu, Liu Bi would be a logical ally of Sun Quan.

53

For a few days at that time, must we now also tell, Cao Cao claimed to be ill and did not appear at court. When Cao Cao smashed Lü Bu at Xiapi, how could he have forseen that Xuande belonged to the imperial house of the Han? He was at loss for a plan.

One day as the emperor was seated in the Emerald Canopy Hall he summoned the Imperial Father-in-law. The emperor said, "Your family, fathers and sons, will enjoy Han stipends for generations." And he bestowed upon him a jade belt. The emperor returned to the rear palaces. When Dong Cheng came out of the inner palace, he ran into Cao Cao who said, "Do you have the jade belt that the emperor bestowed on you?" Dong Cheng gave the belt to Cao to inspect, and when Cao finished looking at it, he said, "You belong to the imperial house, so why shouldn't he bestow a belt upon you?"

When Dong Cheng took it back with him to his mansion, he told his wife what happened. She saw that he was soaked in sweat front and back—it had saturated several layers of clothing! His wife asked him twice, "Why are you sweating?" The Imperial Father-in-law answered her, "The empire of Han is about to be toppled any day." [1b] "What do you mean?" asked his wife. He said, "It's Lord Cao. The palace directors and imperial eunuchs in the inner palace all serve as Cao Cao's eyes and ears. Else, how could he have known that the emperor had offered me a belt as a gift?" When his wife took the belt from him, she saw the end of a tuft of red silk, and when she pulled it out with a golden needle, it held an imperial edict. Frightened, the Imperial Father-in-law and his wife both said, "Our whole family would have been finished if Cao Cao had discovered this in front of the inner gate!"

Dong Cheng saw that the proclamation was addressed to the Imperial Uncle Liu Xuande, the Great Defender before the Palace Wu Zilan, to him and to the two generals Guan and Zhang, as well. When he saw this, Dong Cheng invited Liu Xuande and Wu Zilan so the three of them might sit together and read the edict. The edict stated,

Since We have "let our robes fall into place"[54] to rule the world, buckler and spear have arisen all over the land. Those who grow prickers and thorns[55] will of course have to be cut down and eradicated; those who give rise to treason and flattery truly cannot be borne with tolerance. Long ago when Dan of Yan

---

54. That is, from the story of the ease with which the great sage kings ruled by establishing the proper sumptuary rules for clothing, by simply donning their robes in order to display proper ritual to the world. It comes to mean to rule the world effortlessly and naturally.

55. There seems to be a mistake in this sentence. The common phrase *maoci bu jian* 茅茨不剪 means to be unconcerned with adornment or pretension; that is, in the age of the sage kings, "even the thatch on the roofs was not trimmed." The term does not make much sense here, and we assume that *maoci* may have slipped into the text as an error for *jingji* 荊棘 (thorns and stickers), a common term for miscreants and the rebellious.

was held in ransom in Qin, a horse was born with horns in Qin and so he could escape.[56] When Gaozu was besieged in Xingyang, Ji Xin displayed his loyalty and filiality.[57] Even though We lack virtue We are moved in Our heart by these examples now that We are confronted with the present crisis. As far as the execution of crafty vassals is concerned, Dong Zhuo has already been put to death, but now there is this treacherous hero Cao Cao who holds Us "under his arm" to achieve his own purposes. You must know this. At present the situation for the empire of Han is as urgent as if it was hanging upside down and the situation for the altars for the earth and grain is as perilous as that of piled-up eggs. I encountered no loyal ministers nor yet obtained fine generals. If you receive this edict, you have to eliminate this unscrupulous hero with great decisiveness and announce it everywhere throughout the empire so everyone will fully understand it.

This edict is issued to the Imperial Father-in-law Dong Cheng, the Great Defender before the Palace Wu Zilan, and the Imperial Uncle Liu Xuande, as well as the two generals Guan and Zhang.

On such and such a day of such and such a month of the ninth year of the period Zhongping.[58]

An imperial missive.

When these officials had read the edict, written in the emperor's own hand, the Imperial Uncle said, "We should deliberate carefully. If the two generals Guan and Zhang come to know of this, they surely will go and fight Cao Cao. But no matter what Cao Cao embarks on, he is always accompanied by a hundred thousand troops and a hundred generals, so if both sides confront each other, they will turn Chang'an into a mountain of corpses and a sea of blood." Before he had finished speaking, they heard someone shout outside the window, "You all are quite daring! I will inform Cao Cao!" When the Imperial Uncle opened the door to have a look it turned out to be the Chief Doctor of the Great Court of Medicine, Ji Ping.

The three of them invited him inside the pavilion and discussed how best to kill Cao. Ji Ping said, "The migraines that Cao Cao suffers are called 'tiger headaches.' As soon as that disease manifests itself, I can do him in with a poisoned drug." Dong Cheng replied, "At night Cao Cao sleeps on a headrest [2a]

---

56. He sought his release from Qin, and the King of Qin responded by saying, "I'll assent to it when crows turn white-headed and horses sprout horns." Heaven made it happen in response to Dan's sighs, and he was released.

57. When Liu Bang, the founding emperor of the Han, was besieged in Xingyang, Ji Xin proposed that he dress up as Liu Bang and pretend to surrender to Xiang Yu, the main contender with Liu Bang. The plot worked and Liu Bang made his escape. Xiang Yu burned Ji Xin to death.

58. There is no ninth year of Zhongping. All of the reign periods under Emperor Xian are quite short. Of course, it is a fictional, not historical world that the tale is creating.

stuffed with poison pills and during the day he drinks three cups of wine stirred with the poisonous feathers of the Zhen bird. Can we do him in?" But, said Ji Ping, "My drug is so poisonous that his intestines will all rupture as soon as he swallows it." The officials were pleased.

A month later Cao Cao's disease manifested itself and he sent someone to ask Ji Ping to cure it. But Lord Cao refused to take the drug, saying that it tasted different. Ji Ping then vilified Lord Cao, "You usurping traitor, don't you deserve to die?" He splashed the drug [in his face], but Cao evaded it and immediately arrested Ji Ping and quickly submitted him to torture.

Cao Cao Interrogates Ji Ping

Lord Cao asked him, "Who made you do this?" but Ji Ping didn't say a word. Cao Cao thought to himself, "This must have been a scheme of the Imperial Uncle Liu Bei."

That day he laid out a banquet and invited the Imperial Uncle to his mansion. Cao Cao brought out Ji Ping and asked him again, "Who made you do this?" Ji Ping vilified Cao Cao once again, "Cao Cao is a traitor who has his eyes on the house of Han! Heaven had me poison you." Once again Cao ordered him interrogated under torture but Ji Ping still said, "Nobody made me poison you." He ordered him tortured once more but Ji Ping died. A poem reads,

> Such a treacherous hero as Cao Cao is without precedent in the past;
> Using a drug, Ji Ping tried to murder that traitor.
> Severly tortured under interrogation, he lost his life,
> But to the end he never confessed—a true hero he!

After Cao Cao had beaten Ji Ping to death, he became deeply suspicious of the Imperial Uncle. He said to himself, "My mistake. I should never have brought Liu Bei to court. These three brothers are like tigers and wolves; there is no way to deal with them."

A few days later, Minister Cao invited Xuande to a feast, which was called "A Meeting to Evaluate Heroes." That scared the Imperial Uncle so much he dropped his chopsticks.[59]

---

59. Liu Bei is scared by Cao Cao's casual remark, which means that he considers only Liu Bei a hero on a par with himself, that is, his main rival for power. In the original version of the story in the *Records of the Three Kingdoms*, the dropping of the chopsticks and spoon happened at the moment the remark was delivered.

The meeting disbanded.[60]

One day Cao Cao suddenly made a request of the emperor, "The traitors in the east are too widespread." The emperor responded, "How can we control this?" Cao said, "Send the Imperial Uncle off to guard Xuzhou." The emperor assented to the request.

Xuande left and had been on the road for a month when he reached the inn at Tiekou, about thirty *li* from Xuzhou. All of the officials, yamen personnel, and commoners from Xuzhou came out to greet him.

Let us go back now to tell how Cao Cao had backhandedly also dispatched Che Zhou to be prefect of Xuzhou, with the intent of wresting away the First Ruler's position. Che Zhou also arrived at the inn and asked the First Ruler, "Do you have a proper letter from the prime minister?" The Imperial Uncle said, "I have only the order of the August Emperor; why would I need to have Lord Cao's letter?" Che Zhou immediately went down the stairs and hurried off to Xuzhou by himself. The First Ruler said, "If Che Zhou gets to Xuzhou first and does not come out, what shall we do about it?" Lord Guan said, [2b] "I will go on ahead."

Lord Guan got on his horse and applied the whip, then drew near Xuzhou,

Lord Guan Makes a Surprise Attack on Che Zhou

and attacked Che Zhou by surpise. Che Zhou made one feint, but Guan's "blade dropped and the head fell."

When the First Ruler arrived, the host of officers and the aged notables all welcomed him into the grand yamen. After the banquet given by the officers was over, Xuande said, "My brothers Guan and Zhang, and you officers, prepare your battle garb and armor. Sooner or later Lord Cao's troops will arrive." The host of officers discussed this, and then each of them put their garb, armor, and military weapons in order.

Within a month Cao Cao's army indeed arrived. Lord Guan proposed to the First Ruler, "We should divide our troops in three companies. Let me take your dependents to Xiapi before the fighting starts." The First Ruler agreed to the proposal and Lord Guan took the Imperial Uncle's dependents with him to garrison Xiapi in the east.

---

60. The text here simply says *huisan* 會散. It seems misplaced, or it occurs after a scene that has been deleted, either before or after the dropping of the chopsticks, which may have been the exchange between Cao Cao and Liu Bei. Since no meeting occurs between the invitation to the feast and the "disbanding of the meeting," we assume it is a fragment.

Zhang Fei said, "In my eyes these one hundred thousand troops of Cao Cao are nothing at all!" A messenger informed him, "Cao Cao's army has made camp ten *li* from the city." Zhang Fei laughed and said, "With this scheme of mine I'll send Lord Cao back without a single piece of armor!" When Xuande asked him what kind of scheme, Yide replied, "According to the book on warfare of Master Sun Wu, when fording a river or attacking a wall an army cannot be attacked, but troops in distress can be attacked. So tonight at midnight I will carry out a surprise attack on Cao Cao's camp with three thousand troops and first of all kill Cao Cao." The First Ruler said, "Right!"

But unknown to them in their unit was Zhang Ben, the commander of a company of infantry, who thought to himself, "Earlier my father-in-law Cao Bao told Lü Bu to conduct a surprise attack at night on Xuzhou and he was later killed by Lord Guan. As a son, shouldn't I take revenge for the injustice suffered by my father?" Zhang Ben stealthily left Xuzhou and entered Cao's large camp, where he alerted him about the plan.

About midnight that night, Zhang Fei and the First Ruler led thirty thousand troops to raid the camp. But it was empty and they found themselves surrounded by Cao Cao's army. The troops of Liu and Zhang fought until daybreak and then got out, but not a single piece of armor returned. Nobody knew whether the Imperial Uncle and Zhang Fei were still alive. After Minister Cao had occupied Xuzhou, he comforted the population.

When Cao Cao had taken his seat in his tent, he said to himself, "Liu Bei and Zhang Fei may have died, but at Xiapi there's still Lord Guan. I love that Lord Guan, but how do I obtain him?" Someone in his command said, "Let me go to Xiapi and coax Lord Guan with fine words." The prime minister recognized that it was Zhang Liao and he was very pleased, saying, "If Lord Guan will visit me, all others will surrender." Zhang Liao then took his leave from Lord Cao and soon arrived at Xiapi.

[3a] Her Ladyship Gan as well as Miss Mei, with Aji in her arms, looked up to heaven and wept openly, imploring Lord Guan, "What will become of our family now the Imperial Uncle and his younger brother have died in such a miserable way?" Tears dripping, Lord Guan said, "Sisters, as long as we live we will live together, and if we die, we will die together." Suddenly someone reported, "At present Cao Cao's officer Zhang Liao has reached the city wall and shouted out, 'Open the gate, I have something to say.'" Lord Guan sent someone to invite him in.

When Zhang Liao arrived at the front of the hall, the Lord of the Beautiful Beard[61] asked him, "Has Xuzhou been lost? Do you know the fate of the Imperial Uncle and Zhang Fei?" Zhang Liao replied, "They were killed in the melee." The Lord of the Beautiful Beard wept and said, "I am not afraid of

---

61. Guan Yu.

dying. You must have come here to persuade me [to do so]." Zhang Liao replied, "Not at all. Now the Imperial Uncle and Zhang Fei have been killed by mutinous troops, you don't know how to deal with the family and, should Cao Cao's army arrive below the walls, wouldn't you be at a double loss? Lord Guan, you have studied books since your youth and read the *Springs and Autumns with the Commentary of Mr. Zuo*, how it promotes the wise and good—so how could you not understand our meaning? Cao Cao deeply loves you." Lord Guan said, "But how would Cao Cao treat me were I to join him?" Zhang Liao replied, "He will appoint you to the high rank of general, with a monthly salary of four hundred strings and four hundred stoneweight."[62] Lord Guan then said, "I will submit if he follows my three conditions." "General, just tell them to me," Zhang Liao replied. "Her Ladyship will have one house divided into two courtyards. If I learn any information about the Imperial Uncle, I will visit him. And I submit to the Han but not to Cao Cao. Later I will establish great merit for the prime minister. If he will accept these three conditions, I will immediately submit. If he will not accept them, I would rather fight to death." Zhang Liao laughed and said, "These three conditions are all minor matters." Zhang Liao then returned and saw Lord Cao, to whom he told the whole story.

Within five days Cao Cao's army arrived below the walls. Cao Cao shouted, "Yunchang, come down from the wall so we can talk." "What about my three conditions?" Lord Guan asked. Minister Cao replied, "This is the world of the Han. If you can join me, I will appoint you as Marquis of Shouting with a monthly stipend of four hundred strings and four hundred stoneweight. One house will be divided into two courtyards. If the Imperial Uncle is still alive, you can take his wives and child and go and visit your elder brother. You say you will establish great merit, so you are my trusted friend!" Lord Guan then descended from the wall and met with Cao Cao.

Within a few days he had taken the dependents of the Imperial Uncle westward with him to Chang'an, where he was received in audience by the emperor. When the emperor saw that Lord Guan's curly beard covered this stomach, [3b] he was greatly pleased in his heart and appointed him as Marquis of Shouting with a monthly stipend of four hundred strings and four hundred stoneweight; when "he got on his horse it was gold, when he dismounted it was silver"; one house was divided into two courtyards; every third day there was a small banquet, every fifth day a great banquet.

---

62. Grain was counted in stoneweights: one stoneweight is about 10.5 pounds.

Liu Bei and Zhao Yun

Let's go back now and tell how the Imperial Uncle found himself at a place some fifty *li* from Xuzhou in a forest at the entrance of a valley at Ninemile Mountain. He had in total only a few men with him. In the middle of the group, the Imperial Uncle drew his sword and was about to slit his own throat but his men talked him out of it. Xuande wept, "Xuzhou is lost, and I don't know whether Zhang Fei is still alive or not. And on top of that my beloved younger brother Lord Guan has taken my wives and child to cast his lot with Cao Cao." After he finished speaking, he looked up to heaven and wept with great sorrow.

The Imperial Uncle had nowhere to go, so on the next day he advanced in a northeasterly direction. After traveling for a few days he saw dense groves lit by the sun, and gardens and rice paddies without number. When Xuande asked what this place was, people told him, "This is part of Qingzhou, and our official is Yuan Tan." When the Imperial Uncle arrived on horseback at an inn inside the town, he settled in. The next day, he visited Yuan Tan, who fêted him for several days. The Imperial Uncle said, "Xuzhou is lost, I don't know if Zhang Fei is alive, and Lord Guan has taken my wives and child to cast his lot with Cao Cao. Prefect, allow me to borrow fifty thousand troops so I may kill Cao Cao and retrieve my wives and child." Yuan Tan acceded to his request. A few days later Xuande again raised the topic and Yuan Tan assented but did not ready any troops. About a half a month later, when he returned at night to the inn, the Imperial Uncle was drunk and recited a short song. The song reads,

> All under Heaven is in utter disorder—
>   the Yellow Scarves are everywhere;
> All within the seas are filled with fear—
>   traitors are as numerous as ants.
> Cao Cao has no principles—
>   he intends to become ruler;
> Emperor Xian is bereft of power—
>   he has nothing for support.
> It is right I have the ambition—
>   to restore the house of Liu—
> Yuan Tan lacks all human feeling—
>   there is no end to my sighs!

When he had finished singing, a general in the western corridor gallery, hearing Xuande's song, immediately replied with a perfect match,

I have a long sword—
  which I vainly brandish as I deeply sigh;
When the court is not upright and true—
  bandits resemble vicious dragons.
If stalwart fighters stay hidden—
  there will never be any wind or thunder;
If you wish to raise buckler and spear—
  the court will have that on which to rely.
When heroes meet one with another—
  they will uphold and support the state of Liu;
Beheading and extirpating that traitor Cao—
  they are one body with our lord!

The Imperial Uncle descended the steps and learned that that guest was Zhao Yun, also known as Zilong from Hengshan. After he had met Zhao Yun, he invited him up the stairs where Xuande related to him all the wrongs he had suffered. Zhao Yun said, [4a] "This Yuan Tan of Qingzhou makes decisions but does not follow through. We should go to Xindu and pay our respects to Yuan Shao." The Imperial Uncle and Zhao Yun jumped on their horses and went off, west to Xindu, which nowadays is Jizhou.

Within three days Zhao Yun and the Imperial Uncle had reached Xindu. When they had settled in an inn, Zhao Yun went ahead to see Yuan Shao and told him everything about the Imperial Uncle. The Prince of Ji was greatly pleased and speedily summoned the Imperial Uncle to his presence, so he might meet with the Prince of Ji.

After they had banqueted for a few days, the Imperial Uncle said once again, "Cao Cao bullies the liege lords of the empire, so I would like to borrow some troops to kill Cao Cao and reestablish the house of Han. What do you think, ⚹ Your Majesty?" Yuan Shao acceded to his request and then went on, "I have a brave general, Yan Liang. When he arrives, he will certainly slay that traitor Cao." One grandee, Xu You, reproved him, saying, "Your Majesty, you are mistaken. What gain is there for you to send these troops to their death? Haven't you heard that Cao Cao has a hundred thousand troops and a hundred generals at his side at all times? If you achieve victory you may leave your name to posterity, but if you lose, even Xindu cannot be protected. Your Majesty, please consider this carefully." Xu You said again, "I have recently learned that in the western Taihang Mountains there is bandit general Black Tiger who causes problems for Your Majesty day and night, but you still are unable to even control him." The Prince of Ji was silent. Xu You then went on, "If the Imperial Uncle is to start a campaign you should first take the time to discuss this in detail with your officers. It won't be too late to set out after that." But Yuan Shao could not pardon Cao Cao. He appointed the Tiger-fang Generalissimo

Yan Liang as grand marshal; he appointed the Left General Wen Chou as the commandant of the rear guard and Xu You as the campaign advisor. Leading a hundred thousand troops they arrived to defeat Cao Cao and made camp.

Now let us go back to speak about Cao Cao who was seated in audience when someone reported, "Yuan Shao's army is here and issuing a battle challenge." Astonished, quick as fire the prime minister held a roll call of his army. He immediately appointed Master Bag-of-Tricks Zhang Liao as his field marshal, Xiahou Dun as vanguard, and Cao Ren as generalissimo. That very day Cao Cao set out with a hundred thousand troops. In a few days he had lined his troops up opposite those of Yuan Shao. Cao Cao and Yan Liang engaged in conversation, and a furious Yan Liang said, "Bandit Cao, don't flee!" Holding his lance he gave his horse free rein and attacked Lord Cao head-on. Xiahou Dun rode out on his horse to engage him, but after thirty rounds of battle Xiahou Dun was soundly defeated. Both sides pulled their troops back and, as evening fell, set up camp.

The next day Yan Liang once more issued a challenge. Xiahou Dun again rode out and was defeated once more. [4b] Then Cao Ren rode out to battle Yan Liang, but he too was defeated. Yan Liang made use of the situation to launch an all-out attack, and Cao Cao's army suffered the loss of half of its men. From noon until evening—only then did Yan Liang return to his camp with his troops. When he met with the Prince of Ji, he told him the full story of his victory. Yuan Shao was greatly pleased and rewarded the troops.

Now let us back up and tell how Minister Cao led his defeated troops back to Chang'an. He invited Lord Guan to join him for a banquet and told him about the might of Yan Liang. Even before the banquet was finished, someone reported, "Yan Liang, at the head of his troops, challenges us to battle." Cao Cao said, "The main army will go out first." And he also said, "Lord of the Beautiful Beard, you will follow behind escorting the grain and straw." The prime minister also left and mounted his horse. With his troops he went ahead until they made contact with Yuan Shao's army. Arrayed for battle, the two forces faced each other. Yan Liang rode out to issue a challenge, and Xiahou Dun also rode out. The two of them fought a fierce battle for thirty rounds, but then Xiahou Dun was defeated and returned to his own formation.

Sighing, Lord Cao said, "Yan Liang is a hero. What's to be done about him?" In the midst of his depression someone reported, "Lord Guan is here." Lord Cao hurriedly received him and brought him to the hall, where he explained the awesome power of Yan Liang. Lord Guan laughed, "This guy is a nothing." Lord Guan went out of the camp, got on his horse with his broad blade, and from a high position observed all of the flags and canopies of Yan Liang until he recognized Yan Liang's own parasol. Seeing that a hundred thousand soldiers surrounded and guarded the camp,

Lord Guan Skewers Yan Liang

brandishing his blade, Yunchang spurred alone on his mount toward the encampment. Seeing Yan Liang in the middle of the camp, he caught him completely off-guard, and in a single stroke, he chopped off his head, which fell to the earth. Then he used the tip of his blade to pluck up Yan Liang's head and went out of the encampment and back to his base camp. He met with Lord Cao who was flabbergasted and stroked Yunchang's back, saying, "You plucked Yan Liang's head right out of an army of a hundred thousand as easily as looking at the palm of your hand. You are the bravest of brave generals." "I am not strong," said Yunchang. "My brother could pluck a person's head from an army of a million as easy as looking at the palm of his hand!" Lord Cao said, "So Zhang Fei is even stronger?"

There is an encomium for Guan Yu's shrine that says,

> His brave aura traversed the clouds;
> Truly he was called "A Tiger Officer";
> His bravery equaled that of an entire state of men,
> Called by the enemy "an army of ten thousand."
> Shu and Wu were his wings,
> And yet Wu finished off this magic beast.
> Oh, so cherished! Such bravery—
> Unmatched in the past or future.

Now we speak of Yuan Shao. When the defeated army returned to camp and explained that Lord Guan had slain Yan Liang, Yuan Shao was enraged and cursed the Imperial Uncle, "You and Lord Guan were in communication to make this plan to behead my beloved general Yan Liang. You have destroyed [5a] one of my arms!" He ordered his men to take the Imperial Uncle out and behead him. "Cease your anger my lord," requested Wen Chou, "I want to go out and do battle with Lord Guan to repay this injustice to Yan Liang." Wen Chou led his army forward to face off with Cao's troops. Wen Chou shouted, "Come out, bearded one!" Without uttering a word, Lord Guan went to seize Wen Chou. Wen Chou was defeated in fewer than ten rounds of battle, and he spurred his horse to flee. Angrily, Lord Guan said, "How can you not give me battle!" He pursued him for thirty *li* or more until they reached a ford called Official Ford. As they approached it Lord Guan twirled his blade,

Lord Guan Punishes Wen Chou[63]

spied Wen Chou, and hacked, cutting him into two pieces with arms and all. Wen Chou fell from his horse and died. Minister Cao led his troops in an all-out attack, and seventy or eighty percent of Yuan Shao's army was lost. The defeated army returned to see Yuan Shao and they related in detail how Lord Guan had slain Wen Chou. Yuan Shao was mightily shaken, "He has taken away my second arm. That damned Liu Bei intentionally said that he did not know where Lord Guan was, and now he's destroyed my two generals." He sent his men to round up Liu Bei with the intent of having him decapitated. But unexpectedly someone approached to kneel before him and it was that man from Changshan, Zhao Yun, who said, "In reality, Lord Guan does not know Liu Bei is here. If he knew the First Ruler was here, he would come straight away to join you, great king. The three brothers once swore an oath, 'We need not be born on the same day, but we wish to die on the same day.'" And he went on, "I will guarantee that if Liu Bei and I appear together in front of Cao's battle formation, Lord Guan will immediately cast his lot with us should he see Liu Bei." Yuan Shao was silent. "If you do not believe me, my king, let me leave my family as pawn." Only then did Yuan Shao assent and spare the life of the First Ruler.

The First Ruler and Zhao Yun mounted up and went out of the camp. "If it were not for Zhao Yun," thought the First Ruler to himself, "my life would not have been vouchsafed. Now that brother Yunchang has received a noble title as Marquis of Shouting and has a Han official title, he must have lost his fraternal heart. I have nowhere to turn now. I know that Liu Biao is now the Prince of Jing in Jingzhou. Should I get there, it would be a place to find some security." Without looking back at Zhao Yun, he gave his horse its head and applied the whip to flee off to the southwest.

Zhao Yun pursued him aggressively and asked him, "Where are you going?" Liu Bei was silent. "You have but to say where," said Zhao Yun, "and I will follow." Zhao Yun thought to himself, "The First Ruler is not the image of a common man; [5b] he will eventually rise to an eminent position. And he is also the seventeenth-generation descendant of Gaozu. How can I abandon him?" He caught up with him again and asked him once more. Seeing how aggressively Zhao Yun was pursuing him, the First Ruler told the whole truth and said, "Now there is Yunchang, but he has accepted a salary from the Han without even considering the heart that bound us in righteousness. Now the Prince of Jing, Liu Biao, is residing in Jingzhou." "Since you will stay in Jingzhou," said Zhao Yun, "I will go there with you." "But your family is held as ransom by the

---

63. This is one of a few places in the text when a subheading is missing its enclosing black box.

King of Ji," said the First Ruler. "How can you bear to leave them?" "You are a man of humane virtue," replied Zhao Yun, "and will rise to an eminent position in future days." They went on toward the southwest.

The Reunion of Brothers

Let us go back now to speak of how delighted Cao Cao was, "In a rare act Lord Guan went out on a single horse into an army of one hundred thousand to skewer Yan Liang, and he caught up with Wen Chou at Official Ford. If I can get him to help me, then it's nothing to take on the empire." Cao Cao treated Lord Guan with profound courtesy, giving him a small banquet every three days and a major one every five. He was gifted with gold when he mounted his horse and with silver when he dismounted. He also gave ten beautiful girls to Lord Guan as his personal servants. Lord Guan, upright as always, never paid any attention to them, but lived in the same compound, in two separate court-yards, with his sisters-in-law Gan and Mi. Lord Guan performed morning and evening rituals every day in front of the spirit tablet of the First Ruler.

As that day drew toward evening, he went into the compound of his sisters-in-law where he saw them wailing as they burned incense and offered up sac-rificial wine. He laughed, saying, "Don't cry, sisters; my elder brother is alive." "Are you drunk?" said ladies Gan and Mi. But Lord Guan replied, "I have just heard that brother is with Yuan Shao, the Prince of Ji. Pack up your luggage now, sisters. We will bid Minister Cao adieu tomorrow and head off to Yuan Shao's camp." Lord Guan then returned to his own quarters.

The next day Lord Guan went to take his leave from Minister Cao, but when he got to his headquarters, this sign was hung out—Tenth Day: At Rest.[64] Lord Guan returned to his quarters, but when he went back on the second day, the same plaque was hanging there, so he returned to his quarters. When he went on the third straight day and the plaque was still there, he became angry, "Minister Cao is purposely keeping me from seeing him." So he returned to his quarters again, packed away and sealed up all of the gold and silver he had been given over time, made an official account of their number, sealed them up and turned them all over to the ten beautiful girls. [6a] He had someone prepare the carts and saddle the horses,[65] and then he requested that his two sisters-in-law get on a cart, and he went out of Chang'an bound for the northwest.

---

64. The work and rest cycle in ancient China was one day of rest in every ten. The cyclical sign for that day, *you* 酉, was put out on a banner.

65. Following the emendation suggested by Zhong Zhaohua of 軍程 to 車乘, see Zhong Zhao-hua (1990, 420).

Let us now go back to speak of how angry Minister Cao was, "I can't believe, after I showed Lord Guan how much I relied on him and valued him, that he would be unwilling to stay with me but would go off to Yuan Shao instead." The reason that Minister Cao did not open up his office for three days was because he knew that Lord Guan wanted to go to Yuan Shao's camp to find Liu Bei. He had trusted spies in Guan's quarters, all of whom acted as Cao Cao's eyes and ears. In the few days that the office was not open, Cao Cao deliberated with his officers. One of his advisers, Bag-of-Tricks Zhang Liao, said, "First set out troops in ambush on both sides of Baling Bridge. If Lord Guan reaches there, you offer him a stirrup cup. Lord Guan has but to dismount and you can have Strong-as-Nine-Bulls Xu Chu take Lord Guan into custody. If he doesn't get off his horse then, minister, give him a gift of a ten-patterned brocade silk robe. He has to get off his horse to thank you properly for the gown. Then Strong-as-Nine-Bulls Xu Chu can seize him." Cao Cao was overjoyed, and first sent a company of soldiers to wait in ambush at Baling Bridge. Then Cao Cao, Xu Chu, and Zhang Liao all went to Baling Bridge to wait.

Lord Cao Bestows the Robe

Lord Guan arrived in no time at all, and the minister offered him a stirrup cup. Lord Guan said, "Please do not take offense, minister, but I am not going to drink." He also did not get off his horse. Then the brocade robe was brought out, and Xu Chu was ordered to present it. Again, Lord Guan did not get off his horse, but used the tip of his blade to pluck it up, and then he left, saying, "Thanks for the robe! Thanks for the robe!" Although there were fewer than a hundred men in Guan's retinue, it frightened Lord Cao so much that he dared not strike. Yunchang escorted the carts of sister Gan and sister Mi and went off to the Prince of Ji's camp.

In a few days he had reached the Prince of Ji's camp. The gate guards reported, "A Lord Guan is at the gates." The King of Ji was stunned, "First he destroys my two generals and then he comes here!" Then he thought to himself, "Well, Lord Guan has shown up here, and if I should obtain his services then what worry do I have that Xindu will not be secure?" He ordered someone to ask Lord Guan to come into the camp.

When Yuan Shao met him, he received Lord Guan in the headquarters' tent. The Prince of Ji pressed wine on him, but Lord Guan would not drink it, saying, "I do not see my brother. Where is he?" "He is drunk," replied the King of Ji.

Lord Guan thought to himself, "My brother isn't here." Then he said, "I have my two sisters-in-law outside the gate, we will still have time to drink after they enter the camp." The Prince of Ji [6b] was delighted by this. Lord Guan went out of the camp, mounted up, and then quickly summoned the gate guard.

He grabbed the guard's hair with one hand and brandished his sword with the other. "Is the First Ruler here?" he said. "If you don't answer truthfully, I'll kill you." He scared the gate guard so much he repeated over and over, "Not here! Not here!" And when Lord Guan asked where he had gone, the gate guard replied, "He went off to Jingzhou with Zhao Yun." Only then did Lord Guan release him.

Let us now speak of how Lord Guan, with his two sisters-in-law, went south into the Taihang Mountains in order to go to Jingzhou. It was Lord Guan, alone, who led sister Gan and sister Mi over a thousand mountains and ten thousand rivers.

Lord Guan Travels Alone for a Thousand *Li*

Let us now go back to speak of how the First Ruler and Zhao Yun, leading three thousand troops southward, suddenly heard the sound of gongs and drums and saw a band of robbers. The one in front wore a crimson headscarf, had armor of tempered brass, and held a "mountain-splitting" axe. He cried out, "You must leave a toll for this road." The First Ruler approached him on horseback and said, "What is your name?" When the bandit saw the First Ruler, he quickly dismounted and performed a ritual obeisance, saying, "Xuande! You have been well since our last parting. I am the Han official Gong Gu. I became a brigand here because Dong Zhuo had usurped power." Then he invited the First Ruler, Zhao Yun, and all of their troops to return to his mountain stronghold, where he treated them to beef and wine.

They were just drinking a round when a lieutenant reported, "An envoy from the grand king is here." Gong Gu went out to meet with the envoy. The envoy said, "Now receive the sagely command of the grand king. Since you have offered no payment for three months, I originally wanted your head gone, but I'm temporarily letting you off this time. If you do not send payment again, I will certainly carry it out to the end. But for the time being, I am letting you off." When Gong Gu went back to the tent and saw the First Ruler, the latter asked, "From which state did this envoy come?" Gong Gu replied, "If you reach to the dead center of the mountains ahead, it can be said that I control this little paradise. But recently, someone else with ten riders came here and defeated me, so I have to pay a monthly offering. He is in an old city south of the mountains; he calls himself 'The Grand and Nameless King,' he has built a palace in the city, called Prime Musical Mode, and has instituted a reign title named 'A Bang-up Time.' He uses a magic spear eighteen feet long that ten thousand men cannot match." When the First Ruler heard this, he thought to himself, "Must be Zhang Fei!"

Now Zhao Yun employed a spear that was named "Corners of the Sea and Edge of Heaven Spear," and it was unmatched to the very corners of the sea and to the edge of heaven. [7a] Except for that spear of Zhang Fei's, this was the number one spear mentioned in *Records of the Three Kingdoms*. Zhao Yun wanted to see this Grand and Nameless King, and he rode down the mountain with the First Ruler and all of their troops. When they drew near Old City, Zhao Yun purposely had the gongs and drums sounded.

Let us now speak of how Zhang Fei was sitting in his palace in Old City, when a foot soldier reported, "Someone is outside the walls, challenging you to battle." As soon as Zhang Fei heard this, he gave out a shout, "Who? Which one wants to die?" He quickly ordered his horse prepared, and quick as fire he donned his armor, and then took his spear and mounted his horse. He led several of his cavalry out of the northern gate and saw the First Ruler's army far off.

He flew closer until they were squared off, and Zhang Fei said, "Who is it who dares challenge me to battle?" Zhao Yun came out on his horse holding his spear and Zhang Fei, enraged, wielded his eighteen-foot steel spear to take on Zhao Yun. The two horses joined and the two spears went back and forth like pythons as they joined in hard battle for thirty rounds. Angrily, Zhang Fei said, "Now I've seen plenty of people wielding a spear. But this guy really is a tough one." They joined in battle for thirty more rounds, when Zhao Yun had no more energy, and quit the field to return to his battle line. Zhang Fei spoke angrily, "We were just getting to the fiercest part of the battle—how could he leave off so early?" And giving his horse its head and holding his spear, he chased Zhao Yun.

When he reached the front of the army, and the First Ruler recognized that it was Zhang Fei, he shouted, "Brother Zhang Fei!" Zhang Fei looked at him, and it was his elder brother, so he rolled off the saddle and dismounted, lowered his head, and offered obeisance, saying, "Brother, how did you get here?" Then he remounted and welcomed him, "Come on in the city and be emperor." Everyone entered the city together.

Zhang Fei invited the First Ruler to sit in the main hall, and they held a banquet. Zhang Fei asked, "Where is elder Brother Two?" The First Ruler spelled it out in detail, "Lord Guan aided and abetted Cao Cao, he was enfeoffed as the Marquis of Shouting, he slew two generals of Yuan Shao, and he nearly caused my death. He just has no feelings left for our Peach Orchard oath." After Zhang Fei had listened, he grew enraged, "That good-for-nothing bastard! He said, 'We do not seek to be born on the same day, but we seek to die together.' And now he receives honor and nobility from Cao Cao! If I see him, there's no way he'll get away with it." He urged more wine on the First Ruler.

But let's speak no more about the First Ruler at Old City, but talk instead about Lord Guan who, coming ever nearer Old City, sent someone to report to Zhang Fei. Zhang Fei listened and then shouted, "You bearded son-of-a-bitch! You have some kind of nerve!" [7b] He pressed his men to prepare the horses and strap on armor, and he issued forth with the First Ruler and all the rest.

When Zhang Fei saw Lord Guan, he set his horse galloping, seized his spear, and went straight for Lord Guan. Lord Guan said, "Brother Zhang Fei!" But Zhang Fei didn't heed him and used his spear to thrust at Lord Guan, who quickly parried and blocked it. Seeing that Lord Guan was not going to fight, Zhang Fei pulled up his horse and said, "You are a man of no trust, for you have forgotten the heart that bound us together in righteousness." "Brother," said Lord Guan, "you don't understand. I have come a thousand *li*, bringing my two sisters-in-law and Aji to find you two brothers. Why do you want to kill me now?" "You have received riches and nobility from Cao Cao," replied Zhang Fei, "but have purposely hidden it from us and now pursue the First Ruler." Just as the two were talking, they saw that dust was covering the sun just like rain obscures the sky. As it drew nearer, there were also battle standards with a family name, on which was written "The Han General Cai Yang." Zhang Fei replied to Lord Guan, "You didn't submit to Cao Cao? Now here we have the Han general Cai Yang whom you led to this place on purpose to attack us."

Cai Yang transmitted an order to his multitude to open in formation to strike, then rode out on horseback and said, "You ungrateful soul. I have received the prime minister's order and have come to track you down." Enraged, Lord Guan said, "I forgot no grace, but led my relatives back to find my brother. The great merit that I established for Minister Cao is enough to repay his grace." Then he ordered his men to wave their flags and sound their drums. Cai Yang took up his spear to take on Lord Guan, but Lord Guan gave his horse its head while twirling his blade.

Lord Guan Beheads Cai Yang

By the time the drum had sounded once, Cai Yang's head had been lopped off by Lord Guan's single blade. Cai's army fled in disarray. This is called "Beheading Cai Yang in ten drumbeats."

Seeing that Lord Guan had beheaded Cai Yang, Zhang Fei rolled off his saddle and dismounted, performed the proper rituals, and came forward, saying, "You were not at fault, Brother Two. When I said you were in league with Cao Cao, I never considered your chaste and incorruptible heart." He then lowered his head and paid obeisance. After the ritual was complete, he then invited Lord Guan into the city.

When Lord Guan saw the First Ruler and greeted him, the latter said, "Brother, when you did in those two generals of Yuan Shao, I almost lost my life too. How could I have escaped if it hadn't been for Zhao Zilong? I never thought we would meet each other today." Guan Yu replied, "Brother, I had no idea you were here." He thereupon invited his two sisters-in-law and Aji to come down from the cart. [8a] The three brothers had been reunited. The First Ruler touched his forehead with both hands and said, "If it hadn't been for that pre-ordained meeting I can't imagine how I would have obtained general Zhao Yun. Together with the three thousand troops of Zhao Yun, we have five thousand troops in total." The three of them were very pleased and each day set out a banquet. This is called

The Assembly of the Righteous in the Old City

Moving South

One day the First Ruler said, "Old City is no place to linger long. What would we do if Cao Cao's armies reached here? But now Liu Biao, who is at present Prince of Jing, is in Jingzhou.[66] If I can have an audience with the Prince of Jing and get just one prefecture from him, we could settle there." Guan and Zhang replied, "You are absolutely right!" So they promptly gathered their luggage and selected an auspicious day to start on their journey.

Let's not talk about the ten days spent on the road, for they had already arrived in Jingzhou and had someone go ahead and report their arrival. Liu Biao, Prince of Jing, came out of the city to welcome the First Ruler, and invited them inside, where they were accommodated in a hostel. The Prince of Jing laid out a banquet and said, "I never expected that you, Imperial Uncle, would come here. Here in Jingzhou I have no other relatives, but now I have you and Guan and Zhang to be my trusted companions."

---

66. In the final decades of the Eastern Han, the "province" of Jingzhou covered an extensive area including southern Henan and most of modern-day Hubei and Hunan. The original capital of the area was Hanshou, but Liu Biao moved the seat of administration to the northerly city of Xiangyang, which was strategically located on the Han River. After the battle at Red Cliff, when Liu Bei "borrowed" Jingzhou, the northern part of Jingzhou remained under the control of Cao Cao, so Liu Bei very quickly moved the seat of his administration southward to Jiangling on the Yangzi River. Jiangling was also the place where Guan Yu resided as administrator of Jingzhou. It was common for the seat of administration of a large area, no matter its proper name, to be called by the name of the larger area. Thus Jiangling would also be called Jingzhou.

Also present were Liu Biao's in-laws, Kuai Yue and Cai Mao, who were very much displeased. When the Prince of Jing had gone inside and the officials had all dispersed, Kuai Yue and Cai Mao deliberated, "Now there is this First Ruler Liu to wrest away our power, so we have to do away with him!" Cai Mao said, "Let's get him out of here." The two of them therefore promptly went to court to see the prince, and said, "At present Xinye lacks a prefect. We fear that if Cao Cao's armies arrive, they will first take Xinye and next take Fancheng, and that it will be difficult to stop them. Our advice is to have the Imperial Uncle, along with Guan and Zhang, defend Xinye as prefect, to intimidate Cao Cao ⚹ so he will not cross its borders." The Prince of Jing followed their advice. The two of them delivered a royal command to the Imperial Uncle and Guan and Zhang that ordered them to choose a day for their departure. Kuai and Cai said, "First have Guan and Zhang go there with the members of your family. You, Imperial Uncle, should stay here for a while. Tomorrow is the third day of the third month.[67] First enjoy with us the banquet at the riverside." The First Ruler indeed stayed behind while the two generals left with the members of his family.

Now tell that these two royal in-laws had designed a plan to murder the First Ruler. The two men had decided on a plan to invite the Imperial Uncle to the feast and have him killed by strongmen halfway through the banquet. When the two of them had settled on this plan, they invited the Imperial Uncle because on the third day of the third month all people in the city [8b] would go out and enjoy a riverside banquet. Kuai Yue and Cai Mao took the Imperial Uncle along with them to a banquet outside the walls of Xiangyang. When Kuai Yue secretly gave his orders to the strongmen, one of them noticed that the Imperial Uncle had a face like the full moon, with an aquiline nose and the countenance of a dragon, so he secretly hurried to the Imperial Uncle and whispered the whole truth in his ear. Frightened, the Imperial Uncle had people bring his horse to a thicket of willows. Pretending that he had to relieve himself, the Imperial Uncle left the banquet and got on his horse in the shade of the willows. When people shouted, "The Imperial Uncle is fleeing!" Kuai Yue and Cai Mao were greatly surprised. They quickly ordered their men to bring their horses about and set out in pursuit with their troops.

Fleeing, the First Ruler arrived at a river, namely Sandalwood Creek. The First Ruler looked up to heaven and cried, "Behind of me are enemy soldiers, and in front is this big river—I'm bound to die here in this river!"[68] The First Ruler's horse was called Rogue. The First Ruler leaned forward on his horse

---

67. A celebration of spring that stems from an ancient ablution ceremony. People went to bodies of water to picnic, drink, etc.

68. In the sequence of the five elements, Han is ruled by the element of fire; water quenches fire. So, this may also be understood as "the fate of the dynasty ends with me here in water."

and said, "My fate depends on you, your fate depends on this river. If fate is with us, then jump across this river!" The First Ruler whipped his horse forward, and in one jump it leaped across Sandalwood Creek. When Kuai Yue and Cai Mao arrived in their pursuit and saw how the First Ruler jumped across Sandalwood Creek, they exclaimed, "A true Son of Heaven!" There is a poem that describes this,

> In the third month in Xiangyang the grasses spread evenly;
> All the young nobles go out to Sandalwood Creek.
> Where are the dragon bones of Rogue now buried?
> As before the flowing waters circle the great dike.

Another poem goes,

> On the banks of Sandalwood Creek grow green rushes;
> Every passerby each has a Rogue.
> But don't say that any fine steed can jump across:
> The sagely-bright Son of Heaven was supported by gods.

Let us now speak of when the First Ruler had arrived in Xinye as its prefect and dined and feasted each day with Xu Shu.[69] One day, Xu Shu remarked, "Based upon my observation, Xinye will turn any time now into a mountain of corpses, an ocean of blood!" Zhang Fei didn't believe him and said, "How could that ever happen?"

In a matter of days Cao Ren, also known as Bozhong, the noble son deputed by Cao Cao, led a huge army of a hundred thousand down the road from Xuchang. He had hundreds of famous officers and had come to seize Fancheng and Xinye. The Imperial Uncle was greatly alarmed. Zhang Fei laughed and said, "Let's see, Master, how you will deal with this!" "Rest easy, Imperial Uncle," said Xu Shu. "I'll send Cao Ren back without a single piece of armor." Xu then summoned Zhao Yun and whispered into his ear, explaining a plan to him. Then he invited the Imperial Uncle to the southern gate, saying, "This is a propitious spot." The master then disheveled his hair, took off his shoes, and, using a plate of food and fragrant potage, he performed a sacrifice until it stirred up a whirlwind. Zhao Yun led his troops to circle around [9a] on top of the wall and shoot fire arrows below. Fire arose on all sides and the Cao forces were badly defeated; no one can even guess the number burned to death. Cao Bozhong, with less than a thousand men, escaped with his life and went back.

---

69. A Daoist who had magical powers and who was Liu Bei's field marshal. His sudden appearance here without an account of how he came to help Liu Bei may indicate that this section of the text derives from a different source than the first chapter. Of course, in the world of text based on a circulating oral body of tales, this is both possible and difficult to prove.

The Triple Visit

The Imperial Uncle set out a banquet to honor Xu Shu. But when it was finished on that day Xu thought to himself, "My aged mother at present is in Xuchang, and if Lord Cao learns that I was here and that I killed his troops he will turn into a sworn enemy and there would be no way to guarantee the lives of my mother, wife, and children." That very moment he took his leave of the First Ruler. The latter was not pleased, but Xu Shu said, "If I don't go back, my dependents will be in danger."

So the three, the First Ruler, Guan, and Zhang, accompanied Xu Shu as he began his journey, offering him a farewell cup ten *li* from the city. But because he still could not let him go, the First Ruler accompanied him for another ten *li* and offered him a farewell cup at the long pavilion.[70] Still feeling a deep attachment, the First Ruler asked him, "Master, when will you return?" Xu Shu replied, "I am a person of insignificance, what is there to be fixed on? Now there are two people who know the books of Lü Wang inside out[71] and who, seated in their commanders' tent, can decide a victory at a distance of a thousand *li*—they consider the empire easily won." When the First Ruler asked who these two men might be, Xu Shu replied, "In the south there is Recumbent Dragon, and in the north there is Phoenix Fledgling. Phoenix Fledgling is Pang and Recumbent Dragon is Zhuge, who at present has built himself a thatched cottage on Recumbent Dragon Ridge in Nanyang. His name is Zhuge Liang, and he is also known as Kongming. He employs his troops like a god, and his machinations are unfathomable, even to gods and ghosts. He can be your field marshal." When the First Ruler heard this, he was very pleased, and after he had said goodbye to Xu Shu he went to Xinye.

A few days later the three brothers went to Recumbent Dragon Ridge in Nanyang to invite Zhuge. There is a poem that reads,

---

70. There were rest stops every five miles; those at intervals of five, fifteen, twenty-five, etc., were called "short pavilions," and those at ten, twenty, thirty etc., were called "long pavilions." Thus, this would in fact be the second of the long pavilions.

71. The book in question is the *Six Tactics* (*Liutao*), a handbook of military matters. Its authorship was attributed to Lü Wang, an adviser to King Wen and King Wu, the founders of the Zhou dynasty. Also known as Lü Shang, Jiang Shang, Jiang Taigong, or Jiang Ziya, Lü Wang was a hermit who spent his days angling in Pan Creek until he was brought to court at the age of seventy by King Wen of the Zhou. At the age of eighty, Lü Wang assisted King Wu in his conquest of the Shang and the establishment of the Zhou dynasty. It was only in imperial times (i.e., after 220 BCE) that he was credited with the authorship of this military handbook. His biography is found in translation in "T'ai-kung of Ch'i, Hereditary House 2," in Sima Qian (2006, 31–46).

With a single word they could support family and state,
With a few sentences they could establish a great nation:
Due north you can see in the distance the golden phoenix tail;
But it is better to look southward toward Recumbent Dragon Ridge.

The story goes that in the third month of spring of the thirteenth year of the Zhongping period[72] the Imperial Uncle led three thousand troops and with his two brothers went straight to the Recumbent Dragon Ridge in Dengzhou in Nanyang. They dismounted in front of the hermitage and waited for the man inside to come out.

We must backtrack to explain that Master Zhuge was seated inside his hermitage with his hands on his knees. A face that seemed freshly powdered and lips as if painted red—he was not yet thirty and he read his books every day. His acolyte told him, "There are three thousand troops in front of the hermitage. Their leader, they say, is the new prefect of [9b] Xinye, the Imperial Uncle of the Han, Liu Bei." The master did not say a word, but called the acolyte over and softly whispered something in his ear.

The acolyte went outside and said to the Imperial Uncle, "My teacher left yesterday for Jiangxia to join the drinking party of the Eight Eminences." The Imperial Uncle did not say a word but thought to himself that he would be unable to meet this man. He then ordered someone to grind up some thick ink and wrote a poem on the western wall. The poem reads,

Alone astride a blue simurgh, where does he roam?
Most likely the transcendent beings are meeting at Fairy Isle.
Seeking, but not seeing this gentleman, I go back empty-handed:
Rank grasses and wildflowers fill the land with sorrow.

The prefect returned to Xinye, but in the eighth month Xuande went once again to the thatched cottage to pay his respects to Zhuge. He dismounted in front of the hermitage and had someone knock on the door. Recumbent Dragon once again had his acolyte go outside and declare, "My teacher has left to roam the mountains and enjoy the rivers and he has yet to return." The First Ruler said, "I remember that Zifang reached a ruined bridge when fleeing and met with Lord Yellow Stone; time and again he presented the shoe, and so obtained a heavenly book in three chapters.[73] And Xu Shu, I also remember,

---

72. Another impossible date.

73. Zifang is Zhang Liang, who served Liu Bang in establishing the Han dynasty. But once the dynasty had been established and Liu Bang grew suspicious of his erstwhile supporters, Zhang retired from court, according to legend, to become a hermit. By the end of the Western Han his

said that the Recumbent Dragon was a myriad times better than him—to Zhuge the empire could be had as easily as an arm moving its fingers." Under the influence of his wine the Imperial Uncle was deeply depressed and once again inscribed a poem on the western wall. The poem reads,

Where the autumn wind first rises,
Clouds disperse and the evening sky lowers.
Rain and dew, trees of wilting leaves;
Again and again, geese on sandbanks fly away.
The dark-blue sky is but a single hue;
Traveling oars now urge us on again.
In vain I labored for twenty years:
Neither sword nor armor leaving my side.
Alone I pace in the prefecture of Xinye
But my cold heart has yet to turn to ash.
Those who really understand me are just a few;
I have come to see you, I returned empty-handed again.
I remember how Guan Yu, Zhang Fei, and I
Became sworn brothers in the Peach Orchard
But now our hometown is a myriad *li* away—
Yunmeng is separated by a thousand mountains.
My ambition finds no place of support,
Though I had hoped to connect with a real hero.
Not meeting the Recumbent Dragon
This little one can only go home again.

The Imperial Uncle and his officers mounted their horses and returned to Xinye. Zhang Fei shouted out, "Elder brother, you are wrong! I remember Tigerkeep Pass and how I thrice fought my way out of Xiapi, and how my elder brother Lord Guan skewered Yan Liang, pursued Wen Chou, beheaded Cai Yang, and surprised Che Zhou. In those days we had no 'master'! With a hundred-pound blade I can dispute with this master." The Imperial Uncle simply did not answer.

---

identity as a Daoist was firmly established, and in his eulogy to the "Marquis of Liu, Hereditary House 25" (*Liuhou shijia ershiwu*) in the *Records of the Historian*, Sima Qian expresses some skepticism about the prevailing idea that Zhang received the texts of the Laozi from Laozi himself, which was firmly part of the tradition by that time. See Sima Qian (1993, 99–114). One of the commentarial notes to this passage cites a work that declares, "The Lord of the Wind was the commander of the Yellow Emperor's army, and he later transformed into Laozi, who bestowed his text on Zhang Liang." In later religious traditions Zhang Liang became a Daoist immortal. He once displayed his humility by retrieving a slipper that Master Yellow Stone had thrown down a bridge and the latter instructed him in military strategy, as found in the book entitled *Three Strategies* (*Sanlue*).

But now let us backtrack to discuss Zhuge, who said to himself, "Who am I that I make the prefect return repeatedly to pay his respects? I observe that the Imperial Uncle has the features of a king or emperor: [10a] his earlobes hang down on his shoulders and his hands hang below his knees. Moreover, I have looked at the poems he wrote on the western wall; he is someone who has great ambition." Day in day out the master thought about the last two visits. And then, right when he was sunk in pondering about it, his acolyte reported, "The Imperial Uncle is back again!" The poem reads,

> In an age of chaos while heroes were fighting a hundred battles,
> Kongming was right here, enjoying his plowing and hoeing.
> If the King of Shu had not graced him with a third visit
> Would the master have ever left his old cottage?

The Third Visit to Zhuge

The story goes that the First Ruler had, in the space of four seasons, gone three times to the thatched hut to pay his respects to Recumbent Dragon, but he never got to see him. Zhuge was originally a divine immortal who had studied his craft from his early youth. Now that he had reached middle age, there was no book he had not read; he understood the mysteries of Heaven and Earth and the inscrutable will of gods and ghosts; he could call up the wind and command the rain, create soldiers by scattering beans, and create rivers by waving his sword. Sima Zhongda once remarked, "Advancing, he cannot be stopped; departing, he cannot be held back; and even when in dire straits he cannot be captured—I do not know whether he is a man, a god, or a ghost!" Now, since Xu Shu had recommended Zhuge Liang to Liu Bei, the First Ruler was unshakable in his determination and arrived once again at the thatched cottage. The First Ruler was accompanied by his two younger brothers Guan and Zhang and brought his troops with him. In front of the hermitage they dismounted but he still did not dare announce their arrival. After a while an acolyte came out and the First Ruler asked, "Is your master at home?" The acolyte replied, "My master is reading his texts."

Accompanied by Guan and Zhang, the First Ruler entered the hermitage and, reaching the thatched cottage, performed the rituals of greeting. Zhuge continued to pay attention only to his books. Enraged, Zhang Fei said, "Our brother is the seventeenth-generation grandson of the Han, a descendant of Liu Sheng, the Quiet Prince of Zhongshan. Now he is bending his back in front of your thatched cottage. You deliberately humiliate our brother!" With all his authority Yunchang ordered him to shut up. Zhuge lifted his eyes and looked at them, and then came outside to greet them.

When they had finished the formalities, Zhuge asked, "Who might you gentlemen be?" Xuande replied, "I am the seventeenth-generation grandson of the Han, a descendant of Liu Sheng, the Quiet Prince of Zhongshan, and I currently serve as prefect of Xinye." After Zhuge heard this, he invited the Imperial Uncle into his hermitage, where they sat down. Zhuge said, "I am not really at fault—my acolyte failed to report your arrival." The First Ruler said, "Master, Xu Shu recommends you as an expert in strategy whose skillful schemes surpass those of Lü Wang. I have now come for the third time in four seasons to invite you to leave your thatched cottage; I want you to become my field marshal." Zhuge replied, "Imperial Uncle, will you annihilate Cao Cao [10b] and restore the house of Han?" "Yes," replied Xuande, and he continued to speak, "I have heard that Zhao Gao, chief eunuch, abused his prerogatives, that Dong Zhuo has usurped all power, that Cao Cao is a master of cunning,[74] and Emperor Xian is a fearful weakling. Before long the empire will be mastered by many hegemons, each in their own area. I, Liu Bei, have come here for this reason, to invite you, master, to leave your hermitage and campaign against Cao—but it would be enough if we can simply obtain a single prefecture where we can settle in peace!" "Ever since Emperor Heng and Emperor Ling lost control of the government," replied Zhuge, "the common people have found it hard to survive. And treacherous ministers usurped all of the high positions within the Gates of the Golden Horse.[75] As a result men of virtue have had to flee to mountain and field. Alas! Cao Mengde commands a million troops and thousands of fierce generals. Because he controls the power of the Son of Heaven, there are no liege lords who do not fear him! By guile Sun Quan occupies the geographical advantage of the mountains and rivers of Changsha. His state is wealthy, its people haughty. He rules as the third generation, succeeding his father and elder brother, and the River can hold back a million troops. And then there is you, Imperial Uncle, one who relies on love and righteousness and who builds on heroic action. But also one who lacks even ten thousand troops or a hundred officers! If you wish to restore the empire, Imperial Uncle, you will first have to grasp the opportunity to borrow Jingzhou as your principal, and then later set your eyes on Xichuan[76] as your interest. Now the area of Jing and Chu has the Great River to its north and to its south the southern barbarians;

---

74. To Liu Bei, these would be the "three great treacherous officials." Dong Zhuo is mentioned above; Zhao Gao (d. 207 BCE) manipulated several rulers of the Qin and at the end of the dynasty was instrumental in forging the last testament of the First Emperor of Qin to obviate the First Emperor's plans to have his first son placed on the throne and military power given to his finest general, Meng Tian. Zhao killed Meng Tian; helped the last emperor of the Qin usurp his brother's throne; but was finally killed, along with his clan, by the young emperor he had installed.

75. Metonymy for the central palaces of government.

76. Modern Sichuan.

to its east are Suzhou and Shaoxing, and to its west are Ba and Shu. Haven't you heard about that starving beggar Liu Zhang?[77] He is a fearful weakling as a ruler. As soon as you give the signal to your troops to attack, you can conquer that region in a single day! Once that has happened, you place Guan in command of the armies of Shu, and if you march eastward through Sword Pass to conquer everything west of Hangu Pass it will be as easy as picking up a mustard seed from the floor—why wouldn't the common people welcome you with plates of rice and jugs of brew?" When the Imperial Uncle had found Kongming, he was as happy as a fish that had found water! Let's not talk about outstanding courage, let's not speak about the loftiest hero—heaven's timing, the advantages of topography, or the harmony of people: each of the three kingdoms utilized one of these virtues to establish its state. Xuande thereupon appointed Zhuge as his field marshal. When Zhuge left his thatched cottage, he was twenty-nine.

Zhuge Leaves His Thatched Cottage

When he went to Xinye, he was treated each day to a banquet. One day the Imperial Uncle suddenly asked the field marshal to train the troops. Zhuge opined, "In training the army, whoever disobeys my commands will be beheaded!" Now Zhang Fei had long wanted to get the best of Kongming, so he loudly shouted in front of the hall, "Imperial Uncle, that's impossible! How can a hick cowherd give orders to the troops?" With one hand, Lord Guan pinched Zhang's mouth shut and said, "Zhang Fei, you are too crude! The Imperial Uncle treats the field marshal as the Great Duke!"[78] The First Ruler said, "To me, finding Kongming was like a fish finding water!" The Imperial Uncle invited Zhuge to his office and treated him to a banquet each day.

[12a] A few days more than a month later, someone came to report, "Cao Cao has appointed Xiahou Dun as great marshal and he is going to take Xinye with a hundred thousand troops." Zhang Fei shouted loudly, "Imperial Uncle, for you, finding Kongming was like a fish finding water. My martial prowess is crude and blunted, so let's see how the field marshal will deal with this situation." Immediately Zhuge called out to Lord Guan, "Use my plan!" And he also ordered Zhao Yun, "Act according to my plan!" The other generals too all received their instructions. Zhang Fei asked, "Field Marshal, you haven't employed me, so what am I supposed to do?" The field marshal quickly responded, "General, here are my instructions for you." When Zhang Fei had looked them over, Zhuge said, "General, give it your best!" Within a few days these officers had all dispersed as ordered by the field marshal.

---

77. Who then ruled Yizhou (Sichuan).
78. The Great Duke is yet another name for Lü Wang.

The Field Marshal Executes His Plan

Let us now return to Xiahou Dun, who had set up camp at a distance of thirty *li* from Xinye and ordered his men to explore the situation there. They heard the sound of drums and music, and reported to the great marshal, "The field marshal, executing his plans, has ascended the top of a mountain, and has asked the Imperial Uncle to have a banquet there with music." Xiahou Dun said, "That country hick slights me too much!" He led fifty thousand troops to the high slope. He wheeled to face south, and hoisted his marshal's banner. The Imperial Uncle and the field marshal, accompanied by the officials, raced to the western side. From the upper slope, stones from catapults and rolling tree trunks hit the hillside. Xiahou Dun's horse never had any rest, for he was pursued from behind by two generals. As soon as Zhao Yun emerged from the flank with three thousand troops, Xiahou Dun wanted to return to his camp—but during his absence Ma Gou and Liu Feng had already captured it. Xiahou Dun then fled toward the north and when evening fell, he arrived at an old city. He sent out spies who reported, "There is a limitless supply of grain and straw, wagons, and oxen inside the walls." Everyone explained to Xiahou Dun that these were supplies bound for Xinye, but that the guards there, learning of the impending battle, had fled. Xiahou Dun and his troops entered the town and dismounted at the government office.

The marshal told them to cook food. But just as the rice was done and they were about to eat, troops that had been lying in ambush attacked them on all four sides. Xiahou Dun wanted to flee, but the rope around the corral had been cut. A hundred horsemen emerged to make a direct assault on his formation, and wounded who knows how many. Xiahou Dun said, "This must be the scheme of that cowherd country hick!" With fewer than thirty thousand troops remaining, he fled toward the east. He had gone no more than twenty *li* from the city—it was just a little after midnight—when they all dismounted by the banks of Sandalwood Creek. Xiahou Dun once again told them to make food since the men were exhausted and the horses were worn out. [12b] Officers and soldiers all lay on their backs. When the rice was done, they asked the marshal to eat before any of the officers. Suddenly they heard a sound that echoed like thunder and someone reported to Xiahou Dun, "The water of the Sandalwood Creek is billowing down like a bank of massive white clouds!" The marshal ordered his men to hasten to the top of a hillock, from where he watched as the waters swept the corpses of men and horses downriver. The marshal wept bitterly—not even ten thousand of his troops remained.

When morning came, Xiahou Dun once again went on in a northerly direction, and arrived at a bridge across Sandalwood Creek. His men on the east and west came directly to the south to cross the bridge straight north. But hidden troops emerged to block his way, and he was trapped between Jian Xianhe behind and Lord Guan in front. Xiahou Dun attacked the formations head on and got past, but saw that now he had fewer than three hundred troops left.

Xiahou Dun said, "First rocks rained down all over the hillside, next my camp was occupied, then there was the battle in the old town, and in the end I had to flee because a flood was released to drown my troops." And he went on, "If there is yet another body of troops waiting for me, I will not be able to return to Xuchang!" Before he had finished saying this, less than three *li* ahead of him three thousand troops appeared under the willow trees. Amongst them a drunken general shouted, "The field marshal, the Imperial Uncle, and the other generals all abided by the plan and they shoved me off to this place. And the field marshal said, 'After Xiahou Dun is defeated, he will pass through your hands!'"[79] When Zhang Fei fell silent, someone hurried up to inform him, "Those defeated troops are coming straight east; they're less than three hundred men!" "Who is it?" asked Zhang Fei. "Xiahou Dun," came the reply. Zhang Fei said with a smile, "That field marshal truly is smart!" As soon as his words were finished, Zhang Fei mounted his horse to block Xiahou Dun. The two sides engaged in battle, and Xiahou Dun was soundly defeated.

Let us now tell how Cao Cao had taken his seat in the hall and inquired of his officers, "Xiahou Dun left with a hundred thousand troops and a hundred generals to take Fancheng and Xinye. He has been gone for three months now and there's been no news." Before he had finished these words, one of his underlings reported, "Xiahou Dun and his army have returned." "What," asked Cao Cao, "was the outcome?" The soldier said, "Only twenty or thirty people have made it back." Cao Cao was shaken and ordered Xiahou Dun to present himself. He saw that his armor was covered in blood and that his body showed a number of wounds. Xiaohou Dun prostrated himself on the ground and said, "Please spare my wife and children; I beg to die." Xiahou Dun went on, "A hundred thousand troops beheaded by five generals! Immolated by fire, drowned by a flood, ambushed again and again! And eventually [13a] I was bitterly defeated by that Zhang Fei! It was all the scheme of the country hick Zhuge!"

When Cao Cao heard this, he flew into a rage, "Take Xiahou Dun out and behead him in front of the steps." He heard someone loudly call out before he finished speaking. He recognized that it was Xu Shu, who said, "Prime Minister, Dun has the courage of a prince!" Minister Cao spoke, "What about this Zhuge?" Xu Shu replied, "That man has the ability to fathom Heaven. The whole world is as clear to him as the ten fingers of his hands. If Xiahou Dun managed to escape from Zhuge with his life, he is an outstanding general!"

---

79. The expression has a double meaning, "will pass your way" and "will slip through your fingers." In this text, however, the emphasis is not so much on Zhang Fei's failure as on Xiahou Dun's defeat.

Cao Cao said with a smile, "In my eyes that country hick is nothing. Xu Shu, I will prove you wrong! Leading a million of troops and a thousand of fine officers, I will trample Fancheng and Xinye to pieces and even take Jingzhou!" Immediately he mobilized the troops.

Cao Cao's Great Campaign

But let us turn to the Imperial Uncle, who invited the field marshal and other officers to go to the Xinye yamen for a celebratory banquet and a good time. But someone reported, "Lord Cao is leading a huge army of a million men and a thousand officers and is making his way from afar to Fancheng and Xinye." This scared the Imperial Uncle so much he was stupefied and he asked the field marshal for his advice. The latter replied, "This is simple to deal with!" He immediately wrote a letter and sent someone off to Jingzhou in the southeast to see Liu Biao and borrow three hundred thousand troops. The letter went out that very night and the answer came at full light of the morning, stating that the Prince of Jing had died and that Jingzhou had established Liu Cong, the second son of the Prince of Jing, as ruler. This news moved the Imperial Uncle to tears.

The following day it was again reported that Cao Cao's army was approaching. When the Imperial Uncle questioned Zhuge, the field marshal replied, "This is not a place to oppose Cao Cao," and he invited the Imperial Uncle to flee.

That night in the second watch the officers and troops all fled and proceeded to Jingzhou. Below the city wall they loudly shouted and asked to be admitted into the city. When Liu Cong mounted the wall, he said, "Weep, Imperial Uncle, for my father is dead." Liu Bei responded, "Why didn't you inform me?" Kuai Yue stated, "When the Prince of Jing died, Liu Qi rose in rebellion and he was deposed by the second son. And you, Imperial Uncle Xuande, didn't know?" The Imperial Uncle then said, "Cao Cao is leading a million troops and will arrive below these walls within three days. Dear nephew, please open the gate. As for Cao's fleet, you have your four generals who will grapple with him at the rapids. I am bringing you the two generals Guan and Zhang, and as for someone who understands the civil arts I bring you my field marshal Zhuge." But Liu Cong said, "Jingzhou is too narrow and cramped, there's no space for you here." And Kuai Yue loudly shouted, "These gates will not be opened!" Xuande [13b] was extremely irritated.

By the next day, they were some forty *li* from Jingzhou, where Xuande saw a large grove. When he dismounted and asked about it, he was told, "This is the grave of the Prince of Jing." Xuande offered him food and wine and a plate of fruit in sacrifice, but while he was still bitterly weeping the field marshal informed him, "Cao Cao's army is near."

The next day Xuande heard a great commotion behind them and when he asked who these people were a soldier reported, "These are the common people of Fancheng and Xinye who have caught up with you here." And when Xuande asked, "Why have you come?" one of the group replied, "You, Imperial Uncle, are a man of humanity and virtue. When Cao Cao's troops arrived they killed countless people, so we would rather follow you. We will not regret it, even if it means our deaths." The Imperial Uncle said, "We must march more slowly."

The troops of the Imperial Uncle marched south together with the civilians. On the third day after leaving Jingzhou the field marshal alerted the Imperial Uncle, "The traitor Cao is close and there are families in tow. If that traitor Cao catches up with you because of your concern for these civilians, then what?" Xuande did not respond. Hearing a commotion at the back of the army Xuande asked, "What's happening?" Someone reported, "Cao Cao is killing the civilians at the rear." So he divided his army in three companies and set out.

Let us now relate that the Imperial Uncle, unable to save the civilians, fled due south. One day as the Imperial Uncle was hurrying down the road, someone reported that when Cao's army attacked a great many civilians had been mixed in with the fleeing troops. In the chaos, the Imperial Uncle clung to his saddle as he rode. No one knew the whereabouts of the wives and son of the Imperial Uncle, but Xuande did not say a word.

After they had marched some twenty or thirty *li*, someone told the Imperial Uncle, "Zhao Yun has rebelled!" Xuande asked, "How do you know?" Without looking back the Imperial Uncle went on. The person said it a second time and the Imperial Uncle cut off the mane of his horse with one stroke of his sword, "Take the mane of this horse as example!" These men kept silent and the Imperial Uncle told them, "After I had joined Yuan Shao and Lord Guan had beheaded Yan Liang and executed Wen Chou, the Prince of Ji ordered Zhao Yun to capture me so he could behead and execute me. But Zhao Yun was unwilling to do so. He has accompanied me for three years without any fault. How could he rebel?"

Three *li* further on was a river with a large bridge over it. The mountain grade was particularly steep and it was known as "the long slope of Dangyang." The Imperial Uncle marched past the long slope of Dangyang. There, the field marshal looked back and took note of how high and precipitous this ridge was. He thought that if he could find one stalwart general and a hundred horses to occupy the top, he could hold off the entire million men of Cao Cao's army. [14a] "I made a mistake," said Kongming. "I sent Lord Guan south to the River yesterday to seize the boats so Cao Cao could not cross, and he is still not back." He heard someone shout out loudly—he recognized it to be Zhang Fei,

"Command this bearded Lord Zhang Fei to hold them off!" "I have heard," said the field marshal, "that your eminence's great battle at Tigerkeep Pass and the three exits from Xiaopei were all due to your virtue. Anyone who is brave and staunch enough today to win fame in history by holding up that traitor Cao is surely a great man."

Let us then turn to Zhang Fei, who summoned twenty men, took twenty battle flags, and went north until he reached the long slope at Dangyang.

And then later we will speak of how Zhao Yun went into Cao's troops on a single mount. "We are now over a hundred *li* from the battlefield," he said, "so let me search for the Imperial Uncle's relatives." He made a circuit several times until he saw Lady Gan, with her right hand clutching her ribs and her left holding Aji. Zhao Yun got off his horse and when Consort Gan saw him, tears rained ceaselessly down as she explained, "All relatives were slain by the berserk troops of Lord Cao." She went on, "Zhao Yun, you have come at just the right time. I have been hit in my right ribs by an arrow and when I lift my right hand, my intestines spill out. Our Imperial Uncle is already old but still has no place 'to stand an awl on end.' I'm finished now. You take Aji and turn him over to uncle." When she finished speaking, she went south until she reached a wall and then bade goodbye to Zhao Yun and Aji, and died there below the wall. Zhao Yun pushed the wall over to cover her body. Zhao Yun said, "I will save Aji for our lord from the clutches of Cao's millions!" This instant of bravery won Zhao Yun recognition in history. He held the crown prince as he raced southward, smashing directly through the enemy's formations. There was a later poem,

> How marvelous was this Zhao Zilong:
> A whole heart of loyalty that puts others in awe;
> The First Ruler had been defeated in Jingzhou,
> And his family was unable to follow him.
> With a lifelong disregard for death
> Zhao plunged again into the thicket of tigers and wolves;
> Loyal and filial, he protected the weak little child,
> Daring to challenge a million brave men.
> In the Spring and Autumn era was a Minister Wu,[80]
> And the reign of Han has its Zilong—
> A thousand generations from this point on,
> Who will not look up to these high moral actions?

---

80. Minister Wu is Wu Zixu, whose father and elder brother had been killed by King Ping of Chu. Despite great deprivation he persisted in his determination to take revenge. Eventually he rose to high position in the state of Wu and inflicted a devastating defeat on his old home state.

Zhao Yun Carries the Baby in His Arms

Zhao Yun fled toward the south.

But let us return to Cao Cao, watching from a high vantage point, who thought, "Must be some officer in the hands of Liu Bei!" He then dispatched a host of officers to take Zhao Yun, and their leader, Guan Jing, blocked his way. Zhao Yun twirled his blade and spurred his horse, breaking directly through the formation until, as he reached the bridge, his horse lost its footing and lord and minister were on the ground tightly clutching each other. Behind, Guan Jing was in hot pursuit and drawing near, so Zhao Yun used his stout bow and with a single arrow shot and killed Guan Jing. Carrying the heir apparent in his arms, Zhao Yun then again fled southward. A *li* or so away from the long slope at Dangyang, he saw Zhang Fei far off. "Grand Defender," said Zhang Fei, "you have to save Aji!" Zhao Yun said, "As for the Imperial Uncle's family, the two wives are dead. The crown prince is the only one to survive, and I will take him to the Imperial Uncle." Zhang Fei wept and said, "As a real hero, I just told the Imperial Uncle that I would hold the long slope at Dangyang, to assure that His Majesty makes his escape."

Zhao Yun went on south, and when he had finished the greeting rituals when he saw the Imperial Uncle, he said, "Consort Gan and Consort Mi were both killed by Lord Cao. I was able to rescue the heir apparent from the berserk troops and escape." Zhao Yun then went to see the Imperial Uncle holding the heir apparent. The Imperial Uncle took the child and threw it to the ground. His officers were all startled and remonstrated with the Imperial Uncle. Xuande said, "Because of this 'shameful child of mine,'[81] I almost lost my great general Zhao Yun." When the Imperial Uncle finished speaking, they all praised his goodness. The Imperial Uncle went on southward.

Let us go back and speak of Zhang Fei, who had reached the long slope at Dangyang to the north. He ordered his soldiers to take fifty flags[82] and make a formation of a long horizontal line on a high place to the north. Twenty-some cavalry were to keep lookout over the river to the south. Lord Cao arrived with an army of three hundred thousand. "Respected Sir, why aren't you evading me?" Zhang Fei laughed, "I see no huge army; all I see is Cao Cao." When Cao's cavalry let out a continuous yell, he then shouted, "I am Zhang Yide from Yan, who dares fight to the death with me?" His shout was like thunder in the ears, and the bridge broke completely asunder. Cao's army withdrew some thirty *li* away. There is a eulogy for the shrine to Yide,

---

81. A humble way of referring to one's child.
82. Each flag signified a unit of troops.

When the First Ruler plotted to be king,
And the empire was tripart torn, a tripod[83] bubbling over,
He held the bridge and sent Cao's troops in flight;
His awesome voice sundering the water.
The liege lords trembled in terror;
The soldiers marched to the land of the nine springs.[84]
As stern and forbidding as a god—
The aura of a hegemon!

Zhang Fei Blocks the River and Breaks the Bridge

Let us now explain how Zhang Fei went to catch up to the Imperial Uncle and that evening finally met with him. The Martial Marquis[85] said, "This is a true general! Using flags he stopped Cao Cao's troops cold, so his lord could march on at full speed for fifty *li*. Cao Cao will play right into our hands." The Imperial Uncle was delighted.

The Alliance of Liu Bei and Sun Quan

The next day, the army was marched along the path that led to the land of Wu. There was there a famous general, Lu Su, who was also known as Zijing. When questioned, he replied, "I am on my way to Jingzhou to pay my condolences to the Prince of Jing. Why, Imperial Uncle, have you come here?" Zhuge rode out on his horse to meet with Lu Su, and they greeted each other. Lu Su was greatly surprised, "How could I have guessed that you, the Recumbent Dragon, had joined Liu Bei?" Zhuge said, "Haven't you figured out that traitor Cao reached Jingzhou with a million troops, that Liu Cong surrendered to him, and that that bandit Cao is planning on swallowing up the state of Wu?" Lu Su replied, "So what are your intentions?" "The Imperial Uncle is on his way southward to Downriver Wu and would like to visit his elder brother Liu Bi." Lu Su didn't say a word but thought to himself, "That Liu Bi is a good friend of mine, now the Imperial Uncle and Zhuge should join up with my lord."

---

83. The tripod is a metaphor for the empire now, after Zhuge Liang's suggested plan, to be split into three.

84. The underworld.

85. Zhuge Liang.

When both sides made camp that night Cao Cao was only ten *li* away. Lu Su invited the Imperial Uncle and his officers to a drinking party, and the lanterns shone on the Imperial Uncle, Zhuge, Guan and Zhang, and Zhao Yun. Lu Su thought, "These officers are all brave generals." He also thought, "What worry would our Caitiff-Suppressing General Sun Quan have if he could obtain the Imperial Uncle and his field marshal?"

The next day Lu Su invited the Imperial Uncle to go on to a walled city on the River that was called Xiakou. It was surrounded on three sides by water and they stopped at the north gate. Lu Su said, "I will invite you inside with drums and music." Xuande stayed for a few days in that city, which had an unlimited supply of grain and fodder, wine and meat.

The next day Lu Su was going to take a ship to see the Caitiff-Suppressing General while the First Ruler and his officers would remain in the city. The Imperial Uncle ordered Zhuge to present a letter and go south to visit Sun Quan. The next day he boarded the boat outside the south gate of Xiakou. Xuande spoke to the field marshal, and the latter called Zhao Yun over and whispered in his ear.

Lu Su and the Martial Marquis crossed the River, got on another craft and made the long trip down to Jinling, where they settled down in the inn. The next day Zhuge was received in audience by Sun Quan. After he had entered the yamen and made his bows, Zhuge said, "Lord Cao and his one million three hundred thousand troops have stolen the land of Chu. Now that he has subdued Liu Cong, he will want to take Wu." Sun Quan asked, "How do you know?" He explained, "After Xinye and Fancheng had been lost, Xuande set out for Cangwu with the intention of joining Liu Bi. But Xuande is now at Xiakou." Sun Quan said, "In the beginning, Zhuge made him visit him three times and never met face to face, but now he has joined Liu Bei!" Zhuge presented his letter to Sun Quan, and when the latter opened it to read it, it said,

The undersigned Bei kowtows and petitions the banner of the Caitiff-Suppressing General Lord Sun:

I humbly pray that Your Highest Excellency be assisted and protected by the divinities. Even though I have not yet had the opportunity to pay you a visit, I have learned respectfully [14a] that you, general, vaunt the Way of humanity and virtue, are a meritorious vassal who supports the house of Han, and continue, as the third generation, the rich legacy of your father and elder brother.

At present I am beset by an urgent problem: I am besieged in Xiakou with only a few remaining officers and see no possibility of escape. Cao Cao appropriates to himself the power of the Son of Heaven, leads a million troops, and is killing or injuring the liege lords; the empire of the Han is expected to collapse any day. If the Han is extinguished, he is bound to invade the land of

Wu. But alas, my troops are limited and my officers are few, so I would like to borrow from you, general, the might of wind and thunder for one battle so I may save the living beings of the commanderies and kingdoms from their suffering. Only after the common people find security in their work will peace be reestablished. Paper and brush cannot exhaust Cao Cao's extraordinary fiendishness.

I am now trapped in Xiakou and I have especially ordered my field marshal to take you this letter to transmit my request. I humbly implore you, general, to agree to it. If I will not be refused, I reverentially will listen for reply. Until the moment I may see you I will humbly obey your orders.

Please take good care of yourself.

After Sun Quan read this letter from the Imperial Uncle, he asked his host of officials, "What shall we do?" He saw two people step forward in tandem. These were Zhang Zhao and Wu Fan,[86] who stated, "The Imperial Uncle is besieged in Xiakou and Zhuge has crossed the River to come and visit you, bringing this letter asking for help. Our lord, haven't you heard that Cao Cao's one million troops have already captured Jingzhou? If he gets to the Great River, the officers of the land of Wu should each guard one of the river crossings so Cao Cao's army cannot proceed. If you allow the Imperial Uncle to borrow an army, it's like waving a sharp bare blade over tender meat: we will not be able to put down our armor even after ten years!" When Sun Quan once again asked what should be done, Zhang Zhao once again spoke up, "The liege lords of Shandong and Hebei have all submitted to Cao Cao, and those who fought him have all been defeated." Suddenly they became aware someone shouted—they recognized Zhuge—and he said, "You two only speak of the might of Lord Cao, do you want to surrender? Haven't you heard how Lord Cao, after he had captured the land of Jing and Chu, sent off Liu Cong to a different place and had him killed on trumped-up charges? Do you want to ape the words of the likes of Kuai Yue and Cai Mao who persuaded Liu Cong to surrender to Cao Cao?" This scared Sun Quan to speak out in alarm, "Field Marshal, what you say is right on the mark!"

They debated the problem for three days and still had not yet reached a decision when suddenly someone came to report, "Cao Cao's army of one million three hundred thousand is besieging Xiakou and he has sent someone with a letter to particularly come have an audience with the Caitiff-Suppressing General." Sun Quan ordered someone to summon the envoy before him and present the letter. Sun Quan read it,

---

86. The text and the illustrations consistently write Wu Fan, written in a simplified form in the text as (吴) instead of the actual name Lü Fan (呂).

When in ancient times the August King[87] ruled the court, Chiyou [15a] rose in rebellion, and when King Shun occupied the throne, the descendants of the Miao refused to obey. Now the Yellow Emperor was not a ruler without the Way and Shun of Yu was certainly no inhumane prince. Yet mutinous vassals and traitorous sons turned their back on favors received and abandoned what is right, provoking the fury of heaven and earth as well as the wrath of gods and men. This is the reason why armies take the field and buckler and spear are raised everywhere. I, Cao, have received the imperial directive and bear the emperor's mandate to command this army of a million, to cleanse away the perverted and evil throughout the world. Now I have executed Lü Bu in Xiapi, beheaded Gongsun Zan in Henei, and exterminated Yuan Tan in Qingzhou; when I arrived in Bianliang I immediately arrested Zhang Mao, and when I came to Luoyang I promptly captured Kong Xiu alive.

Should I array formations on the banks of a river or set out my soldiers with their backs to the smallest creek, I depend on the enormous blessings of the Son of Heaven and rely on my own awesome might. Leading a million troops I proceed by both water and land routes, advancing on and adding capital precincts, just as if I were plucking up my robe to wade in the ocean or walking along wide streets. To take the rivers of Wu would be like Mt. Tai crushing an egg. Now I have received an edict ordering me to arrest and capture the rebellious slave Liu Bei. The Suppressor of Caitiffs is a loyal minister of the Han—do not heed his slanderous words. Should you be beclouded and resist me as an enemy, I will take my one million troops right to the Great River, which can be crossed at any time I want. Don't wait for fires of Mt. Kunlun to burst forth to burn both pure jade and simple stone together. Those who lack knowledge and foresight will all and every one be decapitated. I will go no further into detail.

Respectfully submited to the Caitiff-Suppressing General by Cao Cao, Grand Prince of Wei, presently appointed to a position of first advisor, Generalissimo of the Han and concurrently the Grand Marshal of Horse and Foot.

When Sun Quan had finished reading this letter he was so terrified that his body was covered in a cold sweat, his clothes were soaked through, and the hairs on his skin were all standing on end. Zhang Zhao and Wu Fan once again said, "Order your famous generals to take their armies and each hold one of the river crossings. Appoint a grand marshal and have him install a hundred thousand troops on the southern banks of the River so Cao's army cannot cross. And let's not get involved with the Imperial Uncle of the Han."

---

87. This expression here refers to the Yellow Emperor.

This scared Zhuge so much that he was stupefied, "If you don't dispatch troops, my lord in Xiakou is doomed!" As soon as he finished speaking, he knotted up his robe, pulled back his sleeves, raised his sword, and killed that envoy right in front of the steps! Chaos reigned among the officials. Zhang Zhao and Wu Fan said, "Now we see Zhuge's crafty duplicity! Those with understanding will know that Zhuge killed Cao's envoy, but those without will say that Wu troops killed him!" People were ordered to arrest Zhuge, but the latter loudly shouted, "Caitiff-Suppressing General, you make a mistake. If you read the letter again you will see that of the ten liege lords in the empire, most have been killed by Cao Cao—not even one or two remain! My [15b] lord is a seventeenth-generation grandson of Gaozu, a descendant of Liu Sheng, the Quiet Prince of Zhongshan. What crime did he commit? If he comes to kill the Imperial Uncle, he will certainly also harvest the land of the River and Wu. General, carefully consider this." And Lu Su said, "My lord, haven't you heard that everyone in the empire says that all the beheadings do not proceed from Emperor Xian—life and death are determined by Lord Cao alone." Sun Quan then said, "Minister, you are right." And he gave the order to release Zhuge.

That evening Sun Quan, accompanied by Lu Su, went to see Her Ladyship his mother, who invited the two men to sit down. She asked Sun Quan about the state of affairs. The latter told her that Zhuge wanted to borrow an army to take with him to Xiakou in order to save the Imperial Uncle. Then, he went on, "Minister Cao is now on the northern bank with one million three hundred thousand troops." Her Ladyship his mother said, "Haven't you heard how your father and the eighteen liege lords fought their great battles below Tiger-keep Pass? Haven't you seen your father's heroism? Now Cao Cao appropriates the power of the Son of Heaven and abuses and oppresses the liege lords. You should go as quick as you can to Xiakou and rescue the Imperial Uncle to achieve a lasting fame. Just before he died your father said, 'If there is an urgent affair, appoint Zhou Yu as grand marshal.' And if you also make Huang Gai the vanguard, you can defeat Cao Cao." Sun Quan replied, "Mother, you are right." Upon his return Lu Su told what happened to Zhuge who was greatly pleased.

The next day at break of dawn Sun Quan once again asked, "What should we do?" When Zhang Zhao said, "Don't raise troops," Sun Quan raised his sword and cut his table in two, "If anyone says 'Don't send troops!' one more time, he will suffer the same fate as this table." So none of his officials dared raise the issue again.

Sun Quan ordered someone to go to the city of Yuzhang and invite Prefect Zhou Yu, but the latter would not come. When Sun Quan asked Zhuge why Zhou Yu didn't come, Zhuge replied, "I've heard that Lord Qiao has two daughters, Elder Qiao and Little Qiao. Elder Qiao has married your son as his wife, and Little Qiao has become the wife of Zhou Yu. She is young and extremely beautiful, so Zhou Yu is having a great time with Little Qiao everyday. Why would he be willing to come here to become a commander?" Sun Quan thereupon ordered Lu Su and the field marshal to hasten to the city of Yuzhang.

But now let us turn to Zhou Yu, who was having a good time with Little Qiao every day. Someone reported, "The Caitiff-Suppressor has dispatched an official with a ship full of gold and pearls and bolts of silk as a gift for the prefect." Little Qiao was very pleased, but Zhou Yu said, "You don't understand the meaning of this. Zhuge and Lu Su [16a] are coming in person to invite me." In no time at all, Zhuge arrived and Zhou Yu asked, "Who is this man?" Zhuge replied for himself, "I am from Recumbent Dragon Ridge on Mt. Wudang in Nanyang, and my name is Zhuge Liang." Zhou Yu was greatly surprised and asked, "Field Marshal, what is your intention?" Zhuge replied, "Cao Cao is now stationed with a million troops at Xiakou, hoping to swallow Wu and Shu. My lord is in bad straits so I have come to ask for help." Zhou Yu did not say a word. And then he saw a cluster of servings maids and ladies in waiting surrounding Little Qiao as she appeared from behind the folding screen. As she stood next to Zhou Yu she said, "Zhuge, your master is trapped in Xiakou and you don't know how to save him, so you have come all the way to Yuzhang to ask my Zhou Yu to become grand marshal?"

Let's talk for the moment about Zhuge. He was nine feet, two inches tall and just had reached thirty. His beard was raven-black and his nails were three inches long. He was as handsome as could be! After Zhou Yu had treated Zhuge to wine, the servants presented oranges in a golden bowl. Zhuge pushed back his sleeves, held an orange in his left hand, and with his right hand raised a knife. Lu Su said, "Martial Marquis, you offend against propriety." But Zhou Yu said with a smile, "I've been told that Zhuge is from a lowly background. He's just a peasant and simply not used to this." He then divided his orange into three equal parts. Kongming divided his into three parts of different sizes: one large, one small, and one even smaller, and placed them on a silver tray.

Zhou Yu asked, "Field Marshal, what do you mean by this?" Zhuge explained, "The big one is Minister Cao; the smaller one is Caitiff-Suppressing Sun; and the smallest one is my lord, the lonely and desperate Liu Bei. Cao Cao's military might is like a mountain and there is no one who can oppose him. Sun Zhongmou[88] can offer only a bit of resistance. Alas, my lord has limited troops and few officers so we request aid from the land of Wu, but you, Grand Marshal, claim to be too sick." When Zhou Yu remained silent, Kongming shouted with intimidating force, "If Cao Cao now has set his army in motion to come from afar to conquer the lands of the River and of Wu, it is not because

---

88. Sun Quan.

of some fault of the Imperial Uncle. And, you must also know that Cao Cao
has built his Bronze Bird Palace in Chang'an, and is scouring the empire for
beautiful women. If Cao Cao would take the lands of the River and of Wu and
make the two daughters of Lord Qiao his captives, grand marshal, wouldn't that
defile your fine reputation?" Zhou Yu pushed back his sleeves and rose to his
feet and ordered his wife to go return to the rear chambers, as he said, "I am a
real man, I will never be shamed. I will visit the Caitiff-Suppressing General
and be appointed grand marshal. I will kill Lord Cao."

Zhou Yu set out on the road and arrived in a few days. [16b] Sun Quan and
his officers raised Zhou Yu to the high rank of grand marshal and provided him
with the seal of office. After a few days of banqueting, the Caitiff-Suppressing
General saw Zhou Yu off as he set out on the road. He departed with three
hundred thousand troops and a hundred famous officers. He stationed his
troops on the southern bank of the River, bivouacking about at ten *li* from
Chaiye Crossing.

The Battle at Red Cliff

Let us now turn to Cao Cao when he learned that Zhou Yu had become grand
marshal. Some five or seven days later, Lord Cao said while questioning the
event, "The boat with the banner and canopy among those thousand battle
craft on the southern banks of the River must be Zhou Yu's." Cao Cao directed
twenty battle ships and led Kuai Yue and Cai Mao to the middle of the River
for a discussion with Zhou Yu. Zhou Yu was on the south; on the north was
Cao Cao. When the two sides had finished their talks, Zhou Yu's ship went
back, but he was pursued by Kuai Yue and Cai Mao, so he reversed course.
There was Zhou Yu's big ship, and then ten small ships came forward with a
thousand men on each ship, whose arrows stopped Cao's troops. Kuai Yue and
Cai Mao ordered their several thousand men to fire their arrows.

Let us now go back and explain that Zhou Yu used ships with tenting hung
on their sides. As soon as Cao Cao released his arrows and Zhou Yu's ships
were struck on the left side, he would then order the oarsmen to turn the ships
around, so they would be hit on the right side. In no time at all, the ships were
covered with arrows, and when Zhou Yu returned he had obtained a few hundred thousand arrows. Pleased, Zhou Yu said, "Prime Minister, many thanks
for your arrows!" When Cao Cao heard this, he flew into a rage and passed
along the order, "We will battle again tomorrow, and demand our arrows back
from each of Zhou Yu's ships!"

But when they confronted each other the next day Zhou Yu used catapults to bombard Lord Cao's ships with stones and inflicted a heavy defeat on him. When his troops returned to their camp, Cao Cao said, "If it were just on dry land, I would defeat Zhou Yu. But battling on the water I can find no way to get an advantage." Then Cao Cao had an idea, and thought, "Sun Quan has his Zhou Yu, Liu Bei has his Zhuge Liang, but I'm all alone." After discussing it with his officials, he decided to appoint a field marshal.

Followed by a thousand or so men, riding in one plain cart, he took his officials to the River, where he saw a Daoist elder sitting and strumming a zither. "Well," Cao Cao thought to himself, "King Wen found Jiang Taigong[89] and established the Zhou for eight hundred years." Cao Cao quit his conveyance and greeted the man, then invited him to return to his cart for a conversation. "Master," asked Cao Cao, "are you not one of the Eight Eminences of the Lower Yangzi?" "Yes," replied the master.

Cao Cao Appoints Jiang Gan as Marshal of the Army

Cao Cao was elated and took him back to his stronghold, where he feted him for several days.

Cao asked him, "Master, how do we make Zhou Yu withdraw?" [17a] Jiang Gan then launched into a discussion, "Zhou Yu is from Fuchun, in the Jiangnan area, from the same village as me. Let me have an audience with Zhou Yu, ply my words to persuade him, and make him give up on setting his troops in action. Then, at Xiakou on the north bank of the River, first behead Liu Bei, and then drive your troops south across the River and take Wu. It can be had on any day you like." Cao Cao was elated, and looked upon Jiang Gan as a man of the ilk of Jiang Taigong or Zhang Liang. The next day Jiang Gan crossed the river.

Zhou Yu, Lu Su, and Zhuge Liang were engaged in conversation when someone reported, "An elder is here to see the grand marshal." Someone was sent to ask Jiang Gan to enter the camp and all of the officials received him into the tent and offered him a seat. Zhou Yu began, "My old friend, we have been parted many years, and today we meet again." And he went on, "One who 'leaves the family' does not covet fame or benefit. Now Zhou is a grand marshal in Eastern Wu, with a rugged army of three hundred thousand, and a hundred noted generals, and has encamped at the ford at Chaisang. Master, please explain the rights and wrongs of the two states!" With this one sentence Jiang Gan was stumped for a way to reply.

---

89. See note 71.

Now let us speak about how Zhou Yu was in his cups and had asked his host of officers, "Minister Cao is encamped at Xiakou with thirteen hundred thousand troops, and sooner or later Xiakou has to fall. Which of you officers has a plan that can lead to the withdrawal of Cao's army?" From their midst, Huang Gai came forth and said, "Grand Marshal! Send three officers with fifty thousand men to secretly cross at Chaisang, and then follow a small path to a keep some sixty *li* north of Xiakou. There cut off Lord Cao's supplies; then Cao will kill himself in less than a month. This is called 'the plan to cut off the road and stop supplies.'" "Huang Gai," said Zhou Yu angrily, "this plan is worthless!" Lu Su had no plans and the other officers were silent. "Huang Gai is a flatterer and should be put to death!" The host of officers all urged him to be tolerant and Huang was spared death, but he received sixty blows from the bastinado.[90] That night the grand marshal got drunk and his officers dispersed.

In his tent, Jiang Gan said to himself, "From the start, Zhou Yu blocked me from speaking." Huang Gai, full of grief and resentment, went to his tent and said, "Thank you, sir, for being one of the first to urge the marshal to spare me." The master said, "Zhou Yu is not fit to be grand marshal." Huang Gai then opined, "Now there is no one to entrust one's life to and to help." Seeing that they were alone, Jiang Gan spoke of the virtue of Cao Cao. Huang Gai said, "Who can believe that from afar? I should be able to see the noble Cao." Jiang Gan explained, "Minister Cao has appointed me field marshal. I came to persuade Zhou Yu to a different course of action, but he cut me off so that I could not speak about it. Are you, Sir, willing to cast your lot with Cao?" Jiang Gan went on, "There's no need to worry, general, because you would receive a high post or commission." Going on in the same vein, Huang Gai offered, "You are probably not aware that Kuai Yue and Cai Mao have already sent letters and surrendered to Zhou Yu." Jiang Gan was greatly taken aback. Huang Gai said, "The grand marshal gave me the letter." Jiang Gan wanted to read the letter, and after he did he was alarmed, saying, "Minister Cao needs to know about this. I should give the letter to Cao Cao and have those two men executed, so that there is no need for later regret." Huang Gai himself wrote out a letter of surrender, and he said, "When I surrender to Cao Cao, I will offer up five hundred carts of food and fodder to the minister." They spoke until very late. The next day, Jiang Gan was sent off.

But let us speak now about Jiang Gan, who boarded a boat and reached Lord Cao's stronghold that night. On the next day, he had an audience with Minister Cao and explained the whole affair in detail. After reading Huang Gai's letter of surrender, Cao Cao was ecstatic. Jiang Gan then told him about Kuai Yue

---

90. Jiang Gan does not know that the bastinado is part of a plot to make Huang Gai's (feigned) defection to Cao Cao look convincing.

and Cai Mao surrendering to Zhou Yu and then gave the letter to Lord Cao to read; Cao was greatly alarmed.

Let us speak instead of Cao Cao's army of thirteen hundred thousand men. They all had boarded the boats as if they were climbing onto level land. Cao Cao was delighted, and he said, "I have heard of Huang Gai's virtue, but I've never seen him face to face. If he comes, I will certainly rely on him heavily."

Yu Fan came back to the southern bank and had an audience with Zhou Yu in which he related everything in detail. He was also carrying a letter from Cao Cao to Huang Gai. Zhou Yu said, "This great venture is now complete." He gave rewards to Yu Fan and promoted him in rank.

The grand marshal had all of his close top-ranking officials and the general officers read the letter, and Zhou Yu said, "There is a brief window to destroy the million-man army of Cao Cao. I have a plan. If all of you are of the same mind, then bring out a brush and inkstone and write in the palm of your hand. If we all agree, then this plan is the right one. If we don't, then we will discuss it in more detail." "What you say, Marshal," said the officers, "is sure to be right." So they wrote in the palm of their hands, and when finished the officers followed him and ordered the soldiers to move back. When the officers looked at their palms and the palm of the marshal's hand, every character was "fire." All of them were overjoyed. Then Zhou Yu stared at field marshal Zhuge, and said to him, "This plan is 'flaming fire.' It comes from Guan Zhong's 'Pacify the People with Slight Parching Military Strategy.'"[91]

But only the field marshal's hand had the character "wind" written on it. "This," said Zhuge, "is a marvelous plan of yours. On the day that the fire will be set, our [18a] stronghold will be on the southeast, and Cao Cao's on the northwest. How will we defeat Cao Cao if the wind is not in our favor when the time comes?" The grand marshal said, "Why did you write the word 'wind'?" The field marshal repeated, "If all of the general officers employ the word 'fire,' I can aid them with the wind." Zhou Yu said, "Wind and rain are creations of the interaction of yin and yang in the heavens. Are you capable of raising the wind?" Again the field marshal explained, "From the time heaven and earth came into existence, there have been three people who are capable of invoking the wind through sacrifice. The first was the Yellow Emperor, Xuanyuan. He made the Lord of the Wind his marshal and had Wind defeat Chi You. I also heard that Emperor Shun made Gao Yao his marshal and he employed Wind to pin down the San Miao peoples. I have received diagrams and texts, and when

---

91. Guan Zhong (ca. 720–645 BCE) served from 685 BCE as chancellor of the state of Qi, which, under his leadership, became the most powerful state of the Chinese world of that time. In later centuries he was credited with a collection of essays on statecraft that circulated as the *Guanzi* (*Master Guan*).

the day comes, I will aid with a southeasterly wind." None of the officers were happy and Zhou Yu thought to himself, "I come up with a marvelous plan that will allow not a sliver of Cao's army to return, and Zhuge Liang steals my thunder!" The general officers were creating a ruckus when a gatekeeper reported, "There is a gentleman outside who says he would like to see his friend Zhuge." The general officers went out to greet him.[92]

Let us turn now to Zhuge Liang, who met his friend and escorted him up the stairs where they all sat according to their rank. This was Zhuge Liang's elder cousin, Zhuge Jin. They feasted until late and the general officers all left.

Zhou Yu welcomed Zhuge Jin into his own tent to sit and said, "Do you know that Zhuge is dishonorable? The general officers all raised up 'fire' and he talked about sacrificing to the wind." "This Recumbent Dragon of our house," replied Zhuge Jin, "has techniques beyond comprehension." Zhou Yu laughed, "If it makes Cao Cao withdraw and rescues Liu Bei, then I am a prisoner under his aegis!" When he was done talking, he left.

Explain that, several days later Zhuge built a high terrace of rammed earth, with its north side bordering on the River. Then explain that three days after that Huang Gai onloaded a substantial amount of grain and fodder and that there were three boats outside. On that day dozens of Zhou Yu's officers quick-marched groups of marines and went just outside Xiakou city. When Huang Gai's boats reached Xiakou, someone reported to Cao Cao, "Huang Gai is carrying grain and fodder to our camp." Cao Cao welcomed them with smiles and laughter.

Then later explain how the field marshal calculated when the full army would reach Xiakou, and how Zhuge ascended the terrace where he saw fire starting in the northwest.

---

92. In his eagerness to stress Zhuge Liang's contribution to the defeat of Cao Cao at Red Cliff, the author of *Records of the Three Kingdoms in Plain Language* neglects to give a clear exposition of the battle plan. Cao Cao had acquired a river fleet when he conquered Jingzhou (Xiangyang), which would be essential to his plans to cross the River with his troops and attack Wu. To defeat this fleet as it would come downstream on the Han and enter the Yangzi (the River) Zhou Yu proposed the use of ships loaded with combustibles and explosives that would be set on fire when they reached Cao Cao's fleet. For such a plan to be successful, however, these burners would need a strong tail wind to push them against the flow of the River into Cao Cao's thickly packed fleet. Zhuge is described as the only one to perceive the weakness of this battle plan and to provide a solution that will ensure its success. Once panic would have overtaken Cao's fleet, Huang Gai and his ships would then attack Cao's fleet from behind. The omissions are represented in the text, with the imperative use of *shuo* 説, which we have translated as "explain that," which here informs the putative narrator to go on in detail about episodes that are crammed together here, the topics noted to provide cue tags for lengthier descriptions of the individual episodes.

Let us speak now of how Zhuge donned his yellow cape and performed his ritual with disheveled hair and bare feet, holding a sword in his left hand and clacking his teeth, to cause a mighty storm to rise. There is a poem,

> Violent battles at Red Cliff, mighty from antiquity,
> Men of those days were all so in awe of Lord Zhou; [18b]
> But Heaven knew that the eventual tripartition of the tripod's feet
> Was all due to the loyalty of the humble Huang Gai!

Let us now speak of the Martial Marquis crossing the River to Xiakou. On his boat, Cao Cao cried out, "I am dead!" His general officers said, "It's all Jiang Gan's fault." And in a flurry of knives they hacked Jiang Gan into ten thousand pieces.

Cao Cao got on a boat, and hurriedly found a path by which to flee from the confluence of the rivers, and he saw that every boat on all four sides was aflame. He also saw a group of tens of boats on one of which was Huang Gai, who said, "Behead the traitor Cao and make the empire as secure as Mount Tai!" The hundred officers of Minister Cao were ignorant of water battle, and their army was shooting arrows at each other.

Let us now turn to explain that it was too late for Cao Cao to do anything— there was fire on four sides and in front a barrage of arrows. Cao Cao wanted to flee, but Zhou Yu was to the north, Lu Su to the south, Ling Tong and Gan Ning to the west, and Zhang Zhao and Wu Fan to the east. Death lay on all four sides. The Historiographer says, "If it weren't for the fact that Lord Cao's family was fated to produce Five Emperors,[93] he would not have been able to escape."

Cao Cao did escape this peril alive and fled to the northwest. When he reached the bank of the river, his men surrounded Lord Cao as he mounted up. It is said that the fire broke out at dusk and it was noon the next day before he got out. Cao Cao turned around to look and he could still see the smoke and flames from the boats at Xiakou spreading across the sky—not ten thousand men were left from his own army.

Cao Cao fled in a northwesterly direction. After fewer than five li he ran into five thousand troops on the bank of the river and he recognized that is was Zhao Yun from Changshan who blocked his way. All of Cao's officers attacked them together, and Minister Cao broke through their lines and went on. When they had made another ten *li*, they once again ran into two thousand troops, whose leader Zhang Fei blocked their way.

---

93. That is, because his family would go on to establish the Wei dynasty, he was fated to live.

But let us now relate how his officers risked their lives to make a way for him and attack so violently that Cao Cao's helmet was all askew, and his hair had become unbound. He opened his armor and beat his breast, and leaning forward in his saddle he spat blood.

When evening fell they reached a large forest. Cao's troops had no tents at all but could not go forward. Behind him were officers who had split into three routes and were attacking his rear. Minister Cao said, "In front are two roads. One goes straight north. It is the main road to Jingshan, it passes through the land of Chu. The other is called the Huarong road." Cao Cao then thought, "Last time, when my troops reached the long slope of Dangyang, Zhang Fei blocked our way with twenty men and as a result our army could not proceed. If Zhuge has posted his men there again to block our way we will be captured by those bandits because my men are tired and the horses are worn out." So Minister Cao proceeded along the Huarong road, but before he had gone twenty ✳ *li* [19a] he saw five hundred swordsmen: General Guan was blocking his way!

Minister Cao addressed Yunchang with flattering words, "Marquis of Shouting, please consider that I treated you well." But Lord Guan replied, "I am under strict orders of the field marshal." Lord Cao crashed through his lines, but we have to tell that as they were talking they were enveloped by dust and mist, and this enabled Lord Cao to escape. Lord Guan pursued him for a number of *li* and then turned back.

Before he had gone fifteen *li* in an easterly direction he met with Xuande and the field marshal, who said, "That bandit Cao escaped, but it wasn't the fault of Lord Guan." These words made people complain to Xuande and they all asked how this had been possible. The Martial Marquis said, "General Guan is a man of humanity and virtue. In the past he was treated well by Minister Cao, so perhaps he allowed him to escape for this reason." When Lord Guan heard these words he was livid with rage and jumped on his horse, telling his lord that he would pursue him again. But Xuande said, "Younger brother, your nature is not made of stone. You must be tired, aren't you?" And the field marshal said, "I will go too. Be careful to make no mistakes."

The Uneasy Alliance

Next tell that Xuande and his troops marched in an easterly direction and when they had gone thirty *li* straight east, they saw the troops of Wu. The two sides drew up their battle lines, but when they heard them, they said, "These troops that are approaching must be Lord Zhou!"[94] The Imperial Uncle dismounted

---

94. That is, they recognized the dialect of Wu.

and met with Zhou Yu. When the latter saw the Imperial Uncle, he was frightened and said, "I followed the tiger to save the dragon—when will we see great
peace?" When finished speaking, the two of them rode side by side: Zhou Yu
on the left and the Imperial Uncle on the right. They marched on until the evening and then each camped down.

Zhou Yu thought to himself, "Cao Cao is only a usurping vassal, but judging
from Xuande's aquiline nose and dragon face, he has the features of an emperor
or king." Then he thought, "Zhuge with his world-capping talent supports
Xuande, so our hopes for an empire are finished! But with some small trick I
will capture the Imperial Uncle and arrest Recumbent Dragon. With these two
people gone, the empire is basically settled." Lu Su nodded his head and said,
"Grand Marshal, what you say is right."

At daylight of the next day the Imperial Uncle hosted a banquet and the
grand marshal and all his officers were invited. When evening fell, Zhou Yu told
the Imperial Uncle, "On the southern bank there are the Yellow Crane Tower,
the Golden Mountain Monastery, the Queen-Mother of the West Pavilion, and
the Drunken Greybeard Kiosk—all the greatest sights of the land of Wu." The
Imperial Uncle acknowledged this.

The next day Zhou Yu invited the Imperial Uncle to cross the River and
ascend the Yellow Crane Tower for a banquet. The Imperial Uncle crossed the
River and climbed the Yellow Crane Tower. Liu Bei was delighted and viewed
the sites on all four sides. Zhou Yu explained, "Not a hundred *li* to the south
you have the . . . Pass, to the north [19b] you have the Great River, to the west
there is the Lychee Garden, and to the east there is the Hall for Gathering the
Wise." When the officers and the Imperial Uncle had finished the banquet,
Zhou Yu said, "Earlier when Zhuge crossed the River, with flattery he persuaded my lord Sun Quan to action, promoting me to save you." Zhou Yu had
had too much wine and said, "When Zhuge sacrificed to the wind, that was
a union of heaven, earth, and, thirdly, man. By that we were able to save you
in Xiakou—but if it hadn't been for me how could you have escaped? Zhuge
may be strong, but could he have ever made you cross the River?" The Imperial
Uncle was greatly frightened on hearing this, for indeed these were true words
spoken in drunkenness.

Next speak of Zhao Yun in the stronghold of Han, who was in such low spirits
that he sent someone after Zhuge and Lord Guan so they would come back
again. When the field marshal entered the camp, he failed to see the Imperial
Uncle. Zhao Yun explained the transgressions of Zhang Fei to the field marshal.[95] The field marshal intended to have Zhang Fei beheaded, but the officers

---

95. His failure to accompany Liu Bei because he was drunk?

implored him to spare him. Mei Zhu acted as the emissary, and the field marshal had him cross the River by boat.

When Mei Zhu arrived at the Yellow Crane Tower and met with the Imperial Uncle upstairs, he suggested he visit the toilet, where he picked up off the ground a piece of paper with eight words on it, "Eat your fill surely, when he's drunk, leave." After the Imperial Uncle read this, he tore the paper to shreds. Zhou Yu, who had drunk too much, said, "Cao Cao acts the dictator, each liege lord is his own hegemon." When the Imperial Uncle told him, "If you mobilize your army, I will be your vanguard," Zhou Yu was greatly pleased. The Imperial Uncle took brush and inkstone in hand and wrote a short song that he showed to Zhou Yu. The song reads,

> The empire in utter turmoil—
> the house of Liu about to fall:
> Heroes emerged in this world—
> to scorch the four directions.
> At Ravenwood[96] in one fell swoop—
> we annihilated that one who "toppled the strong,"[97]
> Now the house of Han will be restored—
> we will join with the worthy to carry out good actions.
> How worthy is his humanity and virtue—
> how commendable is that Zhou Yu!

An encomium reads,

> How commendable is that Gongjin,
> His birth was a rare occurrence.
> On behalf of Wu he swallowed the hegemon
> And competed with Wei for the prize.
> At Ravenwood he defeated the enemy,
> At Red Cliff he massacred the troop.
> Such brave heroics
> Are matched by none!

Zhou Yu was greatly pleased, "Oh, Imperial Uncle, you are so talented." He then ordered his servants to place his Charred Tail[98] on his knees and intended to

---

96. Ravenwood is located on the north bank of the Yangzi River, opposite Red Cliff.

97. Here the text clearly says *cuigang* (摧剛), which are the first two words of the four-character phrase to "topple the strong and make them weak" (*cuigang weiruo* 摧剛為柔).

98. Charred Tail is the name of a famous zither. One Cai Yong (132–192) deduced from the crackling sound of a fire that a piece of wood that would be perfect for making a zither was

play the Master Kong's *Apricot Altar*.[99] But before the sounds of the zither had finished Zhou Yu was dead drunk and he could not play the piece to the end. The Imperial Uncle said, "The grand marshal is drunk!" The banquet turned into a disorderly crowd, some rising, some sitting down. The Imperial Uncle sneaked away, descended the stairs, and came to the bank of the River. The man at the River crossing asked, [20a] "Where are you going?" And Xuande replied, "The grand marshal is drunk. He has ordered me to prepare a banquet tomorrow. After I cross the River there will be a return banquet in my camp tomorrow and you officers are all invited." The officer guarding the River had no further questions and the Imperial Uncle boarded.

Next explain how, when Zhou Yu woke up from his stupor, he placed his zither on his knees and slowly sat up straight. He asked his servants, "Where did the Imperial Uncle go?" "He went downstairs," they told him, "quite a while ago." Zhou Yu was greatly shaken and immediately called the officer who guarded the River, who explained, "Xuande told us that you, Grand Marshal, had ordered him to cross the River to prepare a banquet."

Let us turn now to tell how Zhou Yu smashed his zither to pieces and loudly cursed out his officers, "As soon as I'm drunk for a moment that slippery slave Liu Bei escapes!" He ordered Ling Tong and Gan Ning to man some battle ships with three thousand troops and pursue the Imperial Uncle—if they caught up with him, they had to bring him the head of the Imperial Uncle.

The Imperial Uncle went on and the troops of Wu chased him. As the First Lord went up the bank, the bandit troops were close behind. Zhang Fei blocked their way and so scared the Wu troops that they didn't try to disembark. They went back and made their report and Zhou Yu sank into a depression. A few days later he led his army across the River, but then he learned that the Imperial Uncle and Zhuge had made camp at Red Cliff Slope some hundred *li* from the River.

Zhou Yu ordered his troops to hasten to the four commanderies around Xiakou,[100] and they first reached Changsha Commandery. The prefect there, Zhao Fan, said, "These four commanderies are attached to Jingzhou, so what are you up to?" The next day Zhou Yu led his troops to battle Cao Zhang, but even after several rounds he could not best Cao Zhang, so the two armies remained at a standoff.

---

burning. He retrieved that piece of wood from the fire and had a zither made that still showed the traces of the fire and was therefore called Charred Tail.

99. Referring to a story from the *Zhuangzi* about Confucius playing the zither at an altar in an apricot forest as his students read their texts. The song that Confucius was playing was retrospectively titled, "Apricot Altar." For the story, see Watson (1968, 344–45).

100. That is, Xiakou and three other commanderies.

The story relates that Lu Su proposed, "To the northeast is Red Cliff Slope; that's where that ungrateful Liu Bei is now; we should ask him for help." He added, "If Xuande, Kongming, Lord Guan, and Zhang Fei come, we definitely will defeat Cao Zhang." He immediately wrote a letter and went to see Liu Bei and Zhuge. After he read the letter, the Imperial Uncle was ready to set out with his troops, but the field marshal said, "You can't do that! At Yellow Crane Tower that bandit general almost did you in." The field marshal summoned Zhang Fei and said, "You go." The field marshal then relayed a little scheme to him.

The next day Zhang Fei led five thousand troops to Changsha Commandery. In the east was Zhou Yu's big camp, in the west was Cao Zhang's big camp, and Zhang Fei's camp was to the north of Changsha. When Zhou Yu learned that Zhang Fei had come to his relief with five thousand troops, he said to his officers, [20b] "When Liu Bei was besieged in Xiakou, our three hundred thousand troops and a hundred famous generals engaged in a fierce battle and we also lost Huang Gai. For killing that Cao Zhang I don't need that Liu Bei." His officers all said, "Right!"

On the next day, Cao Zhang's formations were in the west and Zhou Yu's in the east. Zhang Fei was in the north.

Now let us tell how, when Zhang Fei saw Zhou Yu, he made a deep bow and said, "Zhou Gongjin, I hope you have been well since we parted." Zhou Yu replied, "You bandit general, how do you dare mock me?" He had seen that the banner behind Zhang Fei was inscribed with "Chariot and Horse General."[101] "That drives me mad," said Gongjin. "That cowherd country hick is deliberately poking fun at us. To think that the office of our Sun Quan should be lower than that of Zhang Fei!" Zhou Yu's feeling of hatred for the slight lay in his bosom. The Wu generals and Cao Zhang confronted each other in battle, but even though they fought many rounds, it was a dead standoff.

Let us speak about Zhang Fei, who said, "Wu generals, move back a little and let me behead that Cao Zhang!" The troops of Wu had no idea of the intimidating power of Zhang Fei, but he gave one shout that penetrated beyond the ninth heaven. He fought repeatedly with Cao Zhang and the latter was soundly defeated. Zhou Yu said, "I have been here all this time but I couldn't get the better of Cao Zhang. And now that Zhang Fei has won, how can I not feel shamed?" So Zhou Yu also pursued Cao Zhang, who fired a single arrow that squarely hit Zhou Yu, who fell from his horse. Except for the troops around Zhou Yu, Cao Zhang came close to capturing him.

---

101. At the end of the Han dynasty, this title was an honorary one only awarded to the highest dignitaries at court.

When evening fell, Zhou Yu gathered his troops to return and when they had arrived at the camp, Zhang Fei had also come back. He raced to the camp and shouted, "Grand Marshal, when earlier we were in danger in Xiakou, you came to our rescue. Today is the twentieth day that you have been unable to get an advantage over Cao Zhang. I have defeated him in battle and present you Xiakou's four commanderies to repay you for the favor of Xiakou." Having said that, he left. Zhou Yu put a plaster to the arrowhead wound and put his left arm in a sling. He said, "Both the act of that lonely and desperate Liu Bei turning his back on our favor and Zhang Fei's making me so angry are the work of that Zhuge! So what is the meaning of Zhuge granting me these four commanderies?"

Just a few days later someone reported to Zhou Yu, "The Imperial Uncle and Zhuge now defend Jingzhou with three thousand troops." When Zhou Yu heard this he gave a loud shout and blood flowed from his battle wound. His officers said, "Jingzhou belongs to the land of Wu." So he immediately set out with his troops and within a few days reached Jingzhou. When the Imperial Uncle learned that Zhou Yu was approaching with his troops, he led his officers and formed his army up opposite that of Zhou Yu. Zhou Yu said, "Imperial Uncle and field marshal [21a], how can you not understand this? Jingzhou belongs to the land of Wu, so on what basis did you take it, Imperial Uncle?" The Imperial Uncle replied, "This has nothing to do with me." A general emerged from the doorway made by the parting of battle flags. When Zhou Yu looked closely, he gave a loud shout and fell from his horse. His officers immediately helped the grand marshal reseat on his horse, but blood flowed from his battle wound like a river. He had recognized this general as Liu Qi, the eldest son of the Prince of Jing. Liu Qi loudly shouted, "Grand Marshal Zhou Yu, when my father died, Liu Cong offered up Jingzhou to Cao Cao, but when Cao Cao retreated, this place was reinstated to me thanks to my Imperial Uncle." Zhou Yu had nothing with which to refute this. The Imperial Uncle also said, "Gongjin, join us for a banquet!" But Zhou Yu was so scared that he refused to enter the city lest Zhuge had another of his tricks. Zhou Yu marched his troops back to the southern bank of the River where he stationed them to nurse his illness.

Moreover, for a full three months Lu Su sent people to ascertain the situation in Jingzhou. One came back to report to the grand marshal, "Liu Qi is dead." Zhou Yu thereupon led a hundred thousand troops to take Jingzhou. After marching for a number of days he made camp some tens of *li* from Jingzhou. The day he arrived, the Imperial Uncle rode out on horseback. When Zhou Yu said, "Originally Jingzhou belongs to the land of Wu but you have occupied it," Zhuge replied with a smile, "I'll let you read something." In the space between the two battle formations on a table they placed a cinnabar plate which was covered with a brocade coverlet and had Zhou Yu take a look. When he had done so, he stamped his feet and blood spurted out like a fountain from his wound. His officers hurried to his rescue and covered his battle wound.

Academician of the Hall Zhao Zhiwei presents this addendum: His Majesty, seated in the Jiaming Palace, has heard the memorial presented by the Imperial Uncle and vetted by Prime Minister Cao as guarantor and responds:

Considering that the Imperial Uncle Liu Bei, from the time he defeated the Yellow Scarves, defeated Dong Zhuo at Tigerkeep Pass and followed Prime Minister Cao to jointly execute Lü Bu, has repeatedly established great merit; that his words and demeanor are a model, his humanity and virtue are excellent, and, even when assigned to low rank, he has never shown any arrogance in the performance of his duties,

I hereby promote him to the position of Grand Overseer of the Three Rivers and concurrently Warden of Yuzhou, Grand Marshal of the Fleet, and Pacification Commissioner of the thirteen downriver commanderies, with ten thousand families of tax rights as his source of income. He is also presented with a gold fish pouch to be worn on purple robes of office. The Imperial Uncle is enfeoffed as Prince of Jing. Once the border troubles will have been settled, he will be summoned for further promotion as, one thinks, he will fully understand.

Confirmed on this day of the seventh month, autumn, of the fourth year of the Jian'an period.[102]

Zhou Yu could only lead his troops back.

Let us now speak about the Imperial Uncle residing in Jingzhou. After a few days someone reported, [21b] "The Grand Marshal Attendant Officers Jia Xu, Cao Xiang, and Xiahou Dun are leading fifty thousand troops. They have made camp less than twenty *li* to the northeast of Jingzhou." Zhuge said, "I will lead the two generals Guan and Zhang and go to meet this army of Wei." When they were about to set out on the road he called Zhao Yun and secretly told him his plan. Within three days, the troops departed.

Let us speak of when the Imperial Uncle was prefect of Jingzhou and the common people patted their bellies and sang songs praising his humanity and virtue. One day when evening fell one saw several fully loaded boats at the northeastern water gate (one of six gates of Jingzhou) from which people loudly shouted,

---

102. August–September 199.

"Open the gate! We are traveling merchants!" But from one of the towers in the city wall Zhao Yun replied, "It's too late, you can enter the city tomorrow." But the merchants didn't accept that and said, "Our capital is in these ships and they are fully loaded. We are afraid it isn't safe outside the walls." But Zhao Yun was still unwilling to open the gate. When the first watch of the night had passed, from the third boat someone shouted to Zhou Yu, "I must take Jingzhou."[103] He drew his sword and plunged into the water, ordering everyone to leave their boats and climb the banks. By their accent one could tell they were all officers and troops of the army of Wu.

Originally the grand marshal Zhou Yu used fire arrows to burn down the gate. Zhao Yun said, "This exactly corresponds to the field marshal's plan." The Imperial Uncle ordered his men to shoot at Zhou Yu with the one thousand circular bows that the field marshal had produced, so the officers and troops all fled and twenty *li* from Jingzhou they disembarked. There were also Wu troops that had tried to get the horses.

Next tell that the troops lying in ambush set out, a thousand of them. But Zhao Yun and Jian Xianhe blocked their way. Zhou Yu said, "I fell into that country hick's trap again!" He crashed his way through the troops and fled. When evening fell, at forty *li* from Jingzhou—his troops worn out and his horses exhausted—he again saw an approaching army of more than thirty thousand troops: to the left General Guan, to the right Zhang Fei, and leading was the field marshal. They said, "You should have taken Jingzhou, but you failed in that enterprise. You may be just a general coming our way, but if you reveal who you really are, we will allow you to pass." Zhou Yu was frightened and with his officers made a frontal attack but it took him a long time to make his escape. The field marshal marched his army back and entered Jingzhou with a smile on his face.

The Marriage

Let us speak now about Zhou Yu who reached the bank of the River, where each made camp. He deliberated with Lu Su, and said, "I have a plan!" When Lu Su asked him about it, Zhou Yu said, "The Caitiff-Suppressing General has a younger sister. By this plan to secretely capture the Recumbent Dragon by marrying her off afar to Liu Bei we can kill the Imperial Uncle." The grand marshal had Lu Su [22a] cross the River and see the Caitiff-Suppressor and to explain to madam Sun that she should marry Liu Bei and secretly kill him.

---

103. Following Zhong Zhaohua's parsing of this sentence.

That night Sun Quan took Lu Su to Her Ladyship his mother, who said, "Your grandfather was originally a farmer, but because your ancestors had accumulated unseen virtue, your father became prefect of Changsha. So what prohibits us from becoming the in-laws of the Imperial Uncle?" After Lu Su left the yamen, Sun Quan explained to his mother, "Now Zhou Yu has come up with a scheme: he wants my little sister to kill the Imperial Uncle." Her Ladyship in greatest secrecy asked her daughter for her opinion. The girl had barely done up her hair at fifteen, and said, "My father defeated Dong Zhuo. If I marry Liu Bei and secretly kill the Imperial Uncle I will achieve a lasting fame." Her Ladyship said, "If there are benefits to the ritual, do it; if there are shortcomings to the ritual, don't."

After a few days Lu Su crossed the River and saw Zhou Yu, telling him everything that happened; Zhou was ecstatic. Lu Su made the long journey to Jingzhou to act as the go-between. When he arrived in Jingzhou, he was welcomed by the officers and settled down in the posthouse. Lu Su then raised the issue of the marriage with Zhuge.

When evening fell, Zhuge informed the Imperial Uncle, who said, "A plot by Zhou Yu." "My lord, don't worry," said the field marshal, "it's laughable that Wu would marry the ruler's younger sister off to us." The next day, the Imperial Uncle invited Lu Su, who once again raised the issue of a marriage. The two parties settled on a day.

Lu Su returned to the Great River where he met with Zhou Yu, and then crossed the River to meet with Sun Quan and Her Ladyship, his mother, and then led the young daughter from the land of Wu, across the River, and on the long journey to Jingzhou. Fifty li from there, Lu Su said, "I have five thousand troops with me and among them are hidden twenty officers. If the gates of Jingzhou are opened, we will use that opportunity to take the city." But before he had finished speaking, Zhang Fei appeared for the very purpose of welcoming the young lady. "There's no need for a single soldier, they'll have to make camp outside Jingzhou!" This scared the troops of Wu so much that none of them dared to proceed, and they said, "Lu Su has fouled up Zhou Yu's first plan."

When the young lady entered Jingzhou, Zhang Fei rode by her side. In her carriage the young lady said to herself, "This fellow defeated Lü Bu at Tigerkeep Pass. I've also heard that he thrice fought his way out of Xiaopei. At Dangyang Long Slope his shout made Cao Cao retreat thirty li. This is one stout fellow!" After the young lady's cart had traveled for a few more li, Zhao Yun welcomed her. Zhang Fei told her, "This is the Zhao Yun who saved Aji [22b] from the middle of a million troops!" When she had gone another few li she saw Zhuge who came to welcome her, and she said, "Truly a fine general!"

Later came the Imperial Uncle, leading a few thousands of followers. There were countless numbers of beautiful flowers laid out. When he invited the young lady to enter Jingzhou, she first went to the reception hall within the tent complex. The field marshal invited the young lady to pay her respects and in the hall they had hung the portraits of the ancestors: twenty-four emperors, from Gaozu to Emperor Xian. The young lady said, "I come from a family of farmers, so I have never seen the images of the emperors." The young lady was very pleased.

The next day at the banquet the young lady drank too much, in conformity with Zhou Yu's plans. The young lady immediately made a toast to the Imperial Uncle. All officers were alarmed, but the Prince of Jing said, "Young lady, please make the toast." The young lady saw that Lu Su had had too much to drink and had signaled that he wanted her to kill the Imperial Uncle. But seeing a golden snake coiling on Liu Bei's breast, she could not bear to kill him. She also said, "If respect is feigned it creates rage, and the empire will descend into chaos."

The Imperial Uncle and the young lady enjoyed each other every day for a hundred days. One night, in the second watch, she didn't see him. When she came in from the northwest[104] she saw the Imperial Uncle weeping repeatedly. When she asked him why, the Prince of Jing replied, "Emperor Xian is an incompetent weakling, so Cao Cao acts as a dictator." The young lady encouraged the Imperial Uncle.[105] Over a number of days she repeated time and again, "The Imperial Uncle is the descendant of generations of emperors, so why doesn't he understand the proper marriage rituals? Back home my mother is advanced in years, and also my elder brother is waiting for him to pay his respects to his in-laws." The Imperial Uncle said, "Let me discuss this with the field marshal."

Secretly, the Imperial Uncle discussed the matter of visiting his in-laws with Zhuge,

Young Lady Sun Returns to Her Family

who said with a smile, "Imperial Uncle, just go with the young lady to Jiangnan.[106] Nothing will go wrong." But the Imperial Uncle said again, "I fear this is a scheme of Zhou Yu." The field marshal replied, "My lord, just cross the River. I will encamp fifty thousand troops on the bank of the River, chain up warships,

---

104. The northwest corner of a room, called the *wulou* 屋漏, in ancient times was where the spirit ancestors resided and it was shielded from the rest of the room by tenting; in later times it simply comes to mean the deepest recesses of any structure, permanent or temporary, where one is shielded from public view; a very private place.

105. Following Zhong Zhaohua, and understanding the character *guan* 觀 as a mistake for *quan* 勸.

106. This is a term that literally means "south of the River" but is used as a geographical term for the area that would include modern Jiangxi and Jiangsu; that is, the land stretching for several hundred miles along the southern banks of the Yangtze River.

and have the two generals Guan and Zhang at my sides. This will make it so that the Wu generals won't dare look you straight in the eye."

The Imperial Uncle set out on the road and went to Jiangnan and went on with the young lady to Jiankang Prefecture. The long-distance spies informed Sun Quan, who thought, "Earlier, in that massive battle at Red Cliff we turned back Lord Cao's army of a million troops but lost seventy thousand troops and many officers. Recently, I have found out that that slippery traitor Liu Bei and that cowherd hick [23a] field marshal, Zhuge, have forgotten what they owe us. Time and again Zhou Yu has said that Liu Bei lacks humanity and that he has occupied the thirteen commanderies of Jingzhou." Her Ladyship his mother also had learned about it and asked the Caitiff-Suppressor to visit her. As a very filial son, he went to see his mother, who said, "My son, why do you look so unhappy?" Sun Quan replied, "That Liu Bei snatched away the title of Prince of Jing. We raised three hundred thousand troops and forced that bandit Cao to retreat from Xiakou, but Liu Bei is not a man who shows gratitude. If he comes here, to the southern bank of the River, I intend to kill him!" His mother said, "Your granddaddy grew melons for a living, so you come from farmers. If we later commanded large armies, it was all due to the accumulated blessings of our ancestors. Now your younger sister is married to the Imperial Uncle. If you kill him, who can your sister hope to marry? If the Imperial Uncle comes, you have to treat him properly. If he lacks humanity, you can always kill him later." Sun Quan obeyed his mother's words.

Her Ladyship and Sun Quan welcomed Xuande and after a few days they welcomed him into the city. When the common people observed the features of his face, they were all surprised. After a few days of banqueting in the yamen, Her Ladyship secretly asked Sun Quan, "What do you think of Xuande?" Sun Quan replied, "I observed the Imperial Uncle and he is indeed a Han descendent. His appearance is awe-imposing and later he definitely will be a ruler." Mother and son were both pleased. After they had entertained him for over twenty days, the Imperial Uncle took his leave of Her Ladyship. Sun Quan said, "When the Imperial Uncle came here, he didn't have his own place to sit."[107] Her Ladyship ordered Sun Quan to provide the couple with presents to see them off. After they had been on the road for a few days, they were over twenty *li* from the Great River.

Let us go on to speak of the fact that Zhou Yu had a large stronghold on the southern bank of the River. And when his spies told Zhou Yu what had

---

107. This phrase, *wuzuo zhi chu* 無坐之處, normally means that there is a surfeit of people for a single position or that someone is simply a supernumerary. Its contextual use here would seem to be similar, however, to the aforestated phrase "no place to put the tip of an awl"; that is, he had nothing.

happened, the grand marshal loudly shouted, "I told that young lady Sun of Jiangnan six schemes but not one was accepted." He ordered Gan Ning to lead three hundred troops and to go south and welcome that "lonely and desperate Liu Bei." Gan Ning led his troops to the carriage, where he dismounted to greet the young lady. When she lifted the curtain, she was upset and cursed him out at the top of her voice, "That spineless nitwit Zhou Yu! I am the daughter of the prefect of Changsha and the sister of the Caitiff-Suppressing General. But when I arrive here, he cannot even be bothered. Moreover, I have here the Imperial Uncle the Prince of Jing with me. It can't be that he despises Xuande, this must be because he has absolutely no regard for me." She had but to shout out once and he retreated, saying, "Yes, alright, yes, yes." [23b] When he went back and told Zhou Yu, the latter laughed and shouted, "I'll take thirty thousand troops to her chariot, pull that Imperial Uncle down, and behead that crafty bandit. Then I will have a second talk with that young lady. And for what crime would the Caitiff-Suppressing General condemn me should I see him?"

Zhou Yu and his officers went south to see the young lady, dismounted in front of the carriage, and bowed deeply to show their respect. The young lady said again, "My mother and brother are sending the Prince of Jing across the River, prepare the boats and oars."[108] When Zhou Yu loudly shouted, "Liu Bei is an ungrateful bandit," the young lady smiled, ordered people to pull back the curtain, and told Zhou Yu to look into the carriage again. Zhou Yu shouted in fear and blood flowed from his battle wound like a spurting fountain.[109] His officers helped him to his feet. When the young lady Sun arrived at the northern bank of the River, she had crossed the River together with the Imperial Uncle.

Let us now tell how Zhou Yu nursed his illness for some days, and said, "That young lady Sun deliberately allowed Liu Bei to escape!"

Now tell how the field marshal welcomed the Imperial Uncle back into Jingzhou. Some half a year later someone reported to the Imperial Uncle, "Her Ladyship has ordered Lu Su to come and he has settled down at the posthouse." The next day at a banquet Lu Su said, "We know that Jingzhou for three years on end has had no harvest because of droughts and that dead and starving fill the land. Her Ladyship, the mother of the Caitiff-Suppressing General, sends one million stoneweight of grain all the way to Jingzhou to the Imperial Uncle." The field marshal said, "But the Caitiff-Suppressing General already knew that the harvest had failed in Jingzhou." A few days later a thousand ships brought grain into the city. Lu Su then said, "Three days or so ago Liu Zhang

---

108. Following the emendation of Zhao Zhonghua of *ji* 機 to *ji* 楫.
109. Looking inside the carriage Zhou Yu will observe Liu Bei's true dragon nature.

of Xichuan was appointed as grand marshal, and he took the road to White Emperor City with fifty thousand—he has the intention to topple Wu. The Caitiff-Suppressor has discussed this situation with his officers, so we present this grain to the Prince of Jing to allow us passage so that Zhou Yu can bring Chuan into the fold." The Imperial Uncle agreed, and the field marshal said, "This is no problem at all. But it should be the autumn and the ninth month. Once the farmers have harvested their grain, the grand marshal can lead his troops though our land."

Newly Printed in the Zhizhi Period: The Completely Illustrated Plain Tales—Records of the Three Kingdoms, Part II.

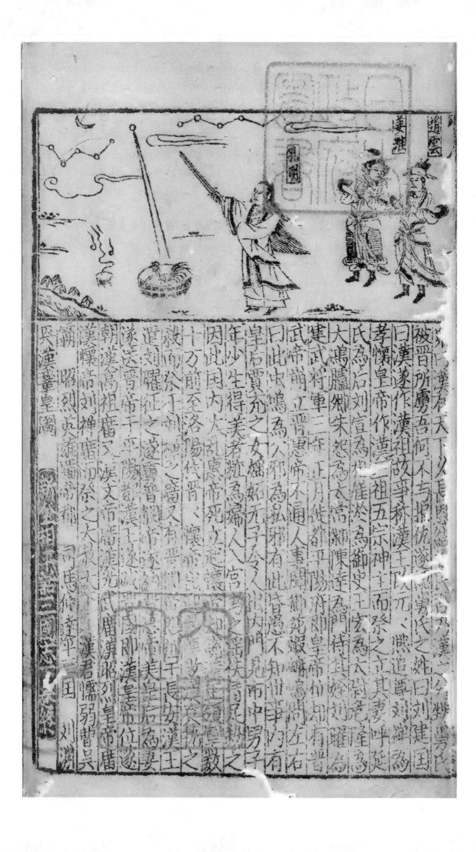

漢有天下火長恩緒□□□□氏名乃漢之分派馬氏之姓曰劉建國
被晉所寓吾阿不与押伏濛漢王元氏熙追尊其妻劉為
孝懷皇帝作漢一祖五宗神主而祭之其妻呼延為
氏為后怨朱怨為太常頼陳達
大鴻臚劉宣為太傅進於為御史王宏為太宰侍其
武帝崩立晉惠帝不通人事聞御苑蝦蟆為官為私耶有
日此虫鳴為八鄉邪郊平陽府即皇帝位即左右
年少生得美者娥為弘農人衆舉愚不知此甚不見而內男子
因此國內大亂東帝死左延德而中男子
皇后賈充之女妬如无子今人及之舉伏
十万前至洛陽代晉人民之吳
殺而於刑羅翟征之遼寧督晉人遂入懷帝
遂送晉帝千平陽晉王遂代漢王
朝懷帝崩劉曜又立武帝屋漢文帝之大赦天下
漢懷帝劉禪英旌都市相守馬術在平
霸漢昭烈帝劉澗閒漢昭烈皇帝位遂
吳漢蔥皇屬漢君懦弱皆吳國劉澗

Newly Printed in the Zhizhi Period:
The Completely Illustrated Plain Tales—
Records of the Three Kingdoms, Part III

The Death of Zhou Yu

[1a] Lu Su crossed the River on the last part of his return journey. In less than two months from that time, Zhou Yu led an army of fifty thousand westward to conquer Sichuan, passing about a hundred *li* south of Jingzhou. As Zhou Yu was marching he came upon an army of ten thousand men, headed by the Imperial Uncle and Zhuge, who said, "You knew that Jingzhou had no harvest for three consecutive years. This year the fields were planted and it is now the middle of the eighth month and—take a look—farmers are harvesting. Your army of a hundred thousand stretches from east to west for more than thirty *li*, and from south to north it is eighty *li* wide. Your soldiers are causing damage and the common people come from far and wide to Jingzhou to complain." Zhou Yu replied, "Earlier we paid you one million stoneweight of grain to buy the right of passage to take Xichuan. How can there be no damage?" And he spoke again, "Field Marshal, you were a farmer in your youth and when you see the damaged fields you must feel upset." The Martial Marquis shouted, "Gongjin, you didn't listen to the words of Lu Su!" Gongjin had no answer to that. His officers pushed aside the formations and the grand marshal marched on west.

But again on the next day when Zhou Yu and his army marched west their way was blocked by another ten thousand troops. Zhang Fei loudly shouted, "I am under strict orders of the field marshal. Grand Marshal, where are you going on your westward march?" After he had said that, each made camp. To block the way, Zhang Fei stationed a lance camp.[110] But in the second watch of the night Zhou Yu used a detour to pass him by. At break of day the grand marshal continued his westward march, and after a few days he reached the territory of Xichuan. Those officials who came to see him but refused to submit were executed on the spot. Zhang Fei's army trailed him from behind him and he reclaimed every province, prefecture, district, or town that had been captured

---

110. This was a camp that was surrounded by *chevaux-de-frise*, and had a protective circle of men armed with lances inside its circumference. This provided a well-fortified and protected area, or headquarters, inside a larger military encampment.

by the grand marshal. Zhou Yu said, "This is another scheme of that cowherd hick!" When he finished speaking, his rage had broken open his battle wound.

He went on for another five days and repeatedly heard the same news until the pain from his battle wound had become so intense that he could bear it no longer. His officers told him that they were about to reach the city of Baqiu.[111] Zhou Yu was so ill he could not even rise to his feet. After some days, he was no longer able to take any food or drink and his face swelled up. He summoned his old friend Lu Su to his side and wept as he told him, "I will meet my end here at Baqiu. Take my remains back to the lands of the River and to Wu. If you see Little Qiao, tell her again, and then again, how much I cared for her." When his words were finished, [1b] the whole city wept.

The day they reached the city, the grand marshal's illness had taken a turn for the worse. Someone reported, "There is a master outside the camp gate who says he and the marshal were close friends in their early days." When Zhou Yu said, "Invite him into the tent," his officers supported him as he sat up. When the master ascended the steps Zhou Yu recognized him as a man from Luocheng in Sichuan—his name was Pang Tong, he was also known as Shiyuan, and his name in religion was Master Phoenix Fledgling. Embracing each other they wept. Pang Tong said, "How did this so unexpectedly happen to you!" Zhou Yu bared his arm so Pang Tong could have a look, and then said, "This is my battle wound." But Pang Tong could not bear to look at it. Zhou Yu then said, "When I die, brother, escort my remains back to Jiangnan."

When Zhou Yu died, Pang Tong fixed the General Star in place.[112] That very night he prepared Zhou Yu's remains. In a few days he started to cross the River, but found his way blocked by the field marshal. The Martial Marquis said, "I knew that Zhou Yu had died and that what fixed the General Star had to be a plot by Pang Tong." When Pang Tong heard these words, he rode out to meet the field marshal, who allowed him to pass with the corpse.

After a number of days he reached Jinling Prefecture. Sun Quan said, "Bury him lavishly." After the rituals of sacrifice, which had gone on for more than a month, ended, Lu Su recommended Pang Tong to Sun Quan. Sun roundly cursed Lu Su, saying, "Earlier, when Liu Biao died, you went to Jingzhou to

---

111. In the *Sanguo zhi*, Zhou Yu perishes in Baqiu, which is located southeast of Jingzhou, as he returns from the capital to make preparations for his campaign against Xichuan. In the *Sanguo yanyi*, he dies in Baqiu while trying to lure Liu Bei out of Jingzhou in order to capture him. This text retains the place name of Baqiu, but since the text has Zhou Yu going westward for five days after entering the border of Xichuan, it is a good example of how freely the *Plain Tales* adapts, changes, and recontextualizes time, place, and people.

112. When a great commander dies, the General Star drops from the sky as a meteor. By pinning down the General Star in its position Pang Tong hopes to mislead enemy diviners into believing that Zhou Yu is very much alive. On the eve of his own death Zhuge Liang will also perform this ritual so his enemies will believe he is still alive even after his death.

offer our condolences, and you took Liu Bei to Xiakou and brought Zhuge with you across the River. With flattering words he enticed us to garrison Chaisang Crossing with three hundred thousand troops and a hundred famous officers. Then he used yet another scheme and in the huge battle at Red Cliff he defeated the one million troops of Cao Cao. But in that battle we lost tens of thousands of troops and also sacrificed several tens of famous officers and Huang Gai as well. Liu Bei then snatched away the thirteen commanderies of Jingzhou and had that country hick kill our beloved general Zhou Yu by rage and frustration. This shattered my heart into ten thousand pieces!" Frightened, Lu Zijing could only retire, muttering "Yes, right, yes, of course. . . ."

New Recruits

Next tell that Lu Su returned to his house and on the third day sent Pang Tong on his way with gifts. When the latter set out on the road, he asked him to dispatch an officer to escort him across the River. Pang Tong pursued his journey and when he reached Jingzhou, he saw that the Emperor Star was shining bright, illuminating the land of Jing and Chu. Pang Tong said, "This still counts as my ruler. Everyone in the empire says that the Imperial Uncle is a man of humanity and virtue." He entered the yamen and met with the Imperial Uncle, who invited him to sit down and asked, "What is your name?" He simply replied, "Pang Tong." The Imperial Uncle understood his intent. He also asked him, "Master, are you acquaintances with [2a] Zhuge?" "Yes, yes," Pang Tong said as he rose to his feet. The Imperial Uncle bestowed upon Pang Tong documents appointing him the district magistrate of Liyang.

Pang did not get what he wanted and for half a month he purposefully made bad decisions on cases brought before him. The common folk all made the long journey to Jingzhou to complain to the Imperial Uncle, who said, "I never knew him, but he said that he was a younger brother of Kongming so I gave him the documents appointing him district magistrate of Liyang. There is no way I would have harmed you!" One of his close servants said, "Zhang Fei just dismounted in front of the yamen." The Imperial Uncle told him to come before him and asked, "Where is the field marshal?" Zhang Fei replied, "In Jingshan District, due north of Jingzhou." When the Imperial Uncle told him about Pang Tong, Zhang Fei said, "I will go to Liyang, drag out that fellow, and present him to you."

The next day Zhang Fei led dozens of men and when he reached Liyang, he dismounted in front of the yamen. To a person, all the common people and the clerks complained about Pang Tong's lack of humanity. With sword in hand,

Zhang Fei went into the yamen. When evening fell, he heard a thunderous snore, and when he slashed a number of times with his sword, blood spurted out like a gushing fountain. He lifted the blanket, and it turned out to be a dog! Zhang Fei said, "Where did that bandit go?"

The next day he went to Jingzhou and told the Imperial Uncle the whole story. The latter said, "The district commander must be a man of worth." Over the course of the next ten days the four commanderies along the River all rebelled. When Xuande questioned Zhuge about this, the field marshal replied, "Don't you remember the words of Xu Shu? 'In the south there is Recumbent Dragon, and in the north there is Phoenix Fledgling.' If you obtain one of these men you can bring peace to the empire. Pang Tong is a man from Luocheng in Xichuan. He is Master Phoenix Fledgling. If they now say that these four commanderies have rebelled, it must be because they have been under the suasion of Pang Tong." The Imperial Uncle replied, "Field Marshal, what you say is right on the mark." The field marshal summoned Zhao Yun, "Take three thousand troops to Changsha Commandery and subdue Zhao Fan."

The next day as the evening fell Zhao Yun set out on the road. Bare-armed and leading a sheep[113] Zhao Fan welcomed Zhao Yun far outside the city. After they entered the yamen, Zhao told him that the rebellion of the four commanderies was all due to the persuasiveness of Pang Tong. They feasted until the evening and Zhao Fan, who had too much to drink, kept with him several tens of women. One of these women was dressed in a crimson gown; she had a charming and lovely appearance, and Zhao Fan had her sit across from Zhao Yun to offer up wine with her own hands. Zhao Fan said, "She is my sister-in-law, I should give her to you as a wife!" Zhao Yun shouted, "You are so common! I'm under the strict orders of the field marshal, what do I care about drink and sex!" [2b] When he finished speaking, he left the yamen. In his cups, Zhao Fan said, "The one who lacks humanity is Zhao Yun!" He took three thousand troops to surround the posthouse and wanted to kill Zhao Yun, but he was struck and killed by Zhao Yun's first arrow. The next day at break of dawn Zhao Yun explained to the officers and the common people that he had killed Zhao Fan and his family. After he had comforted the population he returned to Jingzhou and had audience with the Imperial Uncle, who then told the field marshal, "Zhao Yun has subdued Changsha Commandery."

Zhang Fei, for his part, was one hundred *li* away to the southwest, on his way to Guiyang Commandery. That fellow, Jiang Xiong, prefect there, was an expert in civil as well as martial arts. On the day he arrived, Zhang Fei led his three thousand troops and made camp less than ten *li* from Guiyang. When people reported this to the prefect Jiang Xiong, he said, "Zhang Fei is a coarse fellow. The military writings of Master Sun Wu state that, 'After marching for four

---

113. Conventional symbolic actions of submission.

days cavalry cannot come any nearer and after marching for five days infantry cannot go on; any longer and they will be worn out.' Now Zhang Fei's troops have marched a hundred *li*, so we have discovered that his men are worn out and his horses exhausted. Guan Zhong states, 'An army that comes from afar can easily be surprised and beaten.' If I take advantage of this situation to kill Zhang Fei, it would just be getting rid of one of Zhuge's arms."

Jiang Xiong mustered five thousand troops. They left the city for a surprise attack on Zhang Fei's camp, but they found it empty; troops lying in ambush on the four sides all emerged. Jiang Xiong had wanted to protect Guiyang but it had already been taken by Zhang Fei who, in turn, came back to confront Jiang Xiong. The two armies clashed with each other and the two men fought on horseback. Jiang Xiong was skewered by Zhang Fei and fell from his horse. After subduing Guiyang Commandery, Zhang Fei entered Jingzhou.

Zhuge also had the prince Liu Feng engage Han Guozhong in battle. Guozhong was defeated, but when Liu Feng went up a high slope, he found himself surrounded by water while Han Guozhong fled in a boat. Liu Feng wanted to leave but found his way blocked by a general who was ten feet tall, had round eyes and a long beard, who wielded a long-handled large sword,[114] and on his horse loudly shouted, "This is a scheme to capture the two generals Guan and Zhang. How can Liu Feng stand up to it?" When the field marshal heard about this, he once again questioned the officers. Zhang Fei was again sent out to square off with Han Guozhong. That bearded guy came out again on horseback and Zhang Fei engaged him in battle. But after ten rounds there was no clear winner. After three days or so Zhang sent someone to report to the field marshal and to bring him up the slope.

Zhang Fei welcomed the field marshal into his camp, and told him everything in great detail, "If we can get this man, we will never worry again about the empire of the Han being established." [3a] At break of day, the field marshal climbed a high hill and looked to the southwest; he and his officers saw that the southwestern slope at Guiyang was nothing but water, which was putting Liu Feng in dire straits. On the bank the field marshal saw a lance camp, "Phoenix Fledgling must be in that place." That night the field marshal wrote a letter and had Mei Zhu secretly take it by a roundabout way. When Mei eventually arrived at the small camp, he was arrested by the guards and taken to see Pang Tong. Mei Zhu presented the letter to him. Pang Tong said with a smile, "Zhuge is an old friend of mine." He wrote a letter in reply and gave it to Mei Zhu, who returned to the camp at daylight and presented the letter to the field marshal. After the field marshal read it, he ordered Mei Zhu to take one

---

114. While the text here simply says *shi bing da dao* 使柄大刀, this may refer to the well-known swords called *chang bing da dao* 長柄大刀. On the other hand, it is quite common to drop the numeral "one" before a measure word (*bing*).

thousand troops that evening to the high slope to burn reeds. Then Liu Feng came out to meet with Zhuge.[115]

Next speak about Pang Tong, who that night invited Wei Yan (also known as Wenchang), a famous general from Fufeng in Guanxi. When he was seated, Pang Tong told him in detail about the approaching armies of the house of Han, about the aura of kingliness and power they generated, about Han Guozhong being inhumane, and about things decided but never carried out. He also told him that Xuande was a man of humanity and virtue. "Haven't you heard: 'A noble bird judges the forest before it roosts; a wise vassal chooses the lord he will support.'" When the next day the two armies squared off, Wei Yan decapitated Han Guozhong in front of his horse. After Pang Tong had subdued Wuling Commandery, he joined Zhuge and led his troops straight west to Fuling.[116]

The prefect there, Jin Zu, came out on horseback, leading his troops and arraying them in formation against those of Kongming. Jin Zu ordered a general to ride out. The field marshal was quite stunned and Pang Tong told him, "This is a man from E Commandery and his name is Huang Zhong, also known as Hansheng." The field marshal sent Wei Yan to battle him, but after two days it was a draw. He then sent Zhang Fei to face the enemy and he fought Huang Zhong for ten rounds, but again it appeared to be a draw. Huang Zhong said, "I only recognize Yunchang, I know nothing of any Zhang Fei or Wei Yan!"

For more than ten days they tried to subdue Fuling Commandery. The field marshal said, "Huang Zhong turns out to be made of the stuff of generals. But will the Imperial Uncle be unable to make him surrender?" He sent someone off to Jingzhou to fetch General Guan and five thousand troops to Jinling. The officers welcomed him into the camp.

Within three days General Guan had battled Huang Zhong but there was still no victor. The field marshal asked Pang Tong about Huang Zhong and the latter said, "When I earlier persuaded the four commanderies I also had a conversation [3b] with Huang Zhong and he said, 'I am only a bandit from south of the River, but Jin Zu has treated me extremely well. As long as Jin Zu is alive, I will risk my life to pay him back. If Jin Zu dies, I will select a lord to support.'" Zhuge said, "I've got Huang Zhong."

---

115. We assume here that there is some form of magical battle of wits: Pang Tong had somehow made the water rise to surround Liu Feng and Zhuge Liang had countered this with an equally magical plan; the burning of the reeds may be a play on word magic, it is homophonous with "putting the encirclement in the oven" (爐圍), i.e., "drying up the waters."

116. The text says Jinling, the area along the southern bank of the Yangtze near modern Nanjing. However, since they are traveling west, not east, from Wuling, this is completely unlikely. The nearest major commandery due west of Wuling is Fuling 涪陵, which lies between Wuling Commandery and Yizhou.

A few days later the Martial Marquis and Huang Zhong faced each other on the battlefield. The Martial Marquis feigned defeat and Jin Zu dropped out of formation to pursue him. But after a few *li* Jin Zu found himself blocked again. The Martial Marquis was riding in his four-in-hand, and was seated in that carriage. The field marshal lay back to be out of the line of fire, and all the crossbow arrows were released at once, killing Jin Zu. The field marshal led his troops back to their camp.

A few days later Huang Zhong came to seek revenge. Pang Tong tried to change Huang Zhong's mind, but the latter refused to surrender, saying, "I have this disease. Even if you kill my lord by negligence or mistake, I have to take revenge—how could I surrender?" He fought with Zhang Fei but after they had battled for a hundred rounds no winner emerged. Then the field marshal also had Wei Yan ride out, but even when these two generals combined their forces against Huang Zhong, the latter only grew in might and power. The field marshal said, "That old bandit really flaunts how crazy he is. We have to behead that Huang Zhong!"

The four horsemen were engaged when suddenly a stream of blood spurted out and one general fell from his horse.

So now let us speak about how Huang Zhong's horse had lost its footing but he advanced on foot, twirling his sword, to bring the fight to those three generals. Lord Guan said, "This is a true hero, one without equal in this world!" The field marshal loudly shouted, "You three generals, stay your mounts!" With flattering words, the Martial Marquis persuaded Huang Zhong to surrender to the Han. After Huang Zhong had seen to the burial of Jin Zu, the field marshal led his army back to Jingzhou, where he saw the Imperial Uncle. The Imperial Uncle had a good look at these three new generals. The first of them was Pang Tong, and the Imperial Uncle said, "This is a man of insight." Then he had a good look at Wei Yan. "A man of wise virtue!" And he also said, "But he doesn't measure up to my brother Lord Guan." And when he looked at the third general, it was the old general Huang Zhong.

War in the Northwest

Let us go back now to speak about Minister Cao, seated in the outer hall in Chang'an. He questioned his officials, "I am constantly reminded of two years ago, when we pursued that lonely and desperate Liu Bei to Xiakou. At that time he had only five thousand troops and we still were unable to nab him. Now he has been entrusted with Jingzhou and its thirteen commanderies. He has fifty thousand brave troops and thirty fierce generals. No one can oppose him. As for a man versed in the civil arts he has Zhuge, and as for men versed in the martial arts, he has the two generals Guan and Zhang." He then asked the officials, "How would you deal with this enemy?" The grandee Jia Xu answered the prime minister, saying, "There is this governor of Pingliang Prefecture in Western Wei Province with whom [4a] the former emperor was forced to deal. His name is Ma Teng, and he is a ninth-generation grandson of the Cloud-General Ma Yuan who served under Emperor Guangwu of the Eastern Han. Ma Teng has two sons. The elder one is Ma Chao, also known as Mengqi; the younger one is Ma Da. All of our troops say that each of these three generals has a courage that can match that of ten thousand. So Ma Teng can deal with Zhuge, Ma Chao can deal with Lord Guan, and Ma Da can equal Zhang Fei."

Cao Cao reported this to the emperor, and an edict went out to Pingliang Prefecture in Western Wei. Governor Bian Zhang and Vice-General Han Sui welcomed the envoy into the yamen and they in turn invited Ma Teng to bow before the summons. After the edict had been read aloud, they properly sent the envoy off for his return trip to Chang'an, and Ma Teng made preparations to go to the court.

That night Ma Chao said to his father, "Why are you so unhappy?" Ma Teng replied, "My son, you must have heard how, in the hands of the former ruler the Ten Academicians[117] appropriated the power of the emperor. And that, later, Dong Zhuo did the same. Don't you know this is Cao Cao's empire? Beheadings and quarterings do not come from Emperor Xian, life and death all depend on Lord Cao. If I enter the court and Lord Cao shows humanity and virtue, then all is settled, but if he lacks humanity, then I am going to die in the imperial capital." And he said to his two sons, "If a letter comes that summons you, you must not go to Chang'an, and if I die, you must kill Cao Cao to seek vengeance for me."

The next day, Ma Teng set out on the road at first light. After a few days he arrived in Chang'an where he settled down in the Eternal Gold Meditation Cell. On the third day he was received in audience by the emperor and was granted his old appointment again.[118] After Ma Teng had expressed his gratitude for the sagely grace, he was treated to an imperial banquet for three days.

One day, when His Majesty was seated in the Purple Free and Easy Roaming Guangxuan Palace he summoned his closest ministers to discuss the ordering of the empire. None of the civil officials or military officers said a word. When the emperor directed the question to Ma Teng, the latter replied, "To bring order to the empire one should follow the practices of the sage kings Yao,

---

117. Here, he means the Ten Constant Attendants.

118. Zhong Zhaohua (1990, 487 note 30) suggests this means he was made Chamberlain of the Palace Garrison 衛尉, responsible for protection of the palace.

Shun, Yu, and Tang to make the empire as stable as Mt. Tai. If one follows Jie and Zhou—who were without the Way—one cannot be a ruler to the empire. If your Majesty would heed the following four suggestions of your minister, you should be able to bring great peace to the world." The emperor asked what these were and Ma Teng addressed him again, "Far away, make sure to reward the border troops; close at hand, make sure to dismiss evil ministers; make the grain and corvée taxes light and simple, and repeatedly bestow pardons and grace." And he also said, "Your Majesty, you must have heard of King Ping of Chu. Because he raped the wife of his son, he set the queen, the crown prince, and his grandsons on the path to killing each other. This was masterminded by his prime minister Fei Wuji.[119] Has nobody ever heard of that Huhai of Qin, who [4b] had that grandee Zhao Gao, that traitorous minister?[120] It was through no fault of the rulers that they lost their empires; it was the crimes of their closest ministers." The emperor was silent. One man loudly shouted, "Ma Teng has barely entered the court and speaks in such an unrestrained manner to the emperor! Who do you mean by 'closest ministers'?" After Ma Teng saw who it was, he loudly shouted, "Cao Cao, you are no loyal minister. I hear that every action—praise and blame, summons and consultations, appointments and gifts, assistance and rewards—all proceed from you. This has put the emperor in a position as perilous as if he were hanging upside down and as precarious as a stack of piled-up eggs." Scared, the officials and officers were all drained of color. Emperor Xian said with a smile, "Ma Teng, don't speak nonsense. Cao Cao is a loyal minister." He gifted them with a banquet in order to make peace between these two dignitaries.

That evening Ma Teng returned to the monastery. And that very night Cao Cao dispatched three thousand troops and several officers who, within an hour, had killed Ma Teng and all members of his household. The next morning Cao Cao reported that Ma Teng had suffered a stroke and died of the illness. The emperor was greatly surprised and had him given a state burial. There was no one who knew the truth.

Let us now speak of Ma Chao and Ma Da who had had troubling dreams. Ma Da went to look for news along the road from Chang'an. As he was sitting there with troubled thoughts, he suddenly saw a family servant with his hair unbound, who wept as he reported, "The old Great Defender and his whole family, old and young, have been killed on the orders of Cao Cao." Upon his return Ma Da told this to Ma Chao, who wept bitterly but said not a word.

---

119. Fei Wuji had been sent as envoy to the state of Qin to select a mate for the crown prince. He selected one, but told the emperor how beautiful she was and that "he should take her himself and find another for the crown prince." The emperor did just that.

120. Huhai was the last emperor of the Qin dynasty; he had usurped the throne from his elder brother with the aid of Zhao Gao. See note 74.

The prefect Bian Zhang and Han Sui lent ten thousand troops to Ma Chao. After a few days he arrived in the western edge of Pingliang Prefecture where he made camp. To the east you had Cao Cao. On the stipulated day, the two armies lined up against each other.

Ma Chao rode out on his horse and holding his lance challenged his opponent to battle. When Cao Cao looked at him he was alarmed. He could see Ma Chao's face was as dark as the shell of a living crab, his eyes were like flickering stars, and he was clothed in solemn mourning clothes. Ma shouted out, "Bandit Cao killed my father and mother—but what enmity ever lay between us?" Xiahou Dun rode out on horseback to do battle with Ma Chao. But, after just a few rounds, Ma Chao feigned defeat and, when Xiahou Dun pursued him, he turned around and struck him with an arrow that nearly cost him his life.

The two armies fell upon each other. Ma Chao grabbed a soldier in Cao's army and asked him, "What does that bandit Cao look like?" The soldier, afraid of dying, said, "Lord Cao is a handsome man with a long beard." Ma Chao gave an order, "The one who captures him will be given ten thousand strings' worth of gold and gems." When Cao Cao heard this, he cut off his beard with his sword and changed his clothes. The battle went on until evening, and were it not for the fact that Cao Cao had the "fate of five future emperors," he would have died under a myriad of swords. [5a] Cao Cao managed to escape, but when he arrived in his camp, he could not even eat or drink.

That night he gave the order to ford the Wei River with boats and establish camps both to the east and the west. But on the northern bank were Ma Chao's ten thousand troops who loosed all of their arrows, and on the southern bank were Bian Zhang and Han Sui, who had their thirty thousand troops fire at random. No one knows the number of Cao's troops that drowned in the water.

Let us now speak about how Cao Cao, riding through a narrow defile, got off his horse and covered his face with a saddle pad as he went downstream. At daybreak, the boats reached the southern shore. Lord Cao got a new horse and was about to flee, but in the narrow defile of the Wei River he ran right into Ma Chao. Ma Chao fought Lord Cao in a string of eight battles. Only after three days could Cao Cao escape and then make his camp on a high hill. Ma Chao and his thirty thousand troops made camp to the southeast of him.

Several days later, a master came to visit Ma Chao who asked him, "Who are you?" The master replied, "I am Lou Zijiu,[121] the immortal abbot of the Cloud Terrace Observatory on Mt. Hua. I came her to present you a scheme so you

---

121. The text consistently writes Lou Zijiu 婁子旧 for the well-known strategist Lou Zibo 婁子伯, a scribal confusion of the short form character *jiu* 旧 for the character *bo* 伯. As in other cases where a mistranscription is used consistently, we retain the reading as found in the original publication.

may take vengeance for your father." Ma Chao then said, "Please tell me." "Send Ma Da first with ten thousand troops to enter Chang'an, free Emperor Xian, and kill the relatives of that traitor Cao. It won't be too late if you wait to kill Cao Cao." Ma Chao replied, "This proposal is too farfetched. A real hero should take advantage of the situation to kill the traitor. That's the simplest solution." When Zijiu saw that Ma Chao would not give in, he left the camp.

On the third day after that he paid a visit to Lord Cao. The latter's officials introduced him as Lou Zijiu from Mt. Hua. Lord Cao invited him to sit down next to him. The master said, "Lord Cao, let me present three schemes to you concerning your most troubling concerns." Concerning his first priority, defeating Ma Chao, Cao Cao asked, "You must have heard that Bian Zhang and Han Sui deeply love Ma Chao's talent. Enough, indeed, to make them transfer ten thousand troops to Ma Chao." Lou replied, "A few days ago I learned that Ma Chao has borrowed thirty thousand barbarian troops. If you give those barbarians gold and gems and bolts of silk, they will all disperse. In this way Ma Chao will be unable to advance." Cao Cao was greatly pleased, "Master, what you say is right on the mark." The master then left.

By edict of the emperor Cao Cao wrote, "Lavishly distribute gold and gems to Bian Zhang and Han Sui." After they had left Ma Chao, Cao Cao reclaimed those ten thousand troops. Later this doubled to twenty thousand troops as he returned north to Xinye.[122] Ma Chao lost three thousand men and Cao's army grew by twenty or thirty thousand troops.

Ma Chao, pursued by Cao's army, fled to the west. When he arrived at Sword Pass, he ran into thirty thousand troops led by Zhang Lu. [5b]

Ma Chao Flees West from Cao Cao[123]

Let us now speak about Zhang Lu, who promised to take revenge for Ma Chao. The one hundred and fifty thousand troops of Minister Cao made camp to the east and eyed Zhang Lu like tigers.

After more than a month Zhang Lu said to Ma Chao, "To the west is Sword Pass. I was once forced down and out of that pass by that starving beggar Liu Zhang." Zhang Lu and Ma Chao proceeded westward to the foot of the pass where they looked at the trestle road—the steep inaccessibility of the mountains was beyond words. Zhang Lu had his troops eye Sword Pass like hungry

---

122. There is something garbled in the text here, from the time Lou Zijiu visits Cao Cao to this point. Bian Zhang and Han Sui were both from the western reaches, in the area of modern Gansu, and Cao Cao was stationed in Chang'an; there would of course be no "return" for anyone to Xinye, which is in Hebei.

123. This line seems out of place and redundant here as part of the story. We suspect that it may be a section break that remains unmarked in the text, lacking both the usual spacing before and after and the black box.

tigers but after a few days he took Ma Chao with him to Dongrong Commandery. The foot of the pass was mostly the exclusive dominion of Liu Zhang.

Let us speak now of the generals guarding the pass, Zhang Xiang and Zhang Ren, who had submitted a report to Liu Zhang, who further discussed it with his civil officials and military officers. The grandee Zhang Song said, "In the southeast there is Downriver Wu; in the east there is Liu Bei in Jingzhou; at the foot of Sword Pass you have Zhang Lu and Ma Chao; and then there is Cao Cao in Chang'an. All these liege lords are scheming to obtain Sichuan. You should have a worthy minister request an immediate audience. Then you can put your mind on the same path, and you will then be protected." Liu Zhang asked the grandee Zhang Song, "Who is most powerful?" When he replied, "Cao Cao," the emperor[124] then entrusted Zhang Song with the maps of Xichuan and ordered him to make the long trip to Chang'an by side roads in order to see Cao Cao.

Minister Cao received Zhang Song. But when he saw that he was only five feet, five inches tall, had a sallow and emaciated appearance, and was extremely taciturn, Minister Cao was displeased and went back to his lodging. Zhang Song spoke to himself, "Constant Attendant Yang Xiu is a superior vessel, but he said that Minister Cao looked down upon me."[125] Yang Xiu explained Minister Cao's virtue to Zhang Song. He took out the *Writings of Mengde* in sixteen scrolls, and the *Writings of Master Sun* in thirteen sections.[126] Zhang Song asked to read them, and Yang Xiu gave them to Zhang Song to read: like water pouring from a jug, like the Yellow River at the Ford of Meng flowing eastward![127] Yang Xiu was greatly amazed and told this to Lord Cao, who immediately ordered someone, "Request his presence right now." But, Zhang Song was already gone, and those who pursued him could not find him.

Zhang Song journeyed on in a southeasterly direction but when he saw a burgeoning aura, he made the far trip to Jingzhou. After a number of days he arrived in Jingshan District, ten *li* from Jingzhou, where he settled in at an inn. He informed the district magistrate, who reported that he had come from afar to see the Imperial Uncle.

The next day, when Zhang Song arrived at the city, there were officials, common people, and the Imperial Uncle himself there to welcome him into the yamen. During three days of banqueting, Zhang Song observed the officials: each and every one a dragon or tiger! On the left was Recumbent Dragon, on

---

124. Liu Zhang.

125. Following the suggested reading of Zhong Zhaohua (1990, 461).

126. The *Writings of Mengde* contained the original writings of Cao Cao, who had also composed a commentary to the *Writings of Master Sun*.

127. These metaphors describe the superior ease with which Zhang Song reads these texts that he encounters for the first time.

the right was Phoenix Fledgling, and in the middle he faced the Imperial Uncle. All exuded an aura of nobility that was beyond words. Zhang Song presented the maps of Xichuan [6a] to the Prince of Jing, and said, "The lord of Xichuan is not a proper ruler. Imperial Uncle, if you could occupy the area, the officials would be very pleased." The Imperial Uncle asked Zhuge to compose and take a letter to Liu Zhang in Xichuan.

Zhang Song set out on the road and reached home about a month later. The next day he saw his emperor and told him of Cao Cao's lack of humanity, "Think again of how he earlier obtained Jingzhou and got rid of Liu Cong by beheading him!" The emperor asked, "Who else did you see?" He then spoke of the virtue of the Prince of Jing, Liu Bei, and turned over the letter from the Imperial Uncle for Liu Zhang to read. When the emperor asked his civil officials and military officers for their opinion, there was one superior grandee, Qin Fu, who said, "My lord, you must have heard how Xuande had previously borrowed troops from Downriver Wu and had employed Zhou Yu and this army in a major battle to save the Imperial Uncle in Xiakou. Haven't you also heard how Zhuge thrice drove Zhou Yu mad with rage?" Qin Fu then went on to explain, "That Liu Bei is a man like a crafty barbarian. My Lord, if we invite him to Xichuan,[128] he will make trouble for you." Zhang Song loudly shouted, "Qin Fu, you are mistaken! Earlier we had no one who could oppose Zhang Lu and Ma Chao at the foot of Sword Pass. My lord, you must have heard that the Imperial Uncle belongs to the imperial house of the Han!" The other officials kept silent.

After a few days, Liu Zhang sent Fa Zheng off to Jingzhou to see the Imperial Uncle and Zhuge. After banqueting for a few days, the field marshal said, "As for the southeast, we will send a letter and so deal with Wu. But, Imperial Uncle, you surely know that north of Jingzhou Cao Cao has encamped a hundred thousand troops on the northern bank of the Lian River. And, if we take Xichuan, Cao Cao will cause trouble." The Imperial Uncle asked, "Should we first finish the fight with Cao Cao?" "Afterwards," said Zhuge, "we can conquer Xichuan." And at that moment, he wrote a letter to Lord Cao to set a day to face off in battle so Cao Cao could not give due consideration to crossing the River. They sent someone to take the letter to Lord Cao who, as soon as he finished reading the letter, roundly cursed them.

Liu Bei appointed yet another master as marshal, who claimed he was Pang Tong. When the armies squared off, he was soundly defeated. Cao Cao wanted to ride the tide of this victory to take Jingzhou. He pursued the enemy for thirty *li* until he encountered Zhang Fei. When Cao Cao's troops reached this point, due north of him lay Wei Yan with ten thousand troops, and they inflicted a heavy defeat on Cao Cao, who then fled north. He reached a ridge called

---

128. To fight Ma Chao and Zhang Lu.

Swinestrike Ridge. From the top of the ridge the Imperial Uncle rained down rolling timbers and catapult stones.

As night fell, Cao Cao managed to fight his way out, but fires erupted on the eastern and western flanks. Due north, Guan Yu blocked his way. Cao Cao smashed through the battle lines, but when he reached Yellow Cliff Passage, he found his way blocked by ten thousand troops. With their leader, Huang Zhong, [6b] they attacked. Cao Cao escaped with his life and crossed the Lian River at Xiakou with fewer than ten thousand troops. The armies of the Han were in hot pursuit, and the Martial Marquis intercepted him in front. Lord Cao returned with fewer than five thousand soldiers.

The Sichuan Campaign

Go on to tell about the field marshal entering Jingzhou. A day was chosen for Pang Tong to become marshal and he solicited the Imperial Uncle to conquer Sichuan. Zhuge said, "This year the Great Year[129] is located in the west: we will lose a great general!" But Pang Tong said with a smile, "My fate rests with Heaven, I am not afraid."

The Imperial Uncle led Pang Tong, Huang Zhong, Wei Yan, and other generals to augur a day to set out with the army. They proceeded to Jiaming Pass where the prefect blocked their road and told them, "The grandee Fa Zheng says he bears the sage's directive, but I have not been so informed by His Majesty."[130] Only Fa Zheng was allowed to enter Xichuan, and when he arrived in the imperial capital and saw Liu Zhang, the latter was very pleased. He then asked for opinions from his civil officials and military officers, "I would like to meet the Imperial Uncle at a place a hundred *li* from Chengdu, called the Fu River Meeting."[131] The grandee Qin Fu said, "My Lord, if you go to Fu River

---

129. A nonobservable baleful planet in traditional Chinese astrology, a shadow star across the heavens from Jupiter. It is called the "great year" because it makes a complete circle of heaven, like Jupiter, once every twelve years, moving through the twelve sections of the Chinese zodiac, each marking one year. In the four cardinal directions, the west is the direction of harshness, executions, and death.

130. Liu Zhang.

131. The word *hui* has apparently been copied into the text incorrectly. The term *Fujianghui* can only mean "the meeting at Fu River." The original term might have been an "episode marker"; that is, what follows would be "the episode of [Liu Bei and Liu Zhang] Meeting at Fu River." If this were a narratorial address to the audience/reader then it could be understood as, "'I would like to meet the Imperial Uncle at a place a hundred *li* away from Chengdu.' This is called the Meeting at Fu River."

to meet him, you definitely will end up in a situation as precarious as piled-up eggs." All his generals advised him against his proposal, but Liu Zhang did not follow their advice.

A few days later, the Imperial Uncle led three hundred thousand troops and more than a hundred fierce officers to make camp about twenty *li* east for the Fu River Meeting. At break of day the next day he met with Liu Zhang. At the meeting the two emperors each discussed their lineage and, embracing each other, they wept for a long time.

When the tea and wine were over, Pang Tong raised another cup and signalled Huang Zhong with his eyes. Huang Zhong pulled his sword and wanted to kill Liu Zhang. But Xuande was furious and said, "Don't act in such a wayward manner!" So Huang Zhong didn't dare take action. The officials all raised hell and, since the banquet was over, they asked Liu Zhang to leave for his own camp.

Next speak of Pang Tong telling the Imperial Uncle, "If we don't capture Xichuan today it is not my mistake, it is your fault!" But Xuande said, "He is a member of the Han house, how can we move against him?"

Next speak of Liu Zhang's officials all saying, "Our lord, you nearly didn't get out with your life!" The next day Liu Zhang had Liu Ba invite the Imperial Uncle. Pang Tong told the Imperial Uncle not to go lest he should be detained by those bandits. But he could not persuade him. Wei Yan and Pang Tong were to be constantly by his side and they selected three thousand soldiers to block the gate of Liu Zhang's camp, so those bandits would not even consider entering to cause trouble. When Liu Zhang invited the Imperial Uncle for a banquet on the following day, [7a] Liu Ba, the grand marshal Zhang Ren, and the superior grandee Qin Fu engaged in a dispute with the Imperial Uncle. But Liu Zhang said, "The Imperial Uncle is a man of humanity and virtue, you officers have no right to do this!" The Imperial Uncle left the camp and returned to his barracks.

Next explain that Qin Fu advised Liu Zhang to make the long journey to Bazhou. There the prefect Yan Yan together with the grand marshal Zhang Ren and their fifty thousand troops would capture Liu Bei. Liu Zhang still refused. Zhang Song and Fa Zheng discussed the situation in their own tent, and Zhang Song said, "The Imperial Uncle practices virtue and propriety but he should have trusted Pang Tong." And he also said, "At the Meeting at Fu River he should have killed Liu Zhang. He could have occupied Xichuan at once." Outside his tent a certain Zhao Wen heard this and informed Liu Zhang who immediately arrested Zhang Song and Fa Zheng. But mutinous troops created such a commotion that Fa Zheng was able to make his escape.

Surrounding Zhang Song, the officials took him to see Liu Zhang, who said, "Liu Ba and the superior grandee Qin Fu have been saying that Liu Bei wants to conquer Xichuan and we never believed them. How could we know that these two bandits were his collaborators on the inside and wanted to present Xichuan to that crafty barbarian Liu Bei!" Zhang Song said, "My lord, you must have heard that Sun Quan is scheming for Xichuan. That dictator Cao Cao is scheming for Xichuan. At the foot of the Sword Pass Zhang Lu and Ma Chao in Dongrong Commandery are scheming for Xichuan. My lord, you must have heard that the Imperial Uncle is a man of humanity and virtue and that the people of his country all admire him. He also is a member of the imperial house of the Han. If he captures this region, how can you be denied a commandery in which to spend your final days?" Liu Zhang brutally executed Zhang Song and in a panic ordered someone to go all the way to Bazhou to summon its prefect, Yan Yan.

Next speak about Fa Zheng who, after escaping in the melee and leaving the camp, had audience with the Imperial Uncle and told him everything in detail. Pang Tong said, "Imperial Uncle, it's no fault of mine that you now find yourself in such straits." They immediately set out with the army and fled eastward to Jiaming Pass. Someone informed them that the grand marshals of Shu and Chuan, Zhang Xiang and Zhang Ren, were leading fifty thousand troops to attack their rear. When the Imperial Uncle reached Mianzhou on his eastward march, its prefect Zhang Bangrui blocked his way. After they had grappled for two days, Pang Tong sniffed out a detour that would let them get by. To the northeast was Hanzhou, where Zhang Sheng stopped the Imperial Uncle; on both sides were mountains. Pang Tong dispatched Wei Yan to oppose Zhang Bangrui and sent Huang Zhong to intercept Zhang Sheng. Mianzhou on one side and Hanzhou on the other hemmed in the Imperial Uncle, and for a number of days he could not escape. Zhang Ren [7b] led fifty thousand troops to hold all the strategic positions. Pang Tong told the Imperial Uncle, "There is a city one hundred *li* from here." He immediately led his troops by the back roads all the way to Luocheng, and three days later they were knocking on the city gates. On the walls stood Liu Zhen, a younger brother of Liu Zhang, and when he recognized Pang Tong he ordered all of his officers to tell their archers to shoot.

Pang Tong Is Shot at Luocheng

A poem reads,

> At Luocheng Pang Tong was struck by a bronze arrowhead:
> It was heaven that took this hero's life.
> If Phoenix Fledgling had lived to a ripe old age,[132]
> He'd never have agreed to the tripartition with Cao and Wu.

The defeated troops returned and saw the Imperial Uncle. They told him that Prince Liu Zhen at Luocheng had sent Pang Tong to his death with a volley of arrows. The Imperial Uncle shed tears and as he broke an arrow[133] he said, "One day this enmity will be avenged!" The Imperial Uncle ordered Mei Zhu to take twenty horsemen and find a bypath through Jiaming Pass and go on ahead to Jingzhou and tell the field marshal what had happened. All of the officers wept.

Within ten days the officers had raised an army, and they divided it into three divisions. Zhao Yun would seize the road to Ziwu City. Zhang Fei was ordered to seize the road to Bazhou, and the field marshal would seize the road to Jiaming Pass. There were fewer than a hundred thousand men in these three divisions; in fact, there were only eighty thousand. The Marquis of Shouting would hold Jingzhou.

The troops of the field marshal made camp fewer than twenty *li* from Jingzhou. Zhuge swiftly whispered an order in Zhang Fei's ear. He told Zhang Fei to guard the southeastern exit of Jingzhou at East Market. Zhang led out a thousand troops and lay in ambush along the bank of the small river. Later, in the third watch of the night, an army approached from the north. There were three thousand troops, and in her carriage the young lady Sun held Adou in her arms, and intended to surrender to Eastern Wu. From the saddle of his horse Zhang Fei shouted to her, "Young lady, once you find out the Imperial Uncle is in trouble in Xichuan, you want to escape to the southern bank of the River with Aji!" This one word of reprimand of Zhang Fei made the young lady feel so ashamed that she jumped into the river and drowned.

Zhang Fei caught up with the field marshal and after two days Zhang Fei took the left flank, Zhao Yun took the right, and with the field marshal they went straight west to take Jiaming Pass.

Speak of Zhang Fei now who, after ten days on the road and after going on ahead to Baqiu County, found that all of the civilians there had fled. He went on to the southwest until he reached Bazhou and made his camp some forty *li*

---

132. He was just thirty-six when he was slain.
133. One breaks an arrow when making a vow and swearing an oath.

away. One day, Zhang Fei led his army of thirty thousand off to Bazhou, but about five *li* outside the prefectural city he came to a small confluence of two rivers, where he ordered someone [8a] to probe the water's depth. He forded the river, which was about five *li* wide. Watching him reach the bank, the prefect of Bazhou, Yan Yan, laughingly asked him, "Zhang Fei! Haven't you read Master Sun's *Art of War*? In there it is said, 'Those who are halfway through a river crossing may be attacked.'" Zhang Fei replied, "Haven't you heard about my actions at the long slope of Dangyang? Seeing the million-man army of Cao Cao, I just let out a single shout and they all turned into little recruits. How much less such a little ditch? It doesn't cause me any worry." Zhang Fei spurred his horse up the bank to do battle. Yan Yan fell off his horse in the middle of the panicked troops and was captured by Zhang Fei. When they reached a forest, Zhang Fei dismounted.

Zhang Fei Overawes Yan Yan with Righteousness

He shouted in a loud voice, "I have heard that Yan Yan was a famous general of Xichuan but now I have him. Behead him! Behead him!" When the major general heard this, he laughed, "Zhang Fei is not wise in his ways. I fell, my horse tripped, so he captured me. A great man risks his life as if it were nothing. What's the reason you're beheading me?" Zhang Fei stopped the executioners and said, "Yan Yan, you are a great man!" So he ordered someone to untie his ropes and release him.

Zhang Fei went on, "Liu Zhang of Xichuan is an incompetent and weak ruler. He had Zhang Song go all the way to Jingzhou to fetch the Imperial Uncle, explaining that he needed to capture Zhang Lu and Ma Chao at the foot of Sword Pass. Heeding the clever persuasions of that bandit, he has hemmed the Imperial Uncle in between Mianzhou and Hanzhou and slayed Pang Tong at Luocheng. The field marshal now has divided the army into three divisions to conquer Liu Zhang's Xichuan and will ride on the tide of success to take vengeance for the Imperial Uncle." He also told Yan Yan, "A noble bird evaluates the forest in which it will roost; a wise vassal chooses the lord he will support." Yan Yan replied, "I used to say that the Imperial Uncle's pure virtue was only on the surface and that Zhang Fei was a coarse and boorish fellow, but at a deeper level they both are filled with humanity and virtue. I, Yan Yan, spared from death, will surrender." Zhang Fei felt no trepidation at all when he followed Yan Yan into Bazhou, where they banqueted for three days.

Yan Yan presented a scheme: "A hundred *li* to the northwest you have White Chicken Ridge. I've been thinking that you are a true fellow, and about the fact that the one who guards that strategic terrain is the old general Wang Ping, a good friend of mine." Yan Yan led a hundred horsemen northward to White

Chicken Ridge. The old general knew Yan Yan was coming north and then went together with him to Jiaming Pass, where they learned it had already been taken by the Martial Marquis. When Zhang Fei arrived at the pass he dispatched someone to report to the field marshal, "Zhang Fei has brought Yan Yan for an audience."

The field marshal praised Zhang Fei's accomplishments, and said, "Zhao Yun has not taken Ziwu city." Zhang [8b] Fei asked the field marshal, "Why not?" "In that city is a Xichuan general who calls himself the Iron Arm General Zhang Yi. His attacks are unstoppable and he has defeated Zhao Yun." The field marshal led his troops to Ziwu and Zhang Yi rode out. The field marshal employed a strategy of persuasion through flattering words, but Zhang Yi rejected them and battled with Zhang Fei. For three days no one had a decisive victory even though they had fought more than a thousand times. For a month or more they had not captured Ziwu, nor did they know if the Imperial Uncle was still alive, there between Mianzhou and Hanzhou.

Next speak about the Iron Arm General Zhang Yi who, discussing the situation with his officers, said, "Tighten the noose around the Imperial Uncle. The grand marshal Zhang Ren does not know that the Martial Marquis has captured Jiaming Pass, conquered Bazhou, taken White Chicken Ridge, and accepted the surrender of Yan Yan. He has been in a standoff with the field marshal for over a month and we still cannot force him to withdraw." As he was wondering what to do, a reporting officer said, "The emperor's father-in-law has arrived with a thousand troops to inspect Jiaming Pass and Ziwu."

Zhang Yi said, "The Imperial Father-in-law Zhao Shidao is the greatest traitor at court!" He welcomed the Imperial Father-in-law some thirty *li* from the city and brought him into the yamen, where he was treated with all due courtesy. Zhao Shidao tried to discuss the problem, "Jiaming Pass is the eastern gate to Xichuan but Wang Shouzhong's position there is weak. Will you be able to protect it?" Zhang Yi said, "Each official guards his own town. Now the traitor's troops have already entered our boundaries but are still encamped outside Ziwu. We have been unable to push them back. How can we save Jiaming Pass?" In his cups the Imperial Father-in-law disparagingly berated all of the officers, and he did so three times in a row.

Zhang Yi told his officers, "Liu Zhang is ignorant and deluded; such traitorous ministers act as dictators." He also thought, "Zhang Song and Fa Zheng presented maps of Xichuan to the Imperial Uncle and that is a man of humanity and virtue." That evening all of the officials went with Zhang Yi to kill the emperor's father-in-law. In the latter's party there were people who fled in all directions, and when they were arrested by the Han troops and informed the field marshal, the latter was very pleased. Zhuge dispatched the Attendant

Gentleman of the Ministry of War Yi Ji to persuade Zhang Yi with flattering words and, after he offered up Ziwu and surrendered to the field marshal, Zhang Yi was appointed as attendant grand marshal.

When they proceeded westward to Luocheng, Liu Zhen rode out to give battle, but he was captured by his own officers and then the common folk presented the city to the attackers. The field marshal asked them, "Where is Pang Tong's body?" They found the corpse, killed Liu Zhen, and then made sacrifice to Pang Tong and properly buried him. In a few days, the field marshal led his troops west to Hanzhou. Its prefect [9a] Zhang Sheng met them for battle, but he was captured by Zhang Fei.

Speak now about how Zhang Yi led ten thousand troops to Mianzhou. Its prefect Zhang Bangrui and Zhang Yi engaged in battle. Bangrui suffered a bad defeat and fled. When Zhang Yi had ordered the two armies to do battle, the Xichuanese troops were scattered by the onslaught. After he had saved the Imperial Uncle, he then met with Zhuge and distributed the gold and gems taken in Mianzhou and Hanzhou to the troops, and they banqueted for several days.

In the west, the Imperial Uncle reached the Brocade Washing River, which was a powerful river. There was a bridge that was called the Bridge for Rising to the Realm of the Immortals. Zhuge said, "No one but an immortal can talk about this bridge." The field marshal returned to his camp and discussed the situation with his officers, but for half a month they could make no progress.

Speak now about how Huang Zhong, in the third watch of the night, heard someone calling out his name loudly, "Hansheng!" He asked, "Who is it?" The answer was, "Come out of your tent, I am Pang Tong." And he went on, "I was the one who gave you the four commanderies in order for you to repay the Imperial Uncle. But in the conquest of Xichuan I was wrongly struck by an arrow at Luocheng, so I am now dead. But I would like to express my gratitude to you for killing Liu Zhen to take vengeance for me. At present I have been reborn in heaven, so I have nothing I can give you as a present but this: the Imperial Uncle now wants to conquer Xichuan. Wait for an inauspicious day in the next three days, then you dress in a yellow gown that covers both your head and body. I will assist you; by accomplishing this feat unseen we will capture this bridge on behalf of the Imperial Uncle as a way to repay the grace he has shown us." Huang Zhong woke up and at dawn, he told the field marshal about his dream.

Three days later the Martial Marquis had his officers on that day lead all of their one hundred thousand troops to the eastern side of the Bridge for Rising to the Realm of the Immortals and there set out their battle array.

Pang Tong Helps the Plan

The field marshal sacrificed to the wind. Huang Zhong rode out on his horse. Ten renowned generals followed Huang Zhong up onto the bridge. A resounding sound like thunder rang out and sand and pebbles rose on all sides—those with the wind at their back were victorious; those with the wind against were whipped by torn branches, and they jumped from the towers and into the water, and their temporary battle huts[134] fell into the water. With his sword Huang Zhong hacked the gate open and the officers fought their way in. The Xichuan general, grand marshal Zhang Ren, fought Huang Zhong fewer than three rounds before Huang Zhong beheaded him in front of his horse. The troops of Xichuan withdrew forty *li*. There is a poem that verifies this,[135]

In a nighttime dream Pang Tong presented a strategy,
Sand and pebbles helped in the fight, determining who would be harmed.
At the Bridge of Immortals the army of Xichuan was defeated;
In Brocade Washing River the power of the waters swells.[136]
Temporary battle huts fell into the stream, the wind whipped branches;
Iron sundered, the gate opened: a sword cut the planks.
If he hadn't used the divine teacher's scheme right at this time,
How could he have ever been seated in Chengdu as ruler of the Han?

There is yet another poem,

[9b] In Shu's Brocade Washing River a thousand eternities of sorrow:[137]
On the Bridge of the Immortals the Han king and his liege lords.
If they had only known of Lord Pang's scheme at the time,
They wouldn't have put their heart and soul into arraying battle huts.

After the field marshal had captured the Bridge for Rising to the Realm of the Immortals and had decapitated Zhang Ren, the troops of Xichuan all dispersed. The Imperial Uncle banqueted for a few days then led his troops

---

134. These were called "jumping towers" in the Song, and were moveable temporary structures in the shape of a goose [egg?] that were placed on the top of the city walls for the protection of the defenders.

135. The normal black box is missing here.

136. Because of the blood that was shed.

137. Reading 秋 (autumn) as 愁 (sorrow), although this may also be a case in which both meanings would obtain: "A thousand autumns in the Brocade Washing River of Shu," i.e., the eternal river, and its eternal sorrow. The reader would have automatically made the connection between the two.

westward to Metal's Mouth Pass. Its prefect Ma Shouzhong said, "A great army is about to arrive." Shouzhong also said,[138] "Xichuan cannot maintain its independence." Someone reported, "The Han army is close." Zhang Fei was the one to do battle and he defeated Ma Shouzhong. Huang Zhong finally caught up and so they seized Metal's Mouth Pass.

Huang Zhong Beheads Ma Shouzhong

The prefect was engaged again, and he was beheaded by Huang Zhong in front of his horse. After that the Imperial Uncle went up through the pass. When the field marshal questioned the local people, it turned out that Chengdu Prefecture in Yizhou was fewer than a hundred *li* to the west. They reached the outskirts of Chengdu Prefecture in a few days.

Next explain that Liu Zhang, coming to the conclusion himself that Xichuan could not maintain its independence, led out the common people and, baring their arms and leading sheep, they welcomed the field marshal. Liu Zhang said, "Imperial Uncle, I implore you to take into consideration that I am a member of the imperial family. I beg you for a single commandery where I may live out my last days." The field marshal said, "Your Majesty, don't worry, the Imperial Uncle will certainly spare your life." Zhuge secretly had Liu Zhang locked away. When the Imperial Uncle had taken Chengdu Prefecture, the officers were all happy and banqueted for ten days.

Someone reported, "Zhang Lu and Ma Chao from Dongrong, who had been at the foot of Sword Pass, are leading a hundred thousand troops up Sword Pass. They have also captured Yangping Pass. Behind them there are Cao Cao's two hundred thousand." Within three days the field marshal led fifty thousand troops eastward to Yangping Pass. When he was informed that Ma Chao was approaching with thirty thousand troops, the Martial Marquis had Wei Yan go east to confront Ma Chao. The two armies faced off against each other. Ma Chao feigned defeat and struck Wei Yan with an arrow. The field marshal then sent the grandee Yi Ji to see Ma Chao, and after he surrendered to the field marshal, Zhang Lu went on to defeat Cao Cao.

Also relate that the field marshal brought his army back to Yizhou to see the Imperial Uncle, and they held a banquet.

---

138. Zhong Zhaohua suggests that the words *Shouzhong yan* are superfluous, in which case the line would be understood as, "If a great army is going to reach here, then Xichuan cannot remain independent."

The Imperial Uncle Enfeoffs the Five Tiger Generals

Lord Guan was enfeoffed as Marquis of Shouting, Zhang Fei as Marquis of Xichang, Ma Chao as the Border-Establishing Marquis, Huang Zhong as the Mutiny-Suppressing Marquis, and Zhao Yun as Marquis of Fengli.

The Single Sword Meeting

When the Imperial Uncle ennobled these five tiger generals, the only one who was not present was his beloved younger brother Lord Guan, so he had a trusted follower [10a] take gold and gems to Jingzhou to enfeoff Lord Guan as Marquis of Shouting.

When the envoy arrived in Jingzhou and had seen Lord Guan, the latter expressed his gratitude to the Imperial Uncle. While he was entertaining the envoy the latter said, "Ma Chao is a heroic brave. He has gibbon's arms and is a fine shot.[139] No one can match him." Lord Guan replied, "We have been together for more than twenty years since we became sworn brothers in the Peach Orchard. No one can match the two generals Guan and Zhang." He had someone take a letter to Xichuan for the field marshal.

After half a month the return letter arrived. After Lord Guan had read it, he said with a smile, "The words of the field marshal are right on the mark!" Lord Guan said to his officials, "That Ma Chao—he can be a Zhang Fei or Huang Zhong, but to try and match me? Hard to do."

Whenever the weather was humid Lord Guan suffered from pain in his arm, and he said to his officers, "Earlier on that Wu bandit Han Fu struck me with an arrow and the arrowhead was poisoned." He issued an invitation to Hua Tuo. That Hua Tuo had been a man under the command of that bandit Cao but, judging Cao Cao to lack humanity, he had come to Jingzhou to see Lord Guan. When he arrived in response to the invitation, Lord Guan told him that there was poison in the battle wound on his arm. "Erect a post," Hua Tuo said, "nail a ring to it, and put your arm through it. Then I can cure this pain." Lord Guan laughed loudly and said, "I am a true hero! Why should I fear this?" He ordered his servants to hold up a golden plate. Lord Guan bared his arm and had Hua Tuo scrape away the bone to cure his disease, and all of the poison was removed. Lord Guan never changed his expression at all.

---

139. Long and powerful arms that have the strength to pull a powerful bow; these long arms are referred to as "gibbon's arms."

A plaster was applied to the wound, and it was done with. There is a poem that verifies this,

> In the tripartition of the empire he settled buckler and spear:
> General Guan was a hero, full of manly determination.
> They scraped his bone to cure the wound and eradicate the illness;
> The steel knife cut off his flesh to avoid a severe disease.
> His expression was imperturbable as he entertained the guest from Shu,
> His face remained exactly the same while he sipped his Green Waves.[140]
> It must be that the divine immortals hide their miraculous cures;
> For all eternity the most famous physician is said to be Hua Tuo.

Relate that it took four months for the wound of the Marquis of Shouting to heal after the bone had been scraped away to cure the disease.

One day a spy reported, "Lu Su, Grandee of Downriver Wu, was leading a huge army across the River, and had dispatched someone with a letter inviting Lord Guan to go to a 'single-sword meeting.'" Lord Guan said, "There is surely some plot afoot in this single-sword meeting, but what do I fear?"

When the day arrived Lord Guan, with a light bow and short arrows, and with good mounts and trusted men bearing swords—no more than fifty in all—went south to Lu Su's encampment. The generals of Wu saw that Lord Guan was clothed in absolutely no armor and had but a single sword hanging from his waist. Lord Guan saw that there were three thousand men in Lu Su's retinue, [10b] all in armor, and that each of the officers was wearing a "heart-protecting bronze mirror" on his chest. His lordship thought to himself, "What is this traitor's objective?" When the feast was spread and wine brought forward, Lu Su ordered the army to play music to accompany the feast. The flute made no sound three times in a row and the Grandee shouted out the five notes of the scale, "*gong, shang, jue, zhi, yu!*" And then, three times in a row, he said, "*yu* did not sound." Lord Guan was enraged and clutched Lu Su. Lord Guan said, "You traitor; you set up this feast for no reason and called it a 'single-sword meeting,' then had your troops play music that did not sound the note *yu*. You said, '*Yu* does not sound / *Yu* is clueless,'[141] but today I'll make 'the mirror' be the first to break this sound."[142] Lu Su prostrated himself on the ground and said, "I would not dare." Lord Guan spared his life, got on his horse, and returned to Jingzhou.

---

140. Green Waves is one of the many names for fine rice wine.

141. This is a pun on the homophonic line *yu buming* (the tone *yu* [the same character as Guan Yu's given name] does not sound) and *yu buming* (Yu is clueless).

142. A pun on the syllable *jing*, which can mean both "mirror" and part of Lu Zijing's given name; i.e., "you'll die first."

Later relate how Lu Su sent someone across the River to fetch the fifty thousand troops of grand marshal Lü Meng and they recaptured Changsha and the other three commanderies. When Lord Guan heard this, with all speed he sent someone to Yizhou to request aid. When Zhuge arrived in Jingzhou with his army, Lord Guan guarded Jingzhou while the field marshal led sixty thousand troops and five superior generals to square off with Lü Meng. When the Han troops were defeated, Lü Meng chased them for twenty *li*, but then he found his way blocked by Zhang Fei. When the Wu army in its turn was defeated, the Han troops pursued them. When they had arrived at the border river of Changsha and the other three commanderies, troops that were waiting in ambush emerged on all sides. Zhao Yun rode out to give battle and the Wu army was heavily defeated. When they wanted to make a run for their camp, Huang Zhong blocked their way and they fought yet another battle. When Lü Meng had fled back to his camp, his way was blocked by another three thousand troops and Zhuge rode out to give battle. When Lü Meng reached the River, the Wu troops fled following the River, where Ma Chao blocked their way and engaged in yet another battle. Lu Su and Lü Meng had lost all of their fifty thousand troops, and when they held an inspection, their troops didn't even number three thousand. As for Lü Meng and his officers, they managed to escape with the remaining Wu troops through the reeds on the bank of the River.

Speak of how Lü Meng collected his troops on the southern bank of the River and that the field marshal had returned to the northern side of the River. This standoff lasted for a month. Sun Quan dispatched his son Sun Liang with thirty thousand troops, and he led Lü Meng to cross the River once more to square off with the Martial Marquis. With Heaven as his witness Sun Liang proclaimed the following oath, "Jingzhou and the land of Wu may be states as close to each other as lips and teeth, but they have never cared for each other." The field marshal then defeated Sun Liang in battle. Thereupon he collected his troops and returned to Jingzhou, where he said to Guan Yu, "This is a land of fish and rice.[143] That's why we first borrowed Jingzhou as capital and later schemed for Xichuan as the interest. Only today can conditions make this possible." And the field marshal also said, "In the northwest there's the army of Wei, and in the southeast there's Downriver Wu. [11a] If it weren't you, my lord, nobody else could guard this place."

---

143. A term for the fertile and well-watered land of the south.

Cao Cao's Sichuan Campaign

The field marshal returned with his troops to Chengdu, where the Imperial Uncle treated him to a banquet. Some two months later a soldier came to report, "Cao Cao's army of three hundred thousand has annexed Dongrong commandery. Zhang Lu's army of one hundred thousand troops is coming with him." Zhuge fielded an army of five hundred thousand troops and thirty famous officers, and proceeded eastward to Yangping Pass, where he made camp ten *li* away. Someone informed Cao Cao's army, "The Army of Xichuan is here!" Receiving the field marshal Yi Ji, the prefect of Yangping Pass told him that Cao's army had approached to within forty *li* and made camp. The field marshal said, "After that bandit has captured Sword Pass he will move toward Yangping Pass—he has his mind set on Xichuan. Tomorrow we must fight a decisive battle. Who dares capture that bandit Cao?" One man, looking up to heaven and, deeply moved, said, "My father and mother both died at the hands of that bandit general!" The field marshal recognized him as Ma Chao, and told him his plan.

At daybreak the next day, the two armies lined up against each other. Lord Cao reiterated, "It is Liu Bei who deposed Liu Zhang, but he simply calls others traitorous vassals!" He ordered Xiahou Dun to ride out. Liu Feng engaged him in battle. When evening fell both sides returned with their troops to their camps. Lord Cao said to himself, "With these three hundred thousand troops I will go on to Xichuan to kill Liu Bei. After I have destroyed that country hick, I'll hurry back to do battle."

That night in the third watch, someone announced, "Some old general is delivering grain to the Pass." And, as Huang Zhong was plundering their camp, Cao's troops all fled in the chaos and confusion. Then hidden troops emerged from all four sides and the battle continued all the way to Sword Pass, where they ran smack into Ma Chao who attacked them. By daybreak Lord Cao had managed to escape but in a single day and night he had lost one hundred thousand troops.

Again ten days later Lord Cao sent people out to reconnoiter the situation, and they told him, "The field marshal has once again ordered Yi Ji to guard Yangping Pass together with Ma Chao, and the Martial Marquis has gone through the pass." After ten more days Lord Cao appeared with his army once more before Yangping Pass. Ma Chao was defeated in battle because he was drunk, and Yangping Pass was captured by the Wei general Zhang Liao. Ma Chao didn't dare face the field marshal and sneaked away. When Lord Cao found out, he led his three hundred thousand troops and a hundred famous officers to attack fleeing troops of Yangping Pass from the rear. The prefect

Yi Ji, with fewer than a hundred horsemen, rode three days and nights before he reached Xichuan, and told the field marshal what had happened.

Go on to tell how Cao Cao sent someone out to reconnoiter then went ahead to Ziwu City. Cao Cao said, "Ziwu City is a strategic location in Xichuan." When Lord Cao led his troops to the pass, he could see from far off [11b] that the common people were going about their daily business, and he also saw soldiers amusing themselves in the markets and streets. Lord Cao said, "We must act quickly!" But Zhang Liao told him, "This is a trick of Zhuge. You see these common people of Ziwu City in their cups and those soldiers amusing themselves, but this is called 'furling the flags and resting the drums.' If you go inside these city walls, you won't be able to get out." They fled in a northeasterly direction but were pursued from behind by the Han army. The famous general Wei Yan heavily defeated Cao's army in battle. To his left he had Liu Feng, and to his right he had Zhao Yun, and they continued in pursuit until daybreak, when Zhang Fei blocked their way and attacked them. When they arrived at Yangping Pass, the field marshal had already retaken it, and he also drew on Huang Zhong to launch yet another attack.

Cao Cao fled back to Sword Pass but ran into Ma Chao who also attacked him. Cao Cao dropped his cap and removed his armor, then fled down Sword Pass, managing to escape. More than a month later, the field marshal camped his troops at Sword Pass. Lord Cao again established his camp forty *li* from Sword Pass. A scout found out that Lord Cao had three hundred thousand troops with him and had also dispatched three hundred thousand troops to guard Mt. Dingjun. Xiahou Yuan had another three hundred thousand troops and had built a hundred buildings, where there were five hundred thousand stoneweight of grain—they were hungering like a tiger for Baozhou.[144] This was indeed a strategic place. Yu Xu, the governor of Fenzhou, transported grain and fodder to Mt. Dingjun, where he made a permanent encampment. The field marshal said, "If Lord Cao captures the thirteen prefectures outside Sword Gate, Xichuan cannot enjoy peace." He asked his officers, "Who dares battle at Mt. Dingjun, decapitate Xiahou Yuan, and capture those five hundred thousand stoneweight of grain and fodder?" One man stepped forward. It turned out to be Huang Zhong, who said of himself, "I will decapitate Xiahou Yuan, capture Mt. Dingjun, and requisition those five hundred thousand stoneweight of grain and fodder." The Martial Marquis was delighted. Leading ten thousand troops he cut off Longzhou, captured boats and carts, and expelled Yu Xu.

Speak about how, when Huang Zhong arrived at Mt. Dingjun, Xiahou Yuan said, "I only know of the two generals Guan and Zhang—in an army of

---

144. Perhaps a mistake for Bazhou.

ten thousand Xichuan troops, how dare one old general claim he can capture Mt. Dingjun!" Thereupon he led his troops down Mt. Dingjun and engaged in battle with Huang Zhong.

Huang Zhong Decapitates Xiahou Yuan

In fewer than three rounds Xiahou Yuan had been soundly defeated and fled up the mountain. Huang Zhong said to himself, "Can a real man stand to be below others? If I do not decapitate Xiahou Yuan and if I do not capture Mt. Dingjun, I am not a real man!" He caught up with Xiahou Yuan, engaged him again, [12a] decapitated him in front of his horse, and captured both the grain and fodder and this strategic location. There is a poem by an historian,

> At the foot of Mt. Dingjun he stilled lance and spear:
> All alone Huang Zhong captured Xiahou Yuan.
> He seized the grain, beheaded the general, climbed the highest peak;
> He silenced the drums, stole the banners, crashed through the battle lines.
> Like a hungry tiger he eyed Sword Pass, eradicated the stronghold of Wei;
> A dragon returned to the imperial ward, enthroned in Shu and Chuan.
> His meritorious vassals depicted on the walls of Lingyan Gallery,[145]
> The history books highlight their names, passed on for all eternity.

Speak about how Huang Zhong sent someone to deliver a letter all the way to Zhang Fei, who said, "We brothers all congratulate the old general Huang Zhong on establishing such a major feat. How could he cede to others? Huang Zhong has captured Mt. Dingjun, but he uses that to chide me!" Zhang Fei led his troops in pursuit of Yu Xu, who was resting in front of a forest. People told Zhang Fei, "Yu Xu's troops are coming over from behind the woods." Zhang Fei immediately got on his horse, captured Yu Xu,

Zhang Fei Captures Yu Xu

and went all the way to Sword Pass to report to the field marshal.

Lord Cao had twice tried to invade Sichuan and his six hundred thousand troops and been defeated all in one go. His troops numbered fewer than one hundred thousand, and he had made camp on a high hill. This is what is called, "A ram caught by its horns in a fence: no way forward or back." He was unable to conquer Xichuan, but he was also afraid that Zhuge would attack his rear.

---

145. See note 41.

The field marshal ordered a man to deliver a letter to the prime minister. When the prime minister read the letter, it informed Cao Cao, "Out of the thirteen prefectures outside Sword Pass, I will grant you four commanderies in the area from Shifang to Longzhou." Cao Cao thought to himself, "What could Zhuge be up to?"

For ten days, Cao Cao led his troops to the border of Shifang and the other three prefectures but perceived an aura of war filling the sky. Cao Cao said, "Another trick of Zhuge." He established a large camp on a high hill, kept his troops in armor, but made no move for a month. One day Cao Cao was strolling incognito in a quiet night and saw that his soldiers were bundling up their luggage. When he asked, it turned out that the Constant Attendant in the Ministry of War, Yang Xiu, had ordered his officers to tell the troops to pack their luggage. "What is your intent in fanning the soldiers' doubts?" Yang Xiu replied, "Yesterday after breakfast I saw the prime minister sighing over a chicken bone, saying that there was not enough taste to eat it, but that you still were reluctant to throw it away. Prime Minister, this means that you will withdraw your forces." Cao Cao loudly cursed him out, "When three years ago I was walking in private with you we saw the stele with eight characters for the Beauty Cao.[146] I didn't immediately understand their meaning, and when I asked you, you also didn't understand. It was when I woke up the next morning [12b] that I understood what it meant. 'Yellow silk' meant 'colored thread' 色糸, and that is the character jue 絕; 'infant woman' means a 'young girl' 少女, and that is the character miao 妙; a 'grandson of a different surname' is a 'daughter's son' 女子, and that is the character hao 好; 'pickle mortar' means 'suffering bitterness' 受辛, and that is the character ci 辭. These eight characters were juemiao haoci (exceptionally wonderful fine words)." Cao Cao then roundly cursed him, "When dealing with Zhuge, you don't even dare look him in the eye, but when dealing with me, you treat me like grass and weeds. You must have the desire to usurp my position!" He gave the order to behead Yang Xiu. The other officers could not persuade him otherwise and he beheaded Yang Xiu.

That very night he ordered a retreat. He fled eastward to Purple Forest Crossing. When they marched some twenty li, on the road east there was a bridge across a river running south to north. After the army was fully across, people trailing behind destroyed it and fires arose on both sides.

---

146. Maid Cao was a young girl from Shangyu. After her father drowned in the river and his body was not found, she threw herself into the stream. Five days later her body reemerged, carrying her father in her arms. A stele had been erected that carried an elegy for her by Handan Chun. On the backside of the stele an eight-character line by Cai Yong in praise of the elegy had been inscribed. See Mather (2002, 314–15) for a complete description.

Zhuge Employs a Scheme to Force Cao Cao to Retreat

To the south Wei Yan emerged with ten thousand troops, to the north Zhao Yun appeared with ten thousand more, and from behind they were attacked by the field marshal with three thousand. By daybreak they had made eighty *li* but in front of them appeared three thousand troops, and they were attacked by Huang Zhong and Zhang Fei. Cao Cao could barely make his escape, but his men were worn out and his horses were exhausted, and he could not go on. Again he ran into Ma Chao, and from behind they were attacked by the Martial Marquis and several tens of famous officers. Ma Chao with his thirty thousand men blocked his way and launched an attack.

Cao Cao escaped with his life from Guanzhong, but not five thousand men were left of his main army, and Cao Cao had suffered so much in the fighting that he had pushed back his cap and unbound his hair, and leaning on his saddle spat blood. He reached Chang'an only after a few days on the road.

The Death of Guan Yu and the End of the Han

On the third day back, he was received by the emperor, who fêted him for a number of days. The senior grandee Jia Xu said in secret to Minister Cao, "The son of Emperor Xian has complained to the officials that all appointments to office and gifts and rewards proceed from Minister Cao. Prime Minister, the crown prince wants to kill you." Cao Cao was silent. A few days later, pretending to petition the emperor, he said, "When King Ping of Chu was quite advanced in years, his son Mijian had secretly plotted to usurp the throne and kill his father. Heaven and Earth, however, did not allow it to happen." Emperor Xian again asked, "What do you mean?" Minister Cao lied to him, saying, "The officials at court all say that whenever the crown prince gets drunk, he says over and over that Your Majesty has become too old, and that someone else has a desire to become the ruler. I am afraid that someday the crown prince will cause trouble in the palace." Emperor Xian did not say a word but then thought, "Wang Mang assassinated Emperor Ping to wrest away the empire. My son was born to the empress, yet he still harbors such thoughts!" When he questioned Cao Cao again, the latter proposed that an investigative official [13a] should interrogate the crown prince at the Terrace of Censors. Cao Cao ordered someone he trusted to have the crown prince whipped. Now the crown prince was the son of an emperor and the grandson of a dragon, and he could not bear such pain. Although innocent, he confessed to the crime. Cao Cao reported to Emperor Xian and again mentioned the case of the crown prince. The emperor asked, "How should we handle this?"

Cao Cao Decapitates the Crown Prince

Cao Cao said, "Behead him in the marketplace of the capital." The emperor replied, "My child is the son of an emperor and the grandson of a dragon. How can we behead him in the marketplace?" Cao Cao retorted, "Since ancient times there has been no pardon for those who commit regicide or patricide." The emperor could not refute this and dispatched a palace grand defender to supervise the decapitation of the crown prince in the city's marketplace. The people of the capital said, "The house of Liu has no ruler anymore."

Emperor Xian feared Cao Cao and granted him title as Great King of Wei. The land of Wu then established Sun Quan as Great King of Wu. When this news reached Xichuan, the Martial Marquis told the Imperial Uncle that he should proclaim himself King of Hanzhong. The First Ruler shed tears, as once again he thought of how Gaozu had raised his sword to behead the white snake at Mt. Mangtang, and how over a number of years he had conquered the Qin and eradicated Chu—but now Emperor Xian was an incompetent weakling and Cao Cao acted as a dictator. The murder of the crown prince on trumped-up charges in order to cut off both the root and sprout of the Han was all Cao Cao's scheme. The First Ruler took to bed with an illness for a few days, and then asked Zhuge, "I have two sons. The elder is Liu Feng and the younger is Liu Shan. Who should become the ruler of Xichuan?" Zhuge had the officials discuss this question and, claiming illness, he did not leave his house for a number of days. When the First Ruler sent someone to repeat the question to the field marshal, the latter said, "I am so sick I cannot even move. Let His Majesty go all the way to Jingzhou and ask Lord Guan."

Lord Guan said, "Liu Feng is an adopted son from the Kou family of Lohou, but Liu Shan was born to your main wife." When his return letter reached the First Ruler, the latter said, "What my younger brother says is right on the mark." A few days later Liu Feng was appointed as governor of Jiaming Pass, with Meng Da as his supporting official.

Again a few days later documents of the King of Hanzhong established Liu Shan as the future ruler of Xichuan. When Liu Feng found out, he called Xuande lacking in humanity, but Meng Da said, "This isn't the fault of the Imperial Uncle, it's all the crime of Lord Guan." Liu Feng then broke an arrow and vowed, "Some day this enmity will be revenged."

Now go on to speak about Lord Guan. About a half-year later, someone reported to him, "An envoy from the southern bank of the river has arrived." This senior grandee from Downriver Wu said, "The son of the King of Wu has discovered that the Prince of Jing has a daughter. [13b] What about a marriage alliance between the two families?" Lord Guan, who was in his cups, replied,

"We are the offspring of dragon and tigers! How could we marry her to the grandson of a melon grower?" The envoy then left.

A month or so later the senior grandee Chen Deng arrived all the way from Chang'an, and he had brought his whole family with him to Jingzhou. When Lord Guan was informed of this, he invited them to enter the city. When Lord Guan asked him for his motives, the grandee gave a full account of Cao Cao's lack of humanity: in Chang'an he had built the Bronze Sparrow Palace and had selected the most beautiful women in the empire, and enjoyed their company there every day. "You must have heard that when Cai Yan returned from her marriage to the barbarian, she was taken into this palace by Cao Cao!"[147] Chen Deng then said, "I have one daughter but that bandit Cao hasn't been able to take her in too." Lord Guan said, "Grandee, you did right."

Not a month later and an envoy from Cao Cao came to reclaim Chen Deng, but Lord Guan did not release him. Cao Cao then had a grand marshal Pang De and the assisting officer Yu Jin lead one hundred seventy thousand troops, which they named "The Seven Armies," and each division was comprised of twenty-five thousand men.

Lord Guan Decapitates Pang De

Lord Guan decapitated Pang De in front of his horse and the army of Wei was soundly defeated. A few days later Lord Guan observed that Yu Jin had established his camp downstream on a small river, and when it suddenly started to rain, Lord Guan released the water of that small river and since it had no banks to contain it,

Lord Guan Drowns the Seven Armies

it covered the troops of Yu Jin, who all fell in the water and died. So after two battles not even ten thousand troops remained of the army of Wei.

When Yu Jin returned to Chang'an and provided a full account to Cao Cao, the latter appointed four generals as grand marshals: the first was Prime Minister Jia Xu; the second was Zhang Liao; the third was Xiahou Dun; and the fourth was the Grand Defender Li Dian. And there were several famous officers

---

147. Cai Yan was a daughter of the famous scholar Cai Yong (132–192). She had been abducted by a Xiongnu chieftain who made her his wife. She bore him two children, but she had to leave these two boys behind when she was ransomed by Cao Cao, who had been a good friend of her father. Cao Cao married her off to a certain Dong Si, and when the latter had incurred his wrath, he was spared death at the request of Cai Yan.

involved as they raised an army of a hundred thousand men to go to Jingzhou. Zhang Liao offered up a scheme to establish an alliance with Downriver Wu: if they attacked Jingzhou from two sides it would be smashed.

Zhang Liao crossed the River and was received in audience by the King of Wu. He persuaded Sun Quan with these flattering words, "If the famous general of Wu, Lü Meng, reaches Jingzhou with a hundred officers and a hundred thousand troops,[148] then Jingzhou in the southeast will be attacked by Lü Meng from the land of Wu and in the northwest by the Wei army and Jia Xu."

When Lord Guan learned about this, his son Guan Ping said, "Father, you are getting on in years. You should send a letter to Chengdu Prefecture in Yizhou for the King of Hanzhong. If the field marshal arrives, these bandit troops will disband by themselves without any action by us." Lord Guan replied, "When my elder brother led the officers in the conquest of Shu, we had no part in that achievement. To now go and ask him for reinforcements when [14a] bandit troops enter our territory is not what a real man would do."

After a few days Lord Guan left the city to confront Lü Meng in the southeast but Zhang Liao attacked him from the rear. And when he confronted the army of Wei in the northwest, he was assailed from the rear by Lü Meng. This went on for about half a month but the bandit armies did not disperse. Lord Guan's battle wound split open, and Guan Ping told him, "Prince of Jing, send someone to Xichuan to request reinforcements." When that person arrived at Jiaming Pass, Liu Feng and Meng Da suppressed the letter. Over a month there were three letters requesting reinforcements, and they were all suppressed by Liu Feng and never submitted.

When Lord Guan's battle wound had slightly healed, he made preparations to go into battle the next day. At midnight that day a great storm suddenly started and a sound arose like the thunder. To all of the people of the city it seemed to say that Lord Guan would die. When Lord Guan went into battle the two countries joined forces to besiege him. Lord Guan was encircled on a mountain ridge to the southeast of Jingzhou. After he fell, a heavy rain poured down for several days.

Next tell how the officers of the two countries Wu and Wei arrived at Jingzhou and explained that the Sage had returned to Heaven. By this clever persuasion, they divided up Jingzhou. When Zhang Liao informed Lord Cao in Chang'an, his delight knew no bounds. The defeated troops of Jingzhou fled to Sichuan and informed the field marshal who was shocked; and how could he report it? He suppressed news of the affair.

---

148. Reading *shiwan* 十萬 for *qianwan* 千萬; a common misscription.

Go on to speak of Minister Cao, who told the emperor, "Your Majesty, you are reaching the age of the sages." The emperor said, "And I also have no descendants, so who can be put on the throne?" Cao replied, "Your Majesty surely knows that in the days of Yao, Shun, Yu, and Tang, the one with the most virtue was installed on the throne." And when the emperor asked who might be this person of high virtue, Minister Cao replied, "My son Cao Pi! He is acclaimed by everyone in the empire. He can be enthroned as Son of Heaven." In less than half a year a terrace was built at a place called Phoenix Village, fifty *li* southwest of Chang'an, and this was called the "Terrace for Accepting Abdication." A song reads,

> Cranes, ducks, swallows, rats, foxes, and wildcats shriek;
> Ghosts puff out sickness and death, burn sage and tumbleweeds.
> This terrace may be fine, but its name is not;
> The earth may be piled up high, but virtue is not.
> Tens of feet of yellow earth bury the banners of fire;[149]
> When a horse is startled it must ruin its tailing light.
> He brutalized a widow to obtain a jade seal;
> He intimidated an orphan soul into leaving its native land.
> If a man with gall wants to be Son of Heaven,
> Why talk anymore about playing a child's game?
> Far better to raise your sword and say very clearly,
> "I should be ruler, you should die!"
> The palace fooled itself with this pile of yellow earth;
> To no avail it mightily rose into the sky.
> It ruined forever the tradition of abdication of Tang and Yu; [14b]
> The yellow earth steeply rising up, a marker of this place of sorrow.
> The earth of his grave on the high mount had barely covered him,[150]
> When the Lord of Jin began aping this ritual of Tang and Yu.
> The pile of yellow earth may rise up to the clouds,
> But Heaven bears no brave souls that know it.
> People say, "The terrace is fine, but its name is not,"
> Because it was all evil scheming to usurp the Han.
> In the end, good and evil get their just reward;
> What is gained through evil will be done in by evil.
> The Cao family wished to inherit a thousand-year enterprise,
> But the Simas inherited the throne in just the same way.

---

149. Fire is the agent of the Five Phases that governed the house of Liu.

150. Of Cao Cao.

A poem reads,

> Wrongfully killing the Crown prince, he ended the line of the Han;
> At this fine terrace the Wei ancestor will enthrone their rival lord.
> In total five emperors would be the compensation from the netherworld;
> But when the Simas schemed for kingship, they would kill their own share!

Let us now speak instead of when, following Cao Cao's death, Cao Pi had accepted the abdication, the new lord was congratulated by all officials. Changing the reign period to the first year of Huangchu, he ascended the throne. And after he ascended the throne as Emperor Wen of the Wei, he enfeoffed Emperor Xian as the Duke of Shanyang Commandery, and today the traces of the latter's palace may still be seen to the northwest of the district capital of Xiuwu in Huaizhou.

The Deaths of Zhang Fei and Liu Bei

Let us go back and speak of Sun Quan of Downriver Wu, who had proclaimed himself Great Emperor of Wu and changed his reign title to the first year of Yellow Dragon. When the field marshal learned about this in Xichuan, he informed the King of Hanzhong. The First Ruler said, "The house of Han has weakened and withered; Cao Cao has wrested away the empire; Sun Quan makes himself a hegemon." But the field marshal did not go along with Xuande, and proclaimed him as the August Emperor of Shu and Chuan, changing the reign period to the first year of Jianwu.[151] A banquet was held for several days to congratulate the new ruler. The emperor thought of his sworn brothers of the Peach Orchard, "Since I set out to conquer Sichuan I have been separated from my beloved younger brother Lord Guan and have not seen his face now for several years." He ordered someone to go off to Jingzhou and summon the Prince of Jing. The field marshal could no longer hide or avoid the issue, so he explained Guan Yu's death to the emperor in a calm and slow way. But upon hearing it, the First Ruler immediately collapsed on the floor and was overcome time and again by rage. The First Ruler had masses read for Lord Guan, and after a month he discussed the situation with the field marshal. Zhuge informed him, "In the current transit of the Great Year, the year and the month are bad for a campaign against Wu. Your Majesty, it is unadvisable." But the emperor said, "My thoughts are with the sworn brotherhood of the Peach Orchard: if we three brothers can be together in death, what's 'unadvisable'?" The field marshal could not change his mind.

---

151. It is in actuality the Zhangwu reign (章武), but the text consistently writes Jianwu (建武).

Xichuan fielded an army of four hundred thousand and borrowed another one hundred thousand troops from Meng Huo, the king of the southern barbarians. In the first year of Jianwu, Zhang Fei was appointed as grand marshal to overturn Wu. The Martial Marquis and the crown prince were left in the capital to administer the country. Ma Chao was ordered to hold Sword Pass in the east, and the old general Huang Zhong and Zhao Yun to hold Mt. Dingjun. The field marshal remonstrated with the First Ruler, but to the end he did not heed him. [15a] The emperor chose a day and set out with his troops to overturn Wu.

After a month or so, the emperor reached White Emperor City and set up five camps linked like pearls on a string. After a few days a scout informed him, "To the east, the grand marshal of the army of Wu, Lü Meng, has crossed the River with a hundred famous officers. His army of one hundred thousand has made camp sixty *li* from White Emperor City." The August Emperor said, "Within two days we will go out with the army to do battle and we will behead those bandits from Downriver Wu in order take revenge for Lord Guan." Outside his tent a lone man shouted, "Give me fifty thousand troops and I will behead those bandit generals." The emperor recognized him as his beloved younger brother Zhang Fei. But Zhang Fei had had too much drink, and Xuande said, "Brother, you're old now."

The next day the emperor marched out with the troops and ordered Zhang Fei to guard the camp. He repeated the Sagely Edict three times: Zhang Fei was not allowed to join the battle. "Think of our oath of brotherhood in the Peach Orchard," said Zhang Fei, "we are to die together." He drew his sword and was about to cut his own throat, but the emperor immediately ordered men to hold him back. Zhang Fei showed no proper respect at all for the First Ruler, so the other officers pressed in around him and took him back to camp. Zhang Fei looked up to heaven and, deeply shaken, said, "The First Ruler will not allow me to take revenge for Lord Guan!" Before he had finished speaking, a sound boomed like the thunder and a great wind passed by, snapping in half the pole of Zhang Fei's banner that carried the word, "Marshal." Zhang Fei ordered that his flag-bearer Wang Qiang be given fifty strokes of the bamboo. That night Wang Qiang returned to his own tent unit.

Explain that when Zhang Fei had his meal, the taste of the meat was not to his liking, and in his cups, he ordered the cooks to appear before him. He stared at Zhang Shan and Han Bin. After he uttered a string of curses at them, Zhang Fei ordered that each be given thirty strokes.[152]

---

152. The names in this passage are quite different than in other historical records or vernacular texts; instead of Fan Qiang 范疆 we have here Wang Qiang 王強, and instead of Zhang Da 張達 we have here Zhang Shan 張山.

That night Wang Qiang, Zhang Shan, and Han Bin were drinking wine together and got utterly drunk so they could bear the pain. One of them said, "Today in his stupor Zhang Fei has only picked on minor transgressions!" These three, all unreconciled to their treatment, went to his tent together. After they had killed Zhang Fei they picked up his head and went off to surrender to Wu.

When the emperor learned of this the next day, he collapsed several times from rage. He took to his bed, sick, for several days.

Lü Meng sent someone with a letter to the First Ruler. Within three days the First Ruler led his army to square off with Lü Meng. When the latter feigned defeat and the First Ruler pursued him and had crossed a small river, Lü Meng turned back and again engaged him in battle. The First Ruler was heavily defeated and his troops fought their way westward back to confluence of the small river, but he was brought to a standstill by Lu Xun, the grand marshal of the state of Wu. The First Ruler was defeated again, and the troops of Wu pursued him. Forty *li* after crossing the river, [15b] the First Ruler made camp and let his men cook food. The very moment it was ready, fires started on the bank, and Lü Meng attacked from behind. Then fires erupted on the western side, but ahead and behind they were blocked by troops lying in ambush. They pursued the First Ruler for three days and nights, and when he arrived at White Emperor City his troops numbered fewer than thirty thousand.

The First Ruler nursed his illness in the Precious Woman Palace of White Emperor City, but could not eat or drink and blood flowed from his mouth and nose. He hurriedly dispatched someone to Xichuan to summon the crown prince Liu Shan to come together with the field marshal and the old general Zhao Yun. Within a month the crown prince and the field marshal arrived. When they met with the emperor, he pulled the crown prince to him and held the Martial Marquis tightly. As his tears coursed down he said to the field marshal, "We almost didn't see each other again." Over the next few days the illness of the First Ruler increased. He told the field marshal, "This realm right now could only have been won with you!" He summoned the crown prince to his side and had him bow to the Martial Marquis. The latter wanted him to rise, but the emperor pushed him down. The Martial Marquis protested, "This old official should be sentenced to death!" The First Ruler said, "Field Marshal, you must have heard the story of how Dan the Duke of Zhou carried King Cheng in his arms!" The emperor also said, "Aji is still young and cannot yet be the ruler. If he is fit to be enthroned, enthrone him, but if he is not fit, field marshal, you do it yourself." The Martial Marquis replied, "What virtue do I have that Your Majesty now entrusts your son to me? Even if I were to kill myself, I could never repay this trust." The crown prince knelt down and came forward on his knees then made his bows, and the emperor said, "My son, in any public decision make sure the field marshal agrees." When he had said this, the emperor passed away at the age of sixty-four.

In the second year of Jianwu Liu Shan was enthroned, and the reign period was changed to the first year of Jianxing.

Let us now turn to speak of how the field marshal pinned down the Emperor Star[153] and had ten thousand soldiers and laborers establish a camp twenty *li* east of White Emperor City where they assembled eight piles of rocks, and on each of these piles there were eight times eight, that is sixty-four, flags. When this was reported to Lü Meng, he led his troops to have a look. He summoned the grand marshal Lu Xun, who was stunned. The officers asked what it meant, and Lü Meng replied, "If one arranges trees into formations, it corresponds to the element Fire; if it's a formation of weeds, it corresponds to the element Water. But a formation of rocks creates a puzzle. Officers, don't you see there are sixty-four flags on each pile of rocks? According to the eight trigrams of the Duke of Zhou, I see that Zhuge understands "'the method for making the heavens revolve one circuit,'" and eight hundred times ten thousand times one hundred million star gods are present on these eight piles of rocks."[154] Lü Meng also said, "If you are not Great Duke Jiang, Master Sun Wu, Guan Zhong, or Zhang Liang, you cannot undo it." Before he had finished speaking, a soldier from the rear came to report, [16a] "Zhuge has ordered Wei Yan to make his way through small rocky backways to plunder your main camp, Marshal."

When Lü Meng retreated with his troops, he was pursued from behind by the field marshal with his army. From both sides he was harassed by Ma Chao and Guan Ping and he was heavily attacked by the Martial Marquis from the rear. After Lü Meng crossed the River, the field marshal had a team of four horses pull the carriage carrying the casket. Once the crown prince and the officers had entered Chengdu Prefecture in Sichuan, the First Ruler was buried according to the mourning stipulations for an emperor, and masses were read for one month.

---

153. See note 112.

154. The stars rotate once every year in predictable cycles; this is a method for expelling evil by congregating all the spirits that inhabit the stars in one place simultaneously, assuring the return of normalcy. This is done by an incremental expansion of the eight trigrams, to eight eights and so on, until the full number of astral spirits are present in the formation.

A Threat from the South

A half-year after Liu Shan had mounted the throne, Meng Huo, the king of the southern barbarians, sent a barbarian general to ask for the one hundred thousand troops that the First Ruler had borrowed. "What are your intentions toward us?"[155] The field marshal had him entertained with tea and food, and after half a month gave him gold and gems to send him off. The Young Ruler asked the field marshal, "I'm afraid that this barbarian general will come back again. How will we then handle him?" The field marshal said, "That will be no problem."

In the fourth month of the second year of Jianxing,[156] the Young Ruler banqueted in the Drunk on the Wind Tower, and discussed the state business with the field marshal, "Within one year Meng Huo will field an army of one hundred thousand in order to take Sichuan." The field marshal said, "I will definitely campaign and chastise those southern barbarians." The emperor was stunned and asked, "How?" The field marshal led the emperor to wield the "helping scepter" in the southern direction,[157] and the emperor saw a red aura rise all the way into the Lion Palace.[158] The emperor asked, "What good or bad fortune does this portend?" Zhuge replied, "When your father conquered Xichuan earlier, there was a Grand Defender before the palace named Xiong Kai,[159] who was unwilling to accept the situation. The First Ruler once told me that, when he took Xichuan, Xiong Kai beheaded the prefect of Chuan and the people all bore a grudge against him, so he has now been appointed prefect of Yunnan Commandery, but he's creating trouble."

---

155. This unascribed quote seems out of place here.

156. May–June 224.

157. A puzzling phrase, *yaodi yi nanmian yizhu* 邀帝倚南面翊杵, which Zhong Zhaohua (1990, 475) glosses as, "*yizhu* is a military implement used to conduct dances. *Yi* is 'to fly,' *zhu* is a military implement like the *vajra* (the magical diamond scepter of Tibetan Buddhism), expressing that this passage is involved with military action."

158. That is, the Western constellation Leo. Muslim astronomers had introduced the Twelve Zodiacs of the Greeks into Chinese astronomy by the Northern Song, which is substantiated by the eleventh-century text, *Wujing zongyao*. In that text we find under the heading, "Prognosticating the Five Day Period of the Year" (*zhanhou* 占候), and subheading, "Random Prognostications for Assuring Victory When Sending out an Army," the following passage: "[Solar period] Great Heat, in the sixth month the sun [along the ecliptic] is in the Willow Constellation at five degrees and 28 minutes. Three days later it enters the Constellation Leo. Its spirit is 'ray of victory.'" While a total anachronism, this passage is meant to indicate Zhuge Liang's deep knowledge of the astral phenomena that govern military action on Earth.

159. A mistranscription of the actual name Yong Kai 雍闓, confusing *yong* 雍 and *xiong* 雄. We retain the reading in the text.

Three days later Yi Ji reported, "South of the River three garrisons have revolted. Xiong Kai, the prefect of Yunnan Commandery, has concluded an alliance with Lü Kai, the prefect of Buwei City, and then there is Du Qi, the prefect of Cloud-Gate Pass as well. These three garrisons have concluded an alliance with Meng Huo, the king of the southern barbarians of the Nine Valleys and Eighteen Grottoes. They have all rebelled." The emperor was terrified and asked the field marshal what kind of strategy he might have. The Martial Marquis said, "Meng Huo is the sole reason that these garrisons have revolted. The First Ruler borrowed a hundred thousand troops from him, and therefore he has risen in rebellion. I will lead fifty thousand troops to retake the garrisons and chastise the barbarians."

The emperor granted him authority and within half a month the Martial Marquis had departed with fifty thousand troops and a hundred famous officers. After more than a month he reached Yunnan Commandery and made camp less than ten *li* away. On the third day Xiong Kai came out to give battle, but he was beheaded in front of his horse by Wei Yan. [16b] The field marshal persuaded the common people to surrender the city and pacified them. A few days later they reached Buwei City. The prefect Lü Kai opined, "By dividing his army into five battalions, the field marshal has killed and harmed the common folk." With thirty thousand troops he came out to give battle. Guan Yu's son Guan Suo feigned defeat, and Lü Kai pursued him thirty *li* outside the city. Someone then told him, "Zhuge has employed this plot to capture Buwei City and take your family prisoner." Lü Kai returned and the next day squared off with the Martial Marquis. The Martial Marquis had men armored with swords closely guard Lü Kai's family on all sides. Lü Kai only said, "I may die, but I can plead for my mother's life." Lü Kai was extremely filial. He dismounted from his horse, took off his bow and arrow, and came forward to implore the field marshal, "I will die, but please spare my mother." When the field marshal saw how filial Lü Kai was, he released his family.

In a few more days they reached Cloud-Gate Pass. The rebellious general Du Qi requested a battle, and the old general Wang Ping tried to take Cloud-Gate Pass with three thousand troops. When it had not fallen for a few days, the field marshal decapitated Wang Ping. Embracing the corpse, Lü Kai wept and said, "Alas, prefect, you were my countryman, and now you have been beheaded by the field marshal." The field marshal cursed Lü Kai saying, "You and Wang Ping were both officers of Xichuan. Your guilt today is not implicated in this decision." Because his officers kept imploring him, he released Lü Kai, but that very night the latter got on a horse and fled with a few trusted men southward to Cloud-Gate Pass. Du Qi allowed him into the city and they greatly cursed the Martial Marquis.

The next day the field marshal arrived and Du Qi came down from the pass to square off with him, vilifying him in these words, "Zhuge, you are shameless.

You killed our lord Liu Zhang. We are officers of Xichuan—how can we not rebel?" After the Martial Marquis had employed one of his stratagems to nab Lü Kai and Du Qi and after he had captured Cloud-Gate Pass, he went up the pass to reward the troops and to persuade the common people to surrender and be brought into the fold.

After a few more days, he led his army southward to the territory of the southern barbarians, arriving at Lu River. The overflowing streams of that river were so hot that you could not cross. But the field marshal strummed his zither, and the water of the river cooled itself. The field marshal ordered his troops to cross quickly, saying, "You must have heard of the misty miasmas of the Lu River as one of the barbarian sights. Centipedes and pythons are the poisonous creatures of these barbarian lands."

They made their camp no more than a hundred *li* after crossing the river. Someone reported that Meng Huo challenged them to battle. The next day they squared off against each other and the field marshal ordered Wei Yan to ride out to do battle. The barbarian generals were soundly defeated and Meng Huo was captured. The next day when he met with the Martial Marquis, Meng Huo said, "The First Ruler Liu Bei borrowed [17a] a hundred thousand troops from me, but never had a chance to give them back to me."

Zhuge Captures Meng Huo Seven Times

"Bring me a hundred thousand in gold and gems and I will spare your life." The barbarian generals handed over the gold and gems and ransomed Meng Huo. A few days later, when Meng Huo went off to the Temple of the Weeping Maiden to burn incense, soldiers in ambush emerged on all four sides to nab Meng Huo again, and again he refused to formally surrender. Another hundred thousand in gold and gems and he was again ransomed. The field marshal said, "In just a few days I will capture you in my tent." The king of the southern barbarians didn't believe it. Zhuge had Meng Huo lavishly treated to wine and food. When he arrived in his own camp, the king of the southern barbarians said, "Zhuge is tough. What is his point in releasing me several times?"

But the next day the king of the southern barbarians was laid down by illness and could not rise. He was in great pain for three days.[160] On the third day the field marshal had Guan Ping ask why the king neither surrendered nor gave battle. The king told him that he was suffering from an illness. Guan Ping said, "You know, our field marshal is also very good at medicinal cures." The king of the southern barbarians went along with Guan Ping to see the field marshal. The field marshal had the illness cured with medicinal wine. After he

---

160. As a result of the wine and food, one imagines.

had sipped it, the king immediately felt as he had before the illness. The field marshal asked, "Do you surrender? Today I have captured you in my tent." The king of the southern barbarians refused to surrender, so the field marshal said, "I will lock you in chains and take you to Xichuan. I will decapitate you after I have chastised this barbarian kingdom." Afraid to die, the king of the southern barbarians had himself ransomed once again with gold and gems. The field marshal's officers told him, "That king of the southern barbarians is just a foreigner. But you have released him a number of times." The field marshal said with a smile, "In my eyes this bandit is just like weeds and little seeds. Moreover, our own country of Xichuan was also broke."

Within a few days again the king of the southern barbarians issued a challenge to battle. The Martial Marquis said, "Will you surrender when I capture you this time?" When the two armies squared off against each other, the barbarians took the higher ground and had their men scatter poisonous drugs downhill.[161] The Martial Marquis quickly dismounted, and letting his hair flow and going barefoot, he made a sacrifice to the wind as he held his sword. The king of the southern barbarians was in the south and the Han army was in the north. The wind the field marshal evoked through sacrifice began in the north, and countless numbers of the southern troops fell over backwards. The field marshal captured the king of the southern barbarians once more and again had him ransomed for gold and gems. The field marshal also said, "The next time we meet in battle, I will make you dismount from your horse with a single shout. Will you surrender then?" The king would not credit it.

A few days after he had left, the field marshal and the barbarian army squared off. The field marshal rode out and gave three shouts and, in the southern battle line, the king of the southern barbarians dismounted. When the field marshal reached the camp, [17b] the king still wouldn't surrender. Again he was allowed to be ransomed for gold and gems. When the king of the southern barbarians had returned to his camp, he discussed the situation with his officers, and they sent people to drive out tigers and leopards.

After one full month he again issued a challenge to battle, but the field marshal had a grasp of what he was up to. Within five days the armies squared off and the king ordered his men to drive out those tigers and leopards. As soon as the field marshal gave one shout, it brought forth a thousand men who lined up behind him, one hand holding a shield and one hand raising their swords— this is called "the shield against the southern barbarians." This stirred up the tigers and leopards and they became frightened. The field marshal had the cymbals all sounded at once from behind them, and again he captured the king of the southern barbarians. And again he received five hundred thousand strings' worth of gold and gems as ransom. When the king had returned to his camp,

---

161. The equivalent of using poisonous gas. The verb implies scattering or sifting down.

his officers deliberated, "If he captures you again, will Zhuge be willing to set you free?" The king replied, "I don't ever want to see Zhuge again." That night the king of the southern barbarians slipped away down the southern bank of the Scorching Red River, and settled fifteen *li* away at Reed Pass.

Later tell about the field marshal thinking to himself, "If these barbarian bandits do not surrender they will cause trouble in the future." The field marshal wanted to cross the Scorching Red River with his army, but the heat was unbearable. They all lost their hair, and wore seven-layer turbans. The field marshal marched on for several more days, but it was so hot they could not go on. The Martial Marquis said again, "The Scorching Red River is three *li* wide bank to bank and a hundred feet deep. It's like quenching your thirst by looking at a plum."[162] So again he strummed his zither.

Right there, in the middle of the sixth month of the second year of Jianxing,[163] heavy snow fell, and during that interval the army reached the Scorching Red River, but it was so deep and wide that they had no way to cross. The field marshal ordered his men to make huge kites and they crossed the river on the wind and touched down at Reed Pass, precisely where the king was staying. The king of the southern barbarians said, "Zhuge is no mortal man, he is a celestial divinity." He invited the field marshal into Reed Pass where he entertained him for a couple of days. He presented him with ten carts of gold and gems and, breaking an arrow, he swore an oath that in his lifetime he would never again rebel against the Han. The field marshal also said, "I spare your life. And when I write you a letter, no more than five years hence, you will have to travel all the way to Mt. Qi to come and rescue me."

The Threat from the North

The Field Marshal Sets Out from Mt. Qi Six Times[164]

Speak now of the field marshal taking his army back to Sichuan where, after they arrived in Chengdu Prefecture in Yizhou, he rewarded his troops and comforted the common folk.

Later, halfway through the second month of the fifteenth year of Jianxing,[165] the prefect of Sword Pass reported to the Son of Heaven that Emperor Wen

---

162. That is, we are trying to do something that is impossible.

163. July–August 224.

164. This phrase is not printed white on black in the original, but it is clearly intended to match the earlier "Zhuge Captures Meng Huo Seven Times."

165. April–May 237.

had ascended the throne.[166] In the fourth year of the Qinglong reign period,[167] Emperor Ming of the Wei appointed Meng Da as grand marshal. Leading fifty thousand troops he set his camp forty *li* from Sword Pass, with the intention to conquer Xichuan. The Young Ruler and the field marshal discussed leading fifty thousand troops and a hundred famous officers to set their camp [18a] ten *li* east of Sword Pass.

Zhuge had a trusted servant deliver a letter to Meng Da. When Meng Da opened the letter to read, it said,

> You, grandee, are a man from Xichuan. It was not your fault that Yunchang was earlier brought down in Jingzhou. It was all due to the adopted son Liu Feng, who already has been sentenced. The graves of your ancestors, your village, and your land are all located in Xichuan. You must have heard that a bird from Yue builds its nest facing south, and that horses from the steppe will whinny toward the north.[168] Grandee, if you bring your allegiance back to Xichuan, how can you not be appointed to high office? I will serve as your guarantor, so you will be ranked among the senior grandees.

Meng Da said with a smile, "The field marshal is right." He immediately wrote a letter back to Zhuge. But a few days later Meng Da's second in command, Zhang Sheng, dispatched a report to the Wei emperor, who appointed Sima Zhongda as grand marshal to lead a hundred thousand troops to Sword Pass in the southwest. When Meng Da learned of this, he sent another letter to Zhuge,[169] but Zhuge did not come even though Sima Yi was getting close. When Meng Da again wrote a letter to Zhuge and Zhuge still did not come, Meng Da grasped his intention, and said, "One of Zhuge's tricks!" He then committed suicide by hanging himself.

After Sima's army arrived, he and the field marshal were at a standoff for half a month. Then one day an envoy arrived to report that Emperor Ming had passed away and that his younger brother, Cao Fang, had been enthroned and had changed the reign period to the first year of Zhengshi.[170] Sima Yi then returned with his troops.

---

166. An excellent example of how free the text is with anachronisms. This date actually refers to the inauguration of the third reign name (Jingchu) of Emperor Wen's successor, Emperor Ming.

167. The year 236.

168. These two lines are conventional metaphors for homesickness, as the two animals are looking toward their homes, but also toward their native environments; akin perhaps to the English "fish out of water."

169. Appealing for reinforcements.

170. February 10, 240.

Next tell that when the field marshal had been encamped there with his troops for one month, he led his army to a place more than a hundred *li* from Sword Pass because he wanted to conquer the area known as West of the Pass.[171] This was the first time he set out from Mt. Qi toward the east. The field marshal said, "Ahead of us we have the territory of Qinchuan.[172] I see that for an area of a hundred *li* square there are no grasses or trees at all. So before the army can advance, grain and fodder will have to be brought in. When the army crosses the trestle way wishing to conquer the area to the west of the pass, it will follow the grain and fodder. How can I otherwise conquer Qinchuan if there are no grasses and trees at all?" By the side of the road he saw a fortification built by the King of Wei. When the field marshal had observed Qinchuan, he sent someone to ask the neighboring farmers, "What is the name of the military officer guarding the pass in Qinchuan?" They answered, "His name is Jiang Wei, and he is also known as Boyue. Earlier he was the military commander of Qinchuan but later, on the recommendation of officials and the common people, he became the prefect of Qin." The field marshal said, "So, it turns out he is a capable man. This is a person who can be instructed.'" The field marshal then returned to Sword Pass.

Zhuge Constructs Wooden Oxen and Streaming Horses

From everywhere he summoned carpenters who constructed wooden cattle and streaming horses,[173] more than three hundred in total. The field marshal entered the pass, and for a second time set out from Mt. Qi. [18b] He proceeded to a spot forty *li* from Qinchuan were he made camp.

A few days later Guan Ping led three thousand troops to reconnoiter in Qinchuan. When he arrived at a forest, he dismounted and thought to himself, "The field marshal called Jiang Wei a capable man." When Guan Ping ordered his men to cook their food, Jiang Wei arrived with his troops to attack Guan Ping. But Jiang Wei gathered his troops back in and entered the city.

After a few days he saw the wooden cattle and streaming horses. Jiang Wei said, "Even the Great Lord[174] or Guan Zhong could not have accomplished this!" He then saw Zhuge's wooden cattle and streaming horses pass his city,

---

171. The area west of Tong Pass, near the confluence of the Wei and Yellow Rivers, from Shaanxi into the Gansu Corridor.

172. Roughly the area of modern Shaanxi and the eastern part of Gansu.

173. Despite the illustrations to the original text, which show horses and cattle laden with supplies, these are surely terms for one-wheeled wheelbarrows and two-wheeled pull-carts, perhaps constructed so that the human labor required to move them was concealed from view.

174. See note 71.

and ordered Zhang Zhong to capture them. But when Jiang Wei left the city, he found his way blocked by Wei Yan. Using a trick, the field marshal captured Jiang Wei and also conquered Qinchuan. The field marshal saw that Jiang Wei's appearance was extraordinary as were the surrendered troops and officers they had seized. Jiang Wei honored the Martial Marquis as his father.

A few days later the field marshal led his troops to Jieting Pass—Xichuan could be taken any day! His army remained encamped there for three months but was clueless about how to capture the pass.

Then one day the senior grandee Yi Ji sent someone with a letter all the way to the field marshal.

Go on to say that when that private letter written by the grandee had been read by the field marshal, he hastily ordered his servants to prepare his luggage. The next day he called Jiang Wei in to tell him, "I have to go back to Chuan. I have to go in all haste because I am afraid Xichuan may be lost." Then he whispered something in Jiang Wei's ear. After Jiang Wei had agreed to the scheme, the field marshal set out on the road. When Jiang Wei took command, he said, "The field commander has told me the scheme." And, the next day he led his troops to a location west of Jieting where they made camp.

Next tell that the officer guarding the pass at Jieting was the old general Xiahou Dun, who said, "Jiang Wei has moved his camp to thirty *li* west of Jieting. It is a narrow valley, only three hundred paces wide and a hundred *li* long from south to north. That is a dangerous place to make your camp. I fear only Zhuge. Whoever heard about this stupid little boy, Jiang Wei?" That night he led his troops in a surprise attack on Jiang Wei's camp. But there was no one in there. Then soldiers hidden in ambush emerged on all sides. Wei Yan and the other officers gave Xiahou Dun's army such a beating that they fled straight west. When Jiang Wei later occupied Jieting it turned out that Xiahou Dun had fled in the melee.

Next relate that when the field marshal arrived in Chengdu Prefecture, he was welcomed by all officials. With sword in hand the field marshal entered the inner apartments and straightaway ascended the palace hall. There he saw the [19a] Young Ruler sitting side by side with the eunuch Huang Hao and having a good time. The field marshal gave a shout as loud as the thunder, and roundly cursed Huang Hao, "How dare you, a eunuch servant!" In a panic Huang Hao rose to his feet. Only after the field marshal had given orders to lock him in chains did he formally greet the Young Ruler with the prescribed rituals. The Young Ruler was at a loss about how to answer and simply said, "I wasn't aware that you had arrived." Zhuge took formal leave of the emperor and went to his house.

When the next morning the civil officials and military officers had assembled for the morning audience, the field marshal looked up to heaven and, deeply shaken, confronted the emperor, "And then I remember how the First Ruler gathered troops and defeated the Yellow Scarves—their saddles never left their horses, their armor never left their bodies; for over thirty years. This went on until he could take Chuan—this castrated slave was about to undo it." The field marshal also said, "Your Majesty, you must have heard how Emperor Ling favored the Ten Constant Attendants, and because of those castrated slaves the empire was undone. It's not that I want to bully you, but the late emperor entrusted Your Majesty to me. After my death the loss of the empire will be Your Majesty's fault, but as long as I am alive, the loss of the empire will be mine. Just think about the times of Wu and Yue—because of that beauty Xi Shi, they did not lay down their armor for twenty years. If Your Majesty loves a castrated slave, historians will vilify your name for ten thousand generations." The Young Ruler had no way to answer but simply wept grievously in front of the ancestral tablet of his late father. After the officials and officers had made their prescribed bows, Huang Hao was taken to the marketplace and sliced into ten thousand pieces, while his relations were cruelly executed. The Young Ruler offered his apologies to the field marshal, and the latter replied, "I did this on behalf of my lord's empire!" The emperor set out a banquet and after a few days the field marshal mounted his horse and went out through the pass. This was the third time he had set out from Mt. Qi.

The Song "Daoist Nun," in the Mode of Zhonglü

Hot at dusk, cold at daybreak—
Thrice visited in the thatched cottage:
A man of such great integrity is rare indeed!
Like a cock pecking at its food;
Like a fish finding its stream:
Such nobility that the crowd will never reach.
All alone he went to Dangyang,
Was besieged in Ravenwood,
And greatly crushed Cao Cao at Red Cliff.
He pacified Jing and Chu,
Conquered Xichuan,
And at Mt. Dingjun put Xiahou Yuan to an early death.

Entrusted with the orphan, yielding the throne,
He reestablished peace with the state of Wu;

Seven times he captured Meng Huo—how miraculously!
He subdued Jiang Wei
He was a model of a teacher—
Because of the ingenuity of his wooden cattle and streaming horses!
He morally transformed Dingshan and Rongguo,
Decapitated Wang Shuang,
And made good use of Zhang He and Sima Bao.
How could he know that over the autumnal plain
Only evening clouds and withering grasses would remain.

Later There Was Also a Temple Encomium by Su Dongbo,

Inscrutable as gods and ghosts
As rapid as wind and thunder:
When advancing he could not be stopped,
When retreating he could not be pursued. [19b]
During daylight he could not be attacked;
During nighttime he could not be surprised.
If he was with many, he could not be withstood;
If he was with only a few, he could not be bullied.
In front and behind he understood the situation;
To the left and the right he gave his orders.
He moved the nature of the Five Elements;
He changed the climate of the Four Seasons.
A man? A god? Or an immortal?
I do not know: he was a true Recumbent Dragon!

Now speak about the field marshal who arrived in Jieting after several days and asked the officers about the situation. Wei Yan and Jiang Wei had defeated the Wei army and conquered Jieting; the field marshal was very pleased.

Go on then to speak about how the old general Xiahou Dun went to Chang'an where he was received in audience by the emperor, Cao Fang. The latter appointed Sima Yi as grand marshal and he arrived a month later in Jieting, at the head of two hundred thousand troops, setting his camp some fifty *li* away. Sima Yi did not know Zhuge, and for half a month they were at a standoff. Guan Ping came to challenge Sima Yi to battle but he was soundly beaten. And when Lü Kai challenged Sima Yi to battle, he was also soundly beaten a number of times. Sima said, "I heard that Zhuge is famous throughout the world, but now he is old!"

One day when Zhuge squared off with Sima Yi, Zhuge was heavily defeated, and the Wei troops pursued him more than forty *li* from Jieting until he entered Mt. Qi. They were blocked in front by Wei Yan, by Zhuge in their rear, by Jiang Wei to their left, and by Yang Yi to their right. Soldiers hidden in ambush emerged from all directions. Zhuge battled the Wei army for a full day and night and, from the original one hundred thousand troops, no more than three thousand made their way back. Sima Yi was forced to change his battle dress so that he could flee! Sima Yi made camp at eighty *li* from Jieting but dared not even contemplate looking at the place.

Now our story divides into two.

Let us go back and tell how, in Chengdu Prefecture in Yizhou as the emperor sat in court, a senior grandee said, "Zhuge has rebelled in Jieting!" The emperor questioned his civil officials and military officers, saying, "If the field marshal has rebelled, Xichuan cannot take responsibility for itself!" Yi Ji said to the emperor, "The field marshal will not rebel. Have an envoy go and summon him. If the field marshal comes, he has not rebelled; if he doesn't, he has rebelled." When the emperor sent an envoy to summon him, Zhuge came to court to see the emperor, who told him the whole story. Zhuge said, "This must have been a trick by Sima Yi." The emperor nodded his head, "Your words are right on the mark." The emperor banqueted him for several days.

The field marshal again set out from Mt. Qi: the fourth time. He proceeded to Gemao Pass, which is also known as Jieting. Fifty *li* before he reached the pass all the officers welcomed him, and he went on another forty *li* then made camp. When Zhuge asked them what had happened in Jieting, [20a] the subordinate officers Yang Yi and Jiang Wei said, "Ma Wei lost Jieting." Zhuge was greatly upset, "This is an inaccessible location—how could he lose it?" Jiang Wei replied, "Ma Wei was in his cups, and when Sima Yi issued a battle challenge, Ma Wei wanted to fight him. Wei Yan tried to dissuade him, but was repeatedly vilified, and none of the other officers could make him change his mind either. Ma Wei also cursed the prefect, telling him, 'The field marshal is my fellow townsman. Even if I would lose the city, it wouldn't matter.' The Wei troops first encircled Ma Wei, and when we went out to fight them, we lost Jieting." The field marshal ordered Ma Wei summoned for questioning, and when Ma Wei could say nothing in his own defense, he had him pushed outside and ordered him beheaded.

Zhuge Decapitates Ma Wei

The officers failed to change his mind and Ma Wei was beheaded.

Now tell that Zhuge repeatedly tried to capture Jieting, but without success. He then took a woman's dress and hair ornaments, and called to Sima Yi, "Hey hero, come on down from the wall!"[175] But Sima Yi, seated in armor, did not come out of the city to fight. This standoff lasted half a year.

One day his spies informed him that the emperor's father-in-law was visiting the border. Sima Yi hastily led his officers to welcome him to the city. This man was the Wei general and emperor's father-in-law Zhang He, and they banqueted for half a month.

One day the Martial Marquis led three thousand troops with light bows and short arrows, all well-tested men on fine horses. The field marshal himself rode in a plain carriage and sent someone to curse Sima Yi. Zhang He said, "You are a famous general of Wei, and when Zhuge curses you, there are no officers who dare ride out?" Sima replied, "There are none who can match Zhuge." But Zhang He was in his cups and left the city with thirty thousand men, even though Zhang Yi warned him, "Grand Teacher, you're too old!" But Zhang He said, "I came here at the order of the Sage. When Zhuge challenges you to battle, grand marshal, if you do not go out, you weaken the authority and power of the house of Wei!" The officers could not change his mind and he departed to square off with the Martial Marquis. The Martial Marquis was soundly defeated, and Zhang He's army pursued him for several *li*. When he saw that the Han troops had all dispersed, Zhang He was at the forefront of his army when the Martial Marquis leaned over to look back.

Zhang He Is Shot and Killed by a Hundred Arrows

Zhang He died in front of his army. Minister Sima attacked the Martial Marquis, but he had Yang Yi at his back, and with this trick they captured Jieting. Sima Yi made camp sixty *li* to the northwest of Jieting and looked at Jieting like a tiger.

This standoff had been going on for some days when the field marshal was informed that a secret summons had arrived at the border. After he had read it, he left Jiang Wei in command and hurried on horseback to the court. [20b] When he arrived in Chengdu Prefecture and saw the emperor, he was told, "Sun Quan of the southern bank of the River has died, and Sun Liang has

---

175. He was offering to give Sima Yi the woman's clothing as a gift, to make the point that he refused to come out and fight, but stayed in the city like a woman would stay in her boudoir.

become the ruler of Wu, changing his reign period to the first year of Jian-xing." Zhuge proposed to the emperor, "Send the senior grandee Yi Ji with ten thousand strings' worth of gold and gems to the area of Jiangnan to offer condolences." He also said that he feared that Wu might cause trouble. After he had been treated to imperial banquets for a few days, he bade the emperor farewell and went east to Sword Pass. Once again he set out from Mt. Qi—the fifth time. The field marshal went to Jieting.

Next tell that Sima Yi had taken his formal seat in his tent and discussed the situation with his officers. The grand marshal said, "From past to present no one has seen a marshal like Zhuge. There is nothing that can be done against him!" Again in a few days, the grand marshal and his troops were marching three *li* from his camp, when he saw the Han general Zhou Cang transporting grains with wooden cattle and streaming horses. He sent the infantry general Deng Ai with three thousand troops to capture ten or so of these wooden cattle and streaming horses. The grand marshal ordered the carpenters in his camp to take them apart to measure their size and shape. Then following the pattern, they built several hundred of them. But when he had people raise a wooden mallet and hit them, they would only move a few paces. Sima Yi said, "Zhuge's wooden cattle and streaming horses go three hundred paces every time they are hit and they get on the road to transport grain, but in my camp I only hear the *bengbeng* as they are beaten, but still they don't move. What kind of special method does Zhuge have?"

In a few more days he saw the escorting general and three hundred troops come to the front of his camp. Zhou Cang was in his cups and shouted to the grand marshal, "The field marshal has told me to deliver a letter challenging the grand marshal to do battle; he will meet you in the field to see who is the win-ner. If you don't want to fight, you should surrender. You are a famous general of the state of Wei, why do you close up your gates and stay inside?" The grand marshal said, "Zhou Cang is in his cups!" and ordered his servants to get wine for Zhou Cang, who drank till he was drunk as a skunk. Sima said, "I will give you plenty of gold and gems and money and treasure. If you beat them once with a mallet, Zhuge's wooden cattle and streaming horses will go three hun-dred paces, but the wooden cattle and streaming horses that I made only move a few paces when you hit them. Tell me what method he uses and I will give you millions of strings' worth of gold and gems so your whole family can live in wealth and glory." Zhou Cang said with a smile, "As for the field marshal's wooden cattle and streaming horses—when the men raise their mallets they all recite the *Wooden Cattle Streaming Horses Sutra*." He also said, "Those who beat the wooden cattle and streaming horses are all under my control. Tonight when I go into the camp, grand marshal, I will copy out that *Wooden Cattle Streaming Horses Sutra* for you." [21a] Sima was greatly pleased and he gave

Zhou Cang thirty strings' worth of gold and gems and two fine horses. "Zhou Cang, if you make a copy for me, you will live in indescribable riches and glory."

Zhou Cang returned on the third day. Sima received him hurriedly, and told his servants to take the text from him. After Zhou Cang left, Sima took it and read it, he was flabbergasted: it was in the Martial Marquis' own hand and spelled out,

> Of all generals since ancient times not even five have been able to construct wooden cattle and streaming horses. How can future generations not laugh at you, a famous general of Wei, wanting to learn the *Wooden Cattle Streaming Horses Sutra* from me.

Sima tore the piece of paper to shreds.

The Death of Zhuge Liang

In the seventeenth year of Yanxing[176] the Young Lord summoned Zhuge, saying, "Xichuan is suffering a terrible drought but the Washing Brocade River has overflowed its banks." When Zhuge looked at how much the water had risen, he grasped it portended misfortune. Spurring his horse on, Zhuge hurried to the court to meet with the emperor. All the useless goods that had been made in the palace were sold in the market, the gold and gems that filled the storerooms were given to the officials, and the useless objects there were also sold in the market in order to purchase grain and fodder. In a few days he had acquired rice and grain beyond counting. One half was stored in the imperial capital city and one half was stored at Mt. Dingjun, where a trusted follower guarded the stores.

When he saw the place called Gold Sand Confluence where the Brocade Washing River joined the River, the two banks were more than ten *li* apart: from east to west it was a hundred thousand feet. But when the field marshal sent men to probe the depth of Gold Sand Junction, it was less than ten feet deep. The field marshal thought to himself, "The next time I set out from Mt. Qi those bandits from Downriver Wu might cause problems." He established foundries at fifty places, some for bronze and some for iron, that were to produce a hundred long pillars. On top of each of these pillars was a large eye.

---

176. This would be 263, the final year of the Shu-Han, which is clearly a mistake because, as Zhuge Liang remarks below, the Shu-Han still had some thirty years left. It may be a mistake for the Jianxing reign period, which would make it roughly 223–238.

He also had stone workers produce five hundred stone pillars, and he had iron workers produce iron chains with links of one inch in diameter, and they made a few hundred of these. Fifty thousand people were employed in the production of these articles in bronze, iron, and stone. They worked as one and finished in a year and a half. When put into place, these pillars covered an area seven *li* wide from north to south and twenty *li* long from east to west. And they were all connected with iron chains.

This Was Called the Iron Chain Defense Pond

On the northern and southern banks he stationed twenty thousand troops and four famous generals to guard this strategic entry, because he was secretly afraid that Wu would send its troops and horses into Chuan territory.

When the field marshal had returned to Chengdu Prefecture in Yizhou to see the emperor, the latter [21b] treated him to an imperial banquet for several days. The field marshal said, "Now I want to seize the area of Guanxi and Chang'an in order to restore the Great Han." The emperor was delighted. When they were half drunk, Zhuge suddenly collapsed on the floor, blood streaming from his mouth and nose. The emperor was terrified, and the civil officials and military officers helped him up. Zhuge explained, "From the time I left my thatched cottage forty years ago, I have campaigned on behalf of Your Majesty against Wu and fought with Wei, and this has all broken my one-inch heart into ten-thousand pieces." The emperor said, "Do not try to seize Guanxi. I implore you, field marshal, to summon the border troops back to Chengdu Prefecture." But Zhuge protested, "That is impossible! We will be the laughing stock of later historians! Your Majesty should imitate Yao, Shun, Yu, and Tang, not Jie and Zhou. If we lose the empire, ten thousand generations will curse our names. This year I want once again to try to take the area of Guanxi. If I don't, I will not return." The Young Ruler tried everything he could to make Zhuge stay, but he stubbornly refused, so the emperor could only see him off.

Next speak of Zhuge setting out eastward for Sword Pass. As his wife bade farewell and was about to go back, Zhuge said, "I have a son but he is an incompetent weakling, and I am afraid that if he takes office he will stain my clear name. We have eight hundred mulberry trees and fifty *qing* of fields, and that should be enough to make a living." Zhuge and his wife said goodbye, and then he set out eastward from Mt. Qi with a line of a hundred carts.

After Zhuge had been on the march for a several days, Sima Yi learned about it, and he lay troops in ambush who suddenly emerged on all sides, but the field marshal had the carts form a *carré*, so the troops of Wei could not get near. A few days later Jiang Wei led the officers in welcoming the field marshal into Jieting. For a full month he repeatedly sent battle challenges, but Sima never came out. Zhuge thought, "Sima has made a long-term camp at the foot of a pagoda and over half a month his troops have been on the march, wearing their armor and keeping their padded battle dress on—so many of them must be suffering from sores." He ordered Jiang Wei and Yang Yi to surprise the camp, and they fought so valiantly that Sima Yi's fifty thousand troops dispersed in all directions. The field marshal said, "A heavy rain will fall."[177] He quickly ordered the men to get out oiled capes and umbrellas. That heavy rain fell for over a day before it stopped.

Zhuge led three thousand troops and several famous officers down Jieting for a secret trip. When Jiang Wei asked him why, the field marshal whispered in his ear and told him, "My own Great Year and my major and minor cycles all coincide."[178] When the field marshal had led the three thousand troops under his command about a hundred *li* from Jieting, they came to a large tree, to the west of which they saw a farm. A messenger called out a woman and Zhuge asked directly, [22a] "What district controls this place?" The woman replied, "Fengxiang Prefecture of Qizhou on Mt. Qi. This is Granny Huang's Inn."[179] And when he then asked her, "Has it rained a lot this year?" she replied, "How can it it not rain heavily when a Recumbent Dragon ascends to heaven?" The woman also said, "Sir, don't blame me, you must have heard the old saw, 'When the lord dies at White Emperor, the vassal will die at Granny Huang's.'" The field marshal remembered then that such a saying did exist. When he also asked for the name of the high mountain to their west, the woman said, "It's the Autumn Wind Fifty Feet Plain." When she had said this, the woman turned into a breeze and disappeared, nobody knows where.

The field marshal

Ascended Autumn Wind Fifty Feet Plain to the West

and his troops established camp there. The field marshal thought to himself that the words of that old woman were so inauspicious and he could not get

---

177. Prognosticating his own death; he was a dragon, and traditionally the dragon was associated with water and with rain.

178. It was believed that one's life span (*shou* 壽) was fixed and alloted by heaven. The transit of Jupiter's shadow star marked a twelve-year cycle in a person's life; the major cycle was a ten-year span in which one's life would have a major transformation and it governed one's good and bad luck; the minor cycle governed each year and had the ability to alter the progress of the larger cycle. Here, it means that all of the cycles that govern his life are reaching a simultaneous ending point; he will die.

179. Fengxiang may translated as "soaring phoenix," while Huang is also the term for yellow; the Chinese underworld was called "the yellow springs," like the inn, a resting place.

them out of his mind. He also considered that Sima Yi, who was so skilled at waiting things out, was in fact made of the stuff of generals.

The field marshal was laid up with illness for more than a month and neither the acupuncture needle nor herbal simples could cure him—blood flowed from his mouth and nose. Jiang Wei asked his teacher-father, "You are so adept at medicine. How come you cannot cure your own disease?" Zhuge replied, "From the time I left my thatched cottage at the age of twenty-nine, I have exerted my heart for my ruler for over forty years before we managed to conquer Chuan. This shattered my inch-square heart into ten thousand pieces." Suddenly they heard a commotion outside the gate of the camp, and when Jiang Wei went out to have a look, he saw Wei Yan who entered and said, "If something is wrong with the field marshal, I will look after his seal and tally." The field marshal didn't say a word, but called Wei Yan over and said, "General, it was only thirty years ago that you submitted to the Han, and then only after Jingzhou had subdued the four commanderies to the south of the River. Yet you have repeatedly established great merit for our state. Wei Yan shall be marshal and wear the seal after I die." Wei Yan then left happily.

After another few days he called the Great Defenders Yang Yi, Jiang Wei, and Zhao Yun to his side. Weeping, the field marshal implored them, "Please take my remains back to Chuan when I have died." These men all shed tears.

That night the field marshal, supported by a soldier, held his seal in his left hand and raised a sword with his right; he unbound his hair, and lit a lamp. He used a bowl of water and one black chicken, which he put in the bowl, and so he fixed the General Star. When the Martial Marquis had returned to heaven, Jiang Wei hung up a spirit picture of the former ruler and beheaded Wei Yan. There is a poem later that may serve as evidence,

Where does one seek the shrine of the Prime Minister?
Outside the Brocade Official's City in a dense grove of cypresses.
Darkening the stairs, green grass turns naturally to the color of spring;
Separated by leaves, yellow orioles sing sweet songs in vain.
Repeatedly importuned by triple visits: [22b] a plan for all-under-heaven;
Establishing the enterprise under two rulers: the mind of a seasoned vassal.
But his army not yet victorious, he succumbed first,
Forever causing the tears of heroes to saturate their lapels.[180]

Zhuge's army began to wail as one and their lamentations shook the earth. The common people hastened to inform Sima Yi, telling him that the Martial Marquis had died.

---

180. A poem by the renowned Tang poet Du Fu (712–770), "The Minister of Shu (*Shu xiang* 蜀相)."

When Sima Yi heard this, he came with his troops to steal the corpse of the Martial Marquis. The two armies immediately squared off. Sima said, "The only one I feared was the Martial Marquis. Now that he is dead, you should leave his corpse behind. If you don't, not a single piece of armor will return!" Enraged, Jiang Wei spurred out on his horse, drew his sword, and straightaway took on Sima. The two men engaged in battle, but after a few rounds Jiang Wei was defeated and fled. When Sima pursued him, the cymbals sounded, and from the flanks a division of soldiers attacked him: this was Yang Yi. Sima could not stop him and fled in retreat, but troops hiding in ambush sprung up on all sides. Sima was heavily defeated and lost half of his men. When he had returned to his camp, he dared not come out anymore. In Chang'an the people said of him, "Even a dead Zhuge can set a living Zhongda to flight!" When Zhongda heard this, he smiled and said, "I took his measure when he was alive, but how could I do so in death?"

Let us go back now and tell how the generals escorted Zhuge's casket back to Sichuan. The Han emperor welcomed the cortege and gave himself over to lamentation, his painful weeping never ending. He immediately selected a grave tumulus and buried him, erecting a temple in which to offer sacrifice. He ennobled him as the Loyal and Martial Marquis. When the common people heard about it, it was as if they had lost their own parents. In administering the people, the Martial Marquis was sparing with mutilations and fines and imposed only light taxes and corvées; in commanding the troops, his rewards and fines were strict and his commands and orders were clear. That's why both the military and the people loved him.

Now back to speak of that Sima Yi, who led his troops to have a look at Zhuge's barracks and camp, and sighed, "The most extraordinary talent of our world!" Thereupon he composed a dirge and offered sacrifice. That night, after a fierce storm had passed, he saw a divinity who said, "The field marshal has sent me with a letter." When Sima took the letter to read it, its message was roughly as follows,

> I may have died, but Heaven's Mandate for the Han has another thirty years to run. If the Han disappears, the Wei also will be exterminated, and the Wu will follow. Your lineage is bound to bring about one reunification. But if you stick to your delusions and commit outrageous actions, disaster will strike you!

When Sima had read this he had a mind to pay no attention to it. But the divinity gave a loud shout and Sima said in the most humble way, "I will follow the order of the field marshal." The divinity then pushed Sima to the ground, who wanted to shout but couldn't. When he woke up, it had all been a dream. This is why each time Sima would establish his boundaries he never crossed swords with the Han.

Karma Fulfilled: The World of the Simas

[23a] Sima returned to the court where he found the ruler of Wei's incompetence and stupidity increasing day by day. He was unable to put him on the proper path. The Great Prime Minister Cao Shuang usurped all authority. Sima subsequently mobilized his troops and executed Cao Shuang, deposed the King of Wei, and enthroned the Duke of Gaogui.[181] Sima Yi's power grew and the emperor could not restrain him. The emperor plotted with others to kill him but, when Sima found out about it, he sent Jia Chong to kill the emperor. He then enthroned the young emperor,[182] and all authority over the empire rested with Sima. The young emperor could only sit with folded hands. Subsequently he ennobled Sima as Prince of Jin and then ceded the throne to him, who appointed the young emperor as Prince of Chenliu. When Emperor Xian of the Han heard of this, he laughed until he died.

The Prince of Jin sent Deng Ai and Zhong Hui into Sichuan in a campaign against the Han. The grand marshal of the Han, Jiang Wei, was on a campaign against the state of Xiliang. For this reason Deng Ai's army quickly entered Sichuan. When the Han emperor wanted to surrender, his Prime Minister Wang Zhan[183] admonished the emperor, saying, "We should make fathers and sons, prince and vassals fight together with their backs to the wall, to die together for the sake of the altars of the land and grain, so that we might be able to see the Former Emperor. Why would you want to surrender?" But the emperor did not heed him. Wang Zhan performed a sacrifice and wailed in the temple of the Shining and Valorous Ancestor of the Han.[184] Then he first killed his wife and children, and next sliced his own throat. The Han emperor ordered all of his border generals to surrender. When Jiang Wei received this edict, he and the other officers were furious. He cleaved a rock with his sword, but had

---

181. Cao Mao 曹髦 (241–260), grandson of Cao Pi, who ruled 254–260.

182. Cao Huan 曹奂 (246–303, r. 260–265).

183. The more common term Wang Chen of the northern territory (*beidi* Wang Chen 北地王諶) has been converted here to Prime Minister Wang Zhan (*zaixiang* Wang Zhan 王湛). While the character is different (a scribal error confusing the simplified radical on the left side of the phonetic (i.e., *zhan* 湛 for *chen* 諶), the title is a creation of the author of this text.

184. Liu Bei.

no other option but to surrender. The Prince of Jin appointed the emperor of Han as the Prince of Fufeng Commandery. But Liu Yuan, a son of a daughter of the emperor of Han, escaped, and fled to the north.

Later Sima Yi led the great generals Wang Jun and Wang Hun in a campaign against Wu. Wu was defeated, and Sun Hao, the ruler of Wu, surrendered to Jin. Emperor Wu summoned Sun Hao to a banquet. That villainous minister Jia Chong asked Sun Hao, "I have heard that south of the River you gouge out people's eyes and flay people's skins—now what kind of punishments are those for?" Sun Hao replied, "Those are the punishments applied to ministers who slay their rulers and for disloyal sycophants." When Jia Chong heard these words, he felt deeply ashamed and desisted.

Liu Yuan stood out as exception from his earliest youth. He venerated Confucianism and honored Daoism; he was widely read in the classics and histories and had studied military affairs. When he grew up he was an excellent shot with his gibbon's arms, and his strength surpassed others, so many brave men gathered around him. His son Liu Cong excelled others in daring courage. He was widely conversant with the classics and histories, was an excellent writer, and coud bend a bow of three hundred pounds pull. Noted men in the capital all associated with him, and he assembled around him tens of thousands of the bravest and finest men from the Zuoguo Area. Many in the empire reverted their allegiance to him.

Liu Yuan said to these men, "The Han possessed the empire for a long time and the people are still attached to them because of their grace. I am a grandson of the Han too, so why should I not take revenge for my mother's family that has been enslaved by the Jin?" Thereupon he adopted his mother's family name, called himself Liu, and established a state called Han.[185] He subsequently followed the example of his Han ancestors and called himself King of Han, and changed the reign period to Yuanxi (304–307). He posthumously honored Liu Shan as the Filial and Caring August Emperor, made soul tablets of the Three Progenitors and Five Ancestors, and offered sacrifice to them. He ennobled his wife of the Huyan clan as his empress. Liu Xuan served as minister, Cui Wu as censor, Liu Hong as grand defender, Wei Long as chamberlain for dependencies, Zhu Yuan as chamberlain for ceremonials, and Chen Da as gate attendant, while his nephew Liu Yao served as Jianwu general. In the first

---

185. This would be the Han-Zhao dynasty (304–328), a short-lived dynasty that destroyed the Western Jin under Liu Cong in 316. Although he was always surnamed Liu (his father, a Xiongnu, had early on adopted the surname Liu), the text here refers to the close blood bonds between the Han empire, which sent imperial women as brides to the Xiongnu, and the Xiongnu confederation. Xiongnu families often changed their name to Liu to reify the bond with the Han ruling family.

month of the third year (307) he moved his capital to Pingyang Prefecture in Shanxi and ascended the imperial throne.

Now after Emperor Wu of the Jin had passed away, Emperor Hui of the Jin was enthroned but he was an idiot. When he heard the croaking of frogs in the imperial park, he asked his servants, "Do these frogs croak for public reasons or for private matters?" This was how feeble he was and so ignorant of the world. His empress was a daughter of Jia Chong. She was lascivious, jealous, and barren. She sent her underlings out of the palace, and when they would see any young men in the marketplace who were handsome, they would dress them up as women and take them into the palace, where she would have sex with them. Once her desires were satisfied, she would kill them. Because of this, the country descended into chaos. When Emperor Hui died, Emperor Huai was enthroned.

Let us now speak of how the King of Han first campaigned against the Jin, leading an army two hundred thousand men strong against Jin at Luoyang. Emperor Huai of the Jin came out of the city to meet him in battle but was defeated. When the Han troops captured him, they killed him and sacrificed him in the temple of Liu Shan.

Then there was Emperor Min of the Jin, who ascended the throne in Chang'an. The King of Han dispatched Liu Yao against him, captured Emperor Min of the Jin, and then married Emperor Hui's Empress Yang. Subsequently he sent the Jin emperor to his capital, Pingyang. The King of Han subsequently annihilated the state of Jin and ascended the throne of the emperors of Han. Subsequently he paid his respects in the temple of Gaozu, and also in the temple of Emperor Wen of the Han, in the temple of Guangwu of the Han, in the temple of the Shining and Valorous Emperor, and in the temple of Liu Shan, the Caring Emperor of the Han, offering sacrifice, and he proclaimed a general pardon for the empire.

> The lord of Han weak and cowardly; Cao and Wu both hegemons:
> The Shining and Valorous Hero established his imperial capital in Shu.
> Sima Zhongda pacified the Three Kingdoms,
> But Liu Yuan restored the Han, solidifying the august enterprise.

The New and Completely Illustrated Plain Tales:
Records of the Three Kingdoms, Part III. The End.

Works Cited and Suggested Readings

Publications in Western Languages

Allen, Sarah. 1972–73. "The Identities of Taigong Wang in Zhou and Han Literature." *Monumenta Serica* 30: 57–99.

Besio, Kimberly. 1995. "Enacting Loyalty: History and Theatricality in 'The Peach Orchard Pledge.'" *CHINOPERL Papers* 18: 61–81.

———. 1997. "Zhang Fei in Yuan Vernacular Literature: Legend, Heroism and History in the Reproduction of the Three Kingdoms Story Cycle." *Journal of Sung-Yüan Studies* 27: 63–98.

———. 2007. "Zhuge Liang and Zhang Fei: *Bowang shao tun* and Competing Masculine Ideals within the Development of the *Three Kingdoms* Story Cycle." In Kimberly Besio and Constantine Tung, eds., *Three Kingdoms and Chinese Culture*. Albany: State University of New York Press. 73–86.

———, and Constantine Tung, eds. 2007. *Three Kingdoms and Chinese Culture*. Albany: State University of New York Press.

Bielenstein, Hans. 1986. "Wang Mang, the Restoration of the Han Dynasty, and Later Han." In Denis Twitchett and John K. Fairbank, eds., *The Cambridge History of China: Volume I: The Ch'in and Han Empires, 221 B.C.–A.D. 220*. Cambridge: Cambridge University Press. 223–90.

Børdahl, Vibeke. 2013. *Wu Song Fights the Tiger: The Interaction of Oral and Written Traditions in the Chinese Novel, Drama and Storytelling*. Copenhagen: NIAS Press.

Breuer, Rüdiger Walter. 2001. "Early Chinese Vernacular Literature and the Oral-Literary Continuum: The Example of Song and Yuan Dynasties *Pinghua*," Ph.D. diss., Washington University.

Brewitt-Taylor, C. H. 1925. *San-kuo, or Romance of the Three Kingdoms*. 2 vols. Shanghai: Kelly and Walsh.

Chan, Wing-tsit. 1963. *A Source Book in Chinese Philosophy*. Princeton: Princeton University Press.

Chang, Shelley Hsueh-lun. 1990. *History and Legend: Ideas and Images in the Ming Historical Novels*. Ann Arbor: University of Michgan Press.

Crump, Jr., James I. 1951. "*P'ing-hua* and the Early History of the *San-kuo chih*," *Journal of the American Oriental Society* 71: 249–56.

Cutter, Robert Joe, and William Gordon Crowell. 1999. *Empresses and Consorts: Selections from Chen Shou's Records of the Three States, with Pei Songzhi's Commentary*. Honolulu: University of Hawai'i Press.

De Crespigny, Rafe, trans. 1969. *The Last of the Han: Being the Chronicle of the Years 181–220 A.D. as Recorded in Chapters 58–68 of the Tzu-chih T'ung-chien of Ssuma Kuang*. Canberra: Centre of Oriental Studies, Australian National University.

———. 1970. *The Records of the Three Kingdoms: A Study in the Historiography of San-kuo chih*. Canberra: Centre of Oriental Studies, Australian National University.

———, trans. 1989. *Emperor Huan and Emperor Ling: Being the Chronicle of the Later Han for the Years 157 to 189 AD as Recorded in Chapters 54 to 59 of the Zizhi tongjian of Sima Guang*. Canberra: Faculty of Asian Studies, Australian National University.

———. 1990a. *Man from the Margin: Cao Cao and the Three Kingdoms*. Canberra: Australian National University. http://www.anu.edu.au/asianstudies/decrespigny/morrison51.html

———. 1990b. *Generals of the South: The Foundation and Early History of the Three Kingdoms State of Wu*. Canberra: Australian National University. Internet edition: http://www.anu.edu.au/asianstudies/decrespigny/gos_index.html

———. 1991a. "The Three Kingdoms and the Western Jin." *East Asian History* 1: 1–36. http://www.anu.edu.au/asianstudies/decrespigny/3KWJin.html

———. 1991b. "The Three Kingdoms and the Western Jin." *East Asian History* 2: 143–64. http://www.anu.edu.au/asianstudies/decrespigny/3KWJin.html

———, trans. 1996. *To Establish Peace: Being the Chronicle of the Later Han for the Years 189 to 220 AD as Recorded in Chapters 59 to 69 of the Zizhi tongjian of Sima Guang*. Canberra: Faculty of Asian Studies, Australian National University. http://www.anu.edu.au/asianstudies/decrespigny/peace1_index.html

———. 2010. *Imperial Warlord: A Biography of Cao Cao (155–220 AD)*. Leiden: E. J. Brill.

Diény, Jean-Pierre. 2000. *Les poèmes de Cao Cao (155–220)*. Paris: Institut des Hautes Études Chinoises Collège de France.

Diesinger, Günther. 1984. *Vom General zum Gott: Kuan Yü (gest. 220 n. Chr.) und seine "posthume Karriere."* Frankfurt: Haag & Herchen.

Duara, Prasenjit. 1988. "Superscribing Symbols: The Myth of Guandi, Chinese God of War." *Journal of Asian Studies* 47: 778–95.

Ge Liangyan. 2007. "*Sanguo yanyi* and the Mencian View of Political Sovereignty." *Monumenta Serica* 55: 157–93.

Haar, Barend ter. 2000. "The Rise of the Guan Yu Cult: The Taoist Connection." In Jan A. M. De Meyer and Peter M. Engelfriet, eds., *Linked Faiths: Essays on Chinese Religions and Traditional Chinese Culture in Honour of Kristofer Schipper*. Leiden: Brill. 184–204.

Hansen, Valerie. 1989. "Gods on Walls: A Case of Indian Influence on Chinese Lay Religion?" In Patricia Buckley Ebrey and Peter N. Gregory, eds., *Religion and Society in T'ang and Sung China*. Honolulu: University of Hawai'i Press. 75–113.

Hegel, Robert E. 1998. *Reading Illustrated Fiction in Late Imperial China*. Stanford: Stanford University Press.

Hennessey, William O. 1981. *Proclaiming Harmony*. Ann Arbor: Center for Chinese Studies University of Michigan.

———. 1984. "Classical Sources and Vernacular Resources in *Xuanhe yishi*: The Presence of Priority and the Priority of Presence," *Chinese Literature: Essays, Articles, Reviews* 6: 33–52.

Henry, Eric. 1992. "Chu-ko Liang in the Eyes of his Contemporaries." *Harvard Journal of Asiatic Studies* 52 (2): 589–612.

Hsia, C. T. 1968. *The Classic Chinese Novel*. New York: Columbia University Press.

Hu Ying. 1993. "Angling with Beauty: Two Stories of Women as Narrative Bait in *Sanguo zhi yanyi.*" *CLEAR* 15: 99–112.

Idema, W. L. 1974. "Some Remarks and Speculations Concerning *P'ing-hua.*" *T'oung Pao* 60: 121–72.

———. 1985. *The Dramatic Oeuvre of Chu Yu-tun (1379–1439)*. Leiden: E. J. Brill.

———. 1990. "The Founding of the Han Dynasty in Early Drama: The Autocratic Suppression of Popular Debunking." In W. L. Idema and E. Zürcher, eds., *Thought and Law in Qin and Han China: Studies Presented to Anthony Hulsewé on the Occasion of His Eightieth Birthday*. Leiden: E. J. Brill. 183–207.

———. 2007. "Fighting in Korea: Two Early Narrative Treatments of the Story of Xue Rengui." In Remco E. Breuker, ed., *Korea in the Middle: Korean Studies and Area Studies, Essays in Honour of Boudewijn Walraven*. Leiden: Research School CNWS. 341–58.

Idema, Wilt L., and Stephen H. West. 1982. *Chinese Theater 1100–1450: A Source Book*. Wiesbaden: Steiner.

———. 2012. *Battles, Betrayals, and Brotherhood: Early Chinese Plays on the Three Kingdoms*. Indianapolis/Cambridge: Hackett Publishing Company.

Johnson, Dale R. 1980. *Yuarn Music Dramas: Studies in Prosody and Structure and a Complete Catalogue of Northern Arias in the Dramatic Style*. Ann Arbor: Center for Chinese Studies, University of Michigan.

Johnson, David. 1980. "The Wu Tzu-hsü *pien-wen* and Its Sources: Parts I and II." *Harvard Journal of Asiatic Studies* 40 (1): 93–119; 40 (2): 466–505.

———. 1981. "Epic and History in Early China: The Matter of Wu Tzu-hsü." *Journal of Asian Studies* 40 (2): 255–71.

King, Gail. 1987. "A Few Textual Notes Regarding Guan Suo and the *Sanguo yanyi.*" *CLEAR* 9: 89–92.

———, trans. 1989. *The Story of Hua Guan Suo*. Tempe: Arizona State University Center for Chinese Studies.

Kroll, Paul W. 1976. "Portraits of Ts'ao Ts'ao: Literary Studies of the Man and the Myth." Ph.D. diss., University of Michigan.

Liu Ts'un-yan. 1962. *Buddhist and Taoist Influences on Chinese Novels. Volume 1. The Authorship of* Feng Shen Yan I. Wiesbaden: Kommissionsverlag Otto Harrasowitz.

———. 1980. "Lo Kuan-chung and His Historical Romances." In Winston L. Y. Yang and Curtin P. Adkins, eds., *Critical Essays on Chinese Fiction*. Hong Kong: Chinese University Press. 85–114.

Louie, Kam. 1999. "Sexuality, Masculinity and Politics in Chinese Culture: The Case of the 'Sanguo' Hero Guan Yu." *Modern Asian Studies* 33 pt. 4: 835–59.

Lu Hsun. 1959. *A Brief History of Chinese Fiction*. Translated by Yang Hsien-yi and Gladys Yang. Peking: Foreign Languages Press.

Mair, Victor H. 1988. *Painting and Performance: Chinese Picture Recitation and Its Indian Genesis*. Honolulu: University of Hawai'i Press.

————. 1989. *T'ang Transformation Texts: A Study of the Buddhist Contribution to the Rise of Vernacular Fiction and Drama in China*. Cambridge, MA: Harvard University Press.

Mansveld Beck, B. J. 1986. "The Fall of Han." In Denis Twitchett and John K. Fairbank, eds., *The Cambridge History of China. Volume 1. The Ch'in and Han Empires, 221 B.C.–A.D. 220*. Cambridge: Cambridge University Press. 317–76.

Mather, Richard. 2002. *New Accounts of Tales of the World*. Michigan Monographs in Chinese Studies 98. Ann Arbor: University of Michigan Center for Chinese Studies.

McLaren, Anne E. 1985. "Chantefables and the Textual Evolution of the *San-Kuo-Chih Yen-I*." *T'oung Pao* 71: 159–227.

————. 1995. "Ming Audiences and Vernacular Hermeneutics: The Uses of *The Romance of the Three Kingdoms*." *T'oung Pao* 81: 51–80.

————. 1998. *Chinese Popular Culture and Ming Chantefables*. Leiden: E. J. Brill.

————. 2006. "History Repackaged in the Age of Print: The *Sanguo zhi* and *Sanguo yanyi*." *Bulletin of the School of Oriental and African Studies* 69 (2): 293–313.

————. 2011. "Challenging Official History in the Song and Yuan Dynasties: The Record of the Three Kingdoms." In Lucille Chia and Hilde De Weerdt, eds., *Knowledge and Text Production in the Age of Print: China, 900–1400*. Leiden: Brill. 317–48.

————. 2012. "Writing History, Writing Fiction: The Remaking of Cao Cao in Song Historiograpy," *Monumenta Serica* 60: 45–69.

Mirabile, Paul. 2003. *Ji Bu: l'Épopée chinoise aux Heures Mediévales*. Castres: Imprimerie Contigraph 81.

Moore, Oliver. 2003. "Violence Un-Scrolled: Cultic and Ritual Emphases in Painting Guan Yu." *Arts asiatiques* 58: 86–97.

Ng, On-cho, and Q. Edward Wang, 2005. *Mirroring the Past: The Writing and Use of History in Imperial China*. Honolulu: University of Hawai'i Press.

Owen, Stephen. 1996. *An Anthology of Chinese Literature: Beginnings to 1911*. New York/London: W.W. Norton and Company.

Plaks, Andrew H. 1987. *The Four Masterworks of the Ming Novel*. Princeton: Princeton University Press.

Riftin, Boris L. 1994. "Time as a Factor of Narration in the '*San Kuo Chin P'ing-Hua*.'" *Archiv Orientální* 62: 315–25.

Roberts, Moss, trans. 1976. *Three Kingdoms: China's Epic Drama by Lo Kuan-chung*. New York: Pantheon Books.

————. 1991. *Three Kingdoms: A Historical Novel*. Attributed to Luo Guanzhong. Berkeley: University of California Press.

Ross, Gordon. 1976. "Kuan Yü in Drama: Translation and Critical Discussion of Two Yuan Plays." Ph.D. diss., University of Texas.

————. 1977. "Kuan Yu Travels a Thousand *Li* Alone: A Yuan-dynasty *tsa-chü*." *Literature East and West* 21: 38–50.

Roy, David T. 1990. "How to Read the *Romance of the Three Kingdoms*." In David L. Rolston, ed., *How to Read the Chinese Novel*. Princeton: Princeton University Press. 152–95.

Sawyer, Ralph D., and Mei-chün, eds. 1993. *The Seven Military Classics of Ancient China*. Boulder: Westview Press.

Shen, Simon. 2003. "Inventing the Romantic Kingdom: The Resurrection and Legitimation of the Shu Han Kingdom before the Romance of the Three Kingdoms." *East Asian History* 25/26: 25–42.

Sima Qian (Ssu-ma Ch'ien). 1993. *Records of the Grand Historian. The Han Dynasty I* (Revised Edition). Trans. Burton Watson. A *Renditions*-Columbia University Press Book. Hong Kong/New York: Research Centre for Translation, Chinese University of Hong Kong, and Columbia University Press.

———. 2006. *The Grand Scribe's Records: Volume I: The Hereditary Houses of Pre-Ch'in China.* Translated by Cheng Tsai-fa, William H. Nienhauser, et al. Edited by W. Nienhauser. Bloomington: Indiana University Press.

———. 2008. *The Grand Scribe's Records: Volume VIII: The Memoirs of Han China, Part 1.* Translated by Cheng Tsai-fa, William H. Nienhauser, et al. Edited by W. Nienhauser. Bloomington: Indiana University Press.

Slingerland, Edward, trans. 2003. *Confucius:* Analects. Cambridge, MA: Hackett Publishing Company.

Tillman, Hoyt Cleveland. 1995. "Ho Ch'ü-fei and Chu His on Chu-ko Liang as 'Scholar-General.'" *Journal of Song-Yüan Studies* 25: 77–94.

———. 1996. "One Significant Rise in Chu-ko Liang's Popularity: An Impact of the 1127 Jurchen Conquest." *Chinese Studies* 14 (2): 1–34.

———. 2002a. "Reassessing Du Fu's Line on Zhuge Liang." *Monumenta Serica* 50: 295–313.

———. 2002b. "Historic Analogies and Evaluative Judgments: Zhuge Liang as Portrayed in Chen Shou's Chronicle of the Three Kingdoms and Pei Songzhi's Commentary." *Oriens Extremus* 43: 60–70.

———. 2004. "Textual Liberties and Restraints in Rewriting Chinese Histories: The Case of Ssu-ma Kuang's Reconstruction of Chu-ko Liang's Story." In Tomas C. Lee, ed., *The New and the Multiple: Sung Senses of the Past.* Hong Kong: The Chinese University of Hong Kong. 61–100.

———. 2007. "Selected Historical Sources for *Three Kingdoms*: Reflections from Sima Guang's and Chen Liang's Reconstructions of Kongming's Story." In Kimberly Besio and Constantine Tung, eds., *Three Kingdoms and Chinese Culture.* Albany: State University of New York Press. 53–69.

Waley, Arthur. 1960. *Ballads and Stories from Dunhuang.* London: George Allen and Unwin.

Watson, Burton. 1968. *Zhuangzi.* New York: Columbia University Press.

West, Stephen H. 2003. "Text and Ideology: Ming Editors and Northern Drama." In Paul Jakov Smith and Richard von Glahn, eds., *The Song-Yuan-Ming Transition in Chinese History.* Cambridge, MA: Harvard University Press. 329–73.

West, Stephen H., and Wilt L. Idema. 1995. *The Story of the Western Wing.* Berkeley: University of California Press.

———. 2010. *Monks, Bandits, Lovers, and Immortals: Eleven Early Chinese Plays.* Indianapolis: Hackett Publishing Company.

———. 2014. *The Orphan of Zhao and Other Yuan Plays.* New York: Columbia University Press.

Yang, Winston L. Y. 1980. "The Literary Transformation of Historical Figures in the *San-kuo chih yen-i*: A Study of the Use of *San-kuo chih* as a Source of the *San-kuo-chih yen-i*." In Winston L. Y. Yang and Curtin P. Adkins, eds., *Critical Essays on Chinese Fiction*. Hong Kong: Chinese University Press. 45–84.

———. 1981. "From History to Fiction: The Popular Image of Kuan Yü." *Renditions* 15: 67–79.

Chinese and Japanese Secondary Sources

Anonymous. 1954a. *Xinbian Wudaishi pinghua* 新編五代史平話. Shanghai: Zhongguo gudian wenxue chubanshe.

———. 1954b. *Xinkan Da Song Xuanhe yishi* 新刊大宋宣和遺事. Shanghai: Zhongguo gudian wenxue chubanshe.

———. 1956. *Quanxiang pinghua wuzhong* 全相平話五種. Beijing: Wenxue guji kanxingshe.

———. 1959. *Sanguo zhi pinghua* 三國志平話. Beijing: Zhonghua shuju.

———. 1971. *Quanxiang pinghua Wuwang fa Zhou shu* 全相平話武王伐紂書. Taipei: Guoli Zhongyang tushuguan.

———. 1989. *Quanxiang pinghua Sanguozhi* 全相平話三國志. In Zhong Zhaohua 1990. 371–501.

———. 1990a. *Sanfen shilüe* 三分事略. In Liu Shide 劉士德, Chen Qinghao 陳慶浩, and Shi Changyu 石昌渝, eds. *Guben xiaoshuo congkan* 古本小説叢刊, seventh series. Beijing: Zhonghua shuju.

———. 1990b. *Sanfen shilüe* 三分事略. In *Guben xiaoshuo jicheng* 古本小説集成, vol. 1. Shanghai: Shanghai guji chubanshe.

———. 1999. *Sanfen shilüe* 三分事略. In Chen Xianghua 陳翔華, ed. *Yuanke jiangshi pinghua ji* 元刻講史平話集. Beijing: Beijing tushuguan chubanshe.

Ashida Kōshō 蘆田孝昭. 1974. "*Sangoku heiwa no kōzō to buntai*" 三國平話の構造と文体. In *Mekata Makoto hakase koki kinen Chūgoku bungaku ronshū* 目加田誠博士古稀記念中国文學論集. Tokyo: Ryūkei shosha. 409–27.

Ban Gu 班固. 1962. *Hanshu* 漢書. 12 vols. Beijing: Zhonghua shuju.

Chen Shou 陳壽. 1959. *Sanguo zhi* 三國志. 5 vols. Beijing: Zhonghua shuju.

Chen Xianghua 陳翔華. 1990. *Zhuge Liang xingxiangshi yanjiu* 諸葛亮形象史研究. Hangzhou: Zhejiang guji chubanshe.

———. 1995. "Sanguo gushiju kaolüe" 三國故事劇考略. In Zhou Zhaoxin, *Sanguo yanyi congkao* 三國演義叢考. Beijing: Beijing daxue chubanshe. 363–435.

Cheng Yizhong 程毅中. 1980. *Song Yuan huaben* 宋元話本. Beijing: Zhonghua shuju.

Ding Xigen 丁錫根, ed. 1990. *Song Yuan pinghua ji* 宋元平話集. 2 vols. Shanghai: Shanghai guji chubanshe.

Fan Ye 范曄. 1965. *Hou Han shu* 後漢書. Volume 8. Beijing: Zhonghua shuju.

Gao Mingge 高明閣. 1986. *Sanguo yanyi lungao* 三國演義論稿. Shenyang: Liaoning daxue chubanshe.

Gu Qing 顧青. 2005. "Shuo pinghua" 説平話. *Zhongguo gudai xiaoshuo yanjiu* 1: 51–59.

Guan Siping 關四平. 2009. *Sanguo yanyi yuanliu yanjiu* 三國演義源流研究. 3rd ed. Harbin: Heilongjiang jiaoyu chubanshe.

Han Weibiao 韓偉表. 2007. "*Sanguo yanyi yu jiangshi pinghua yuanyuan guanxi yanjiu shuping*" 三國演義與講史平話關係研究述評. *Zhejiang haiyang xueyuan xuebao.* March: 14–18.

Hu Ji 胡忌. 2008. *Song Jin zaju kao* 宋金雜劇考. Rev. ed. Beijing: Zhonghua shuju.

Hu Shiying 胡士瑩. 1980. *Huaben xioashuo gailun* 話本小説概論. Beijing: Zhonghua shuju.

Huang Yi 黃毅. 2007. "*Sanguozhi pinghua yu Yuan zaju Sanguoxi: Sanguo yanyi xingchengshi yanjiu zhi yi,*" 三國志平話與元雜劇三國戲:三國演義形成史研究之一. *Ming Qing xiaoshuo yanjiu* 4: 80–92.

Inoue Taizan 井上泰山 et al. 1989. *Ka Kan Saku den no kenkyū* 花關索傳の研究. Tokyo: Kyuko shoin.

Ji Dejun 紀德君. 2002. *Zhongguo lishi xiaoshuo de yishu liubian* 中國歷史小説的藝術流變. Beijing: Zhongguo shehui kexue chubanshe.

Jiang Dianyang 姜殿揚. 1996. "*Sanguozhi pinghua xu*" 三國誌平話序. In Vol. 2, pp. 745–46, Ding Xigen 丁錫根, ed. *Zhongguo lidai xiaoshuo xuba ji* 中國歷代小説序跋集, 3 vols. Beijing: Renmin wenxue chubanshe.

Jiangsusheng shehui kexueyuan Ming Qing xiaoshuo yanjiu zhongxin江蘇省社會科學院明清小説研究中心, eds. 1990. *Zhongguo tongsu xiaoshuo zongmu tiyao* 中國通俗小説總目提要. Beijing: Zhongguo wenlian chubanshe.

Kim Bunkyō 金文京. 1993. *Sangokushi engi no sekai* 三國志演義の世界. Tokyo: Tōhō shohō.

———. 2008. "*Sangokushi heiwa no ketsumatsu ni tsuite no shikiron*" 三国志平話の結末についての試論. In Sangokushi gakkai 三国志學會, ed. *Sangokushi ronshū* 三国志論集. Tokyo: Kyuko shoin. 401–6.

Li Fuqing 李福清. 1997a. (Boris Riftin), *Guangong chuanshuo; Sanguo yanyi* 關公傳説三國演義. Taipei: Hanzhong.

———. 1997b. (Boris Riftin), *Sanguo yanyi yu minjian wenxue chuantong*三國演義與民間文學傳統. Trans. Yin Xikang 尹西康 and Tian Wei 田大畏. Shanghai: Shanghai guji chubanshe.

Li Yiya 李宜涯. 2002. *WanTang yongshishi yu pinghua yanyi zhi guanxi* 晚唐詠史詩與平話演義之關係. Taipei: Wenshizhe chubanshe.

Liu Haiyan 劉海燕. 2004. *Cong minjian dao jingdian: Guan Yu xingxiang yu Guan Yu chongbai di shengcheng yanbian shilun* 從民間到經典：關羽形象與關羽崇拜的聲稱演變史論. Shanghai: Shanghai Sanlian shudian.

Liu Shide 劉世德. 1984. "Tan *Sanfen shilüe*: ta he *Sanguozhi pinghua* de yitong he Xianhou" 談三分事略它和三國志平話的異同和先後. *Wenxue yichan* 4: 99–111.

Lu Shihua 盧世華. 2009. *Yuandai pinghua yanjiu: yuanshengtai di tongsu xiaoshuo* 元代平話研究：原生態的通俗小説. Beijing: Zhonghua shuju.

Luo Xiaoyu 羅筱玉. 2010. *Song Yuan jiangshi huaben yanjiu* 宋元講史話本研究. Beijing: Zhongguo shehui kexue chubanshe.

Meng Yuanlao 孟元老 et al. 1962. *Dongjing meng Hua lu (wai sizhong)* 東京夢華錄外四種. Beijing: Zhonghua shuju.

Nikaidō Yoshihiro 二階堂善弘 and Nakagawa Satoshi 中川諭, trans. and ann. 1999. *Sangokushi heiwa* 三国史平話. Yokohama: Kōei.

Ning Xiyuan 寧希元. 1988. *Yuankan zaju sanshizhong xinjiao* 元刊雜劇三十種新校. 1st ed. 2 vols. *Lanzhou daxue gujisuo guji zhengli congkan*. Lanzhou: Lanzhou daxue chubanshe.

Ogawa Yōichi 小川陽一. 1982. *Sangon Nihaku honji ronkō shūsei* 三言二拍本事論 考集成. Tokyo: Shintensha.

Ōtsuka Hidetaka 大種秀高. 1995. "Guan Yu de gushi" 關羽的故事. In Zhou Zhao-xin, ed., *Sanguo yanyi congkao* 三國演義叢考. Beijing: Beijing daxue chubanshe. 236–67.

———. 1997. "Kan U to Ryū En: Kan U zō no seiritsu katei" 関羽と劉淵:関羽像 の成立過程. *Tōyō bunka kenkyūjo kiyō* 134: 1–17.

———. 1998. "Kan no monogatari kara Tō no monogatari e: *Sangokushi heiwa ni megutte*" 漢の物語から唐の物語へ：三国志平話にめぐつて. In *Chūgoku tsūzoku bungei e no shiza* 中国通俗文藝への視座. Tokyo: Toho shoten.

Shanghai bowuguan 上海博物館 and Shanghai wenwu baoguan weiyuanhui 上海文物保管委員會, eds. 1973. *Ming Chenghua shuochang cihua congkan* 明成化説唱詞話叢刊. Shanghai: Shanghai bowuguan.

Shen Bojun 沈伯俊 and Tan Liangxiao 譚良嘯, eds. 2007. *Sanguo yanyi dacidian* 三國演義大辭典. Beijing: Zhonghua shuju.

Shi Changyu 石昌渝. 1994. *Zhongguo xiaoshuo yuanliulun* 中國小説源流論. Beijing: Sanlian shudian.

Shōji Kakuitsu 莊司恪一. 1991. "*Sangokushi heiwa* ni tsuite" 三国志平話について. *Tōyō bunka kenkyūjo kiyō (Mukyūkai)* 11: 95–109.

Sun Kaidi 孫楷第 1965. "*Sanguozhi pinghua yu Sanguo zhizhuan tongsu yanyi*" 三 國志平話與三國志傳通俗演義. In Sun Kaidi, *Cangzhou ji* 滄州集. Volume 1, 109–20. Beijing: Zhonghua shuju.

Tan Fan 譚帆 a.o. 2013. *Zhongguo gudai xiaoshuo wenti wenfa shuyu kaoshi* 中國古代 小説文體文法術語考釋. Shanghai: Shanghai guji chubanshe.

Tan Luofei 譚洛非. 1992. *Sanguo yanyi yu Zhongguo wenhua* 三國演義與中國文化. Chengdu: Ba Shu shushe.

Tatsuma Shōsuke 立間祥介, trans. 2011. *Zensō Sangokushi heiwa* 全相三国志平話. Tokyo: Ushio shappansha.

Tu Xiuhong 涂秀虹. 2009. "*Sanguozhi pinghua* xushi de yuanze yu shijiao" 三國志平 話敍事的原則與視角. *Wen shi zhe* 2: 45–53.

Ueda Nozomu 上田望. 1995. "Mingdai tongsu wenyi zhongde Sanguo gushi: yi *Fengyue jinnang* suoxuan *jingxuan xubian sai quanjiajin Sanguozhi daquan* wei xian-suo" 明代通俗文藝中的三國故事：以風月錦囊所選精選續編賽全家錦三 國治大全為線索. In Zhou Zhaoxin, ed. *Sanguo yanyi congkao* 三國演義叢考. Beijing: Beijing daxue chubanshe. 347–62.

Wang Lijuan 王麗娟. 2007. *Sanguo gushi yanbian zhong di wenren xushi yu minjian xushi* 三國故事演變中的文人敍事與民間敍事. Jinan: Qi Lu shushe.

Xiao Xiangkai 蕭相愷. 1997. *Song Yuan xiaoshuo shi* 宋元小説史. Hangzhou: Zhe-jiang guji chubanshe.

———. 2005. *Song Yuan xiaoshuo jianshi* 宋元小説簡史. Taiyuan: Shanxi renmin chubanshe.

Xu Qinjun 徐沁君. 1980. *Xinjiao Yuankan zaju sanshizhong* 新校元刊雜劇三十種. Beijing: Zhonghua shuju.

Yan Chunxin 閻春新. 2003. "Shilun Zhuge Liang wenhua xingxiang de yansheng: Zhuge Liang wenhua xianxiang chubu xingcheng de lishi kaocha" 試論諸葛亮文化形象的衍生: 諸葛亮文化現象初步形成的歷史考察. *Tianfu xinlun* 4: 108–12.

Zeng Yongyi (Tseng Yong-yih) 曾永義. 2003. *Suwenxue gailun* 俗文學概論. Taipei: Sanmin shuju.

Zhang Bing 張兵. 2005. *Huaben xiaoshuo jianshi* 話本小説簡史. Taiyuan: Shanxi renmin chubanshe.

Zhang Shengyun 張生筠 and Wei Chunping 魏春萍. 2006. *Sanguo yanyi yu Zhongguo xiqu* 三國演義與中國戲曲. Changchun: Jilin daxue chubanshe.

Zhang Yong 張永. 2003. *Yuan Ming xiaoshuo fazhan yanjiu—yi renwu miaoxie wei zhongxin* 元年明小説發展研究：以人物描寫為中心. Shanghai: Fudan daxue chubanshe.

Zhang Zhenglang. 1948/2008. "Jiangshi yu yongshishi" 講史與詠史詩. In *Zhang Zhenglang wenshi lunji* 張政烺文史論集. Beijing: Zhonghua shuju. 119–65.

Zhao Wangqin 趙望秦 and Pan Xiaoling 潘曉玲. 2008. *Hu Zeng Yongshishi yanjiu* 胡曾詠史詩研究. Beijing: Zhongguo shehui kexue chubanshe.

Zhao Wanli 趙萬里. 1957. *Xue Rengui zheng Liao shilüe* 薛仁貴征遼事略. Shanghai: Gudian wenxue chubanshe.

Zheng Qian 鄭騫. 1962. *Jiaoding Yuankan zaju sanshizhong* 校訂元刊雜劇三十種. Taipei: Shijie shuju.

Zheng Zhenduo 鄭振鐸. 1961. "Sanguozhi yanyi de yanhua" 三國志演義的演化. In *Zheng Zhenduo, Zhongguo wenxue yanjiu* 中國文學研究. Hong Kong: Guwen shuju. 166–239.

Zhong Zhaohua 鍾兆華. 1990. *Yuankan quanxiang pinghua wuzhong jiaozhu* 元刊全相平話五種校注. Chengdu: Ba Shu shushe.

Zhou Wen 周文. 2009. "Yuankan quanxiang pinghua wuzhong jiaozhu zhaji sanze" 元刊全相平話五種校注札記三則. *Hubei di'er shifan xueyuan xuebao* 1: 4–5.

Zhou Zhaoxin 周兆新. 1990. Sanguo yanyi kaoping 三國演義考評. Beijing: Beijing daxue chubanshe.

———. 1995a. "Yuan Ming shidai Sanguo gushi de duozhong xingtai" 元明時代三國故事的多種形態. In Zhou Zhaoxin, ed. Sanguo yanyi congkao 三國演義叢考. Beijing: Beijing daxue chubanshe. 301–46.

———, ed. 1995b. Sanguo yanyi congkao 三國演義叢考. Beijing: Beijing daxue chubanshe.

Zhu Yixuan 朱一玄, ed. 1997. *Ming Chenghua shuochang cihua congkan* 明成化説唱詞話叢刊. Zhengzhou: Zhongzhou guji chubanshe.

———, and Liu Yushen 劉毓深, eds. 1983., *Sanguo yanyi ziliao huibian* 三國演義資料匯編. Beijing: Baihua wenyi chubanshe.

Zuojia chubanshe bianjibu 作家出版社編輯部. 1957. *Sanguo yanyi yanjiu lunwenji* 三國演義研究論文集. Beijing: Zuojia chubanshe.

Glossary

The entries are arranged in alphabetical order. The Chinese characters provided are those used in the *Records of the Three Kingdoms in Plain Language*. When these characters depart from the more usual forms, these are also provided.

Adou 阿斗
ai 艾
Aji 阿計
Anxi 安喜
August Emperor Guangwu of the Han 漢光武皇帝

Ba 巴
Baling 霸陵
Ban 班
baojuan 寶卷
Baozhou 包州
Baqiu 巴丘
Bazhou 巴州
beidi Wang Chen 北地王諶
Bian Zhang 邊璋
Bianliang 汴梁
Boyue 伯約
Bozhong 伯忠
Bu 布
Buwei 不危

Cai 蔡
Cai Mao 蔡瑁
Cai Yan 蔡琰
Cai Yang 蔡陽
Cai Yong 蔡邕
Cangwu 滄吳/蒼梧
Cangzhou 滄州
Cao 曹
Cao Bao 曹豹
Cao Bozhong 曹伯忠
Cao Cao 曹操
Cao Fang 曹芳
Cao Huan 曹奐

Cao Mao 曹髦
Cao Pi 曹丕
Cao Ren 曹仁
Cao Shuang 曹爽
Cao Xiang 曹相
Cao Zhang 曹璋
Chaisang 柴桑
chang bing da dao 長柄大刀
Chang'an 長安
Changsha 長沙
Che Zhou 車冑
Chencang 陳倉
Chen Da 陳達
Chen Deng 陳登
Chen Gong 陳宮
Chenliu 陳留
Chen Shou 陳壽
Cheng 成 (King Cheng)
Chengdu 成都
Chibi fu 赤壁賦
Chibi huaigu 赤壁懷古
Chi You 蚩尤
chu 初
Chu 楚
Chu Chou 楚酬 (→Fan Chou 樊稠)
Chu Pingwang (King Ping of Chu) 楚平王
Chuan 川
ci 辭
cihua 詞話
ciwen 詞文
cuigang 摧剛
cuigang weiruo 摧剛為柔
Cui Lian 崔廉
Cui Yu 崔淤

Da Liang Wang 大梁王
Dan 丹
Dan 旦 (Duke of Zhou)
Dangyang 當陽
Dasang 大桑
Deng Ai 鄧艾
Dengzhou 鄧州
Deran 德然
Dezhou 德州
Di Renjie 狄仁傑
dianjun xiaowei 殿軍校尉
dianku 典庫
Diaochan 貂蟬
Ding 丁
Ding Jianyang 丁建陽
Dingjun 定軍
Dingzhou 定州
Dong Cheng 董成
Dong Zhuo 董卓
Dongrong 東戎
Du Fu 杜甫
Du Qi 杜旗
Duan Gui 段珪
Dunhuang 敦煌

E 鄂
Epang 阿房

Fa Zheng 法正
Fancheng 樊城
Fan Chou 樊稠
Fan Qiang 范疆
Fanyang 范陽
Fan Ye 范曄
Fei Wuji 費無忌
Fenzhou 汾州
Feng 豐
Fengxian 奉先
Fengxiang 鳳翔
Fu 符 (符江)
Fuchun 富春
Fufeng 扶風
Fu Huanghou (Empress) 伏皇后
Fuling 涪陵

Gan 甘
Gan Ning 甘寧
Gansu 甘肅
Gaogui 高貴 (Duke of Gaogui)
Gao Yao 皋陶
Gaozu 高祖
Gemao 隔茅
gong 宮
Gong Gu 鞏固
Gongjin 公瑾
Gongsun Zan 公孫贊(→公孫瓚)
guan 觀
Guan 關
Guan Hanqing 關漢卿
Guan Jing 關靖
Guan Ping 關平
Guan Suo 關鎖
Guanxi 關西
Guan Yu 關羽
Guan Yunchang 關雲長
Guan Zhong 管仲
Guanzhong 關中
Guang 光
Guangdong 廣東
Guangning 廣寧
Guangwu 光武 (Emperor)
Guangxi 廣西
Guiyang 桂陽
Guo Qian 郭潛
Guo Si 郭嗣(→郭汜)

Haizhou 海州
Han Bin 韓斌
Han Fu 韓甫
Han Guozhong 韓國忠
Han Sui 韓遂
Han Xin 韓信
Hansheng 漢升
Hanshou 漢壽
Hanzhong 漢中
Hanzhou 漢州
hao 好
Hebei 河北
Henei 河內
Hengshan 恆山

Honghai 洪海
Hou Cheng 侯成
Hou Han shu 後漢書
houshuo 後説
Hu Zeng 胡曾
Hubei 湖北
Huhai 胡亥
Hua 華
Hua Guan Suo zhuan 花關索傳
Hua Tuo 華佗
huafen liangtou 話分兩頭
huafen liang shuo 話分兩説
Huai 淮
Huaidi (Han) 懷帝
Huaiyin 淮陰
Huaizhou 懷州
Huang 黃
Huangchu 黃初
Huangfu Song 皇甫嵩
Huang Gai 黃蓋
Huang Hao 黃皓
Huang Zhong 黃忠
Huarong 華容
Huidi (Jin) 晉惠帝
huisan 會散
Huizong 徽宗 (Song)

Ji 冀
ji 楫
ji 機
Ji Ling 紀靈
Ji Ping 吉平
Ji Xin 紀信
Jia 賈
Jia Chong 賈充
Jia Xu 賈許 (→賈詡)
Jiaming 嘉明
Jian Xianhe 簡獻和
Jian'an 建安
Jiang Taigong 姜太公
Jiang Wei 姜維
Jiang Wu 江吳
Jiankang 建康
Jianwu 建武
Jianxing 建興

jianxiong 奸雄
Jianyang 建陽
Jiang Gan 蔣幹
Jiang Shang 姜尚
Jiang Xiong 蔣雄
Jiang Ziya 姜子牙
Jiangnan 江南
jiangshi 講史
Jiangsu 江蘇
Jiangxi 江西
Jiangxia 江下
Jie 桀
Jieting 街亭
Jin Zu 金族
Jing 荊
jing 鏡
Jingchu 景初
Jingdi (Han) 景帝
jingji 荊棘
Jingshan 荊山
Jingzhou 荊州
Jinling 金陵
Jiujiang 九江
Jiujiang Wang 九江王
Jizhou 冀州
ju tao wang zhi zuo 舉討王之作
juan 卷
jue 絕
jue 角
juemiao haoci 絕妙好辭

Kaifeng 開封
Kong 孔
Kong Xiu 孔秀
Kongming 孔明
Kuai 蒯
Kuai Che 蒯徹
Kuai Wentong 蒯文通
Kuai Yue 蒯越
Kunlun 昆侖

Langya 琅玡→琅耶
Laozi 老子
Li 李
li 里

Li Dian 李典
Li Guang 李廣
Li Jue 李傕
Li Ru 李儒
Li Su 李宿→李肅
Lian 漣
Lianggong jiu jian 梁公九諫
Lianjiang 連江
Lintao 臨洮
Lingdi (Han) 漢靈帝
Ling Tong 凌統
Lingyan 凌煙
Liu 劉
Liu Ba 劉巴
Liu Bang 劉邦
Liu Bei 劉備
Liu Bi 劉璧
Liu Biao 劉表
Liu Cong 劉琮
Liu Deran 劉德然
Liu Feng 劉封
Liu Hong 劉宏
Liu Qi 劉琦
Liu Shan 劉禪
Liu Sheng 劉勝
Liutao 六韜
Liu Xiu 劉秀
Liu Xuan 劉宣
Liu Yao 劉曜
Liu Yuan 劉淵
Liu Zhang 劉璋
Liu Zhen 劉珍
Liyang 歷揚
Long Ju 龍且
Longzhou 隴州
Lou Zibo 婁子伯
Lou Zijiu 婁子舊
Lu 瀘
Lu Su 魯肅
Lu Xun 陸遜
Lu Zhi 盧植
Lu Zijing 魯子敬
Luocheng 落城→雒城
Luoyang 洛陽
luwei 爐圍

Lü Bu 呂布
Lü Fanan 呂範
Lü Hou 呂后 (→Lü Taihou)
Lü Kai 呂凱
Lü Meng 呂蒙
Lü Shang 呂尚
Lü Taihou (Dowager Empress) 呂太后
Lü Wang 呂望

Ma Chao 馬超
Ma Da 馬大→馬岱
Ma Gou 馬垢
Ma Shouzhong 馬守忠
Ma Teng 馬騰
Ma Wei 馬畏→馬謖
Ma Yuan 馬援
Mangtang 芒湯→芒碭山
maoci bu jian 茅茨不剪
Mei Fang 梅芳 (→靡芳)
Mei Zhu 梅竹 (→糜竺)
Meiwu 郿塢
Meiyang 梅陽
Meng Da 孟達
Meng Huo 孟獲
Meng Tian 蒙恬
Mengde 孟德
Mengqi 孟起
Mi Fang 靡芳
Mi Zhu 糜竺
Mijian 彌建
Mianzhou 綿州
miao 妙
Miao 苗
Mindi (Jin) 晉愍帝
Mingdi (Wei) 魏明帝
mingyue 名日

Nanjing 南京
Nanyang 南陽
Niu Xin 牛信

Pang 龐
Pang De 龐德
Pang Tong 龐統
Pangu 盤古

Pei 沛
Pei Songzhi 裴松之
Peng Yue 彭越
Pingdi (Han) 平帝
pinghua 評話
Pingliang 平涼
Pingyang 平陽
Pingyuan 平原
Puzhou 莆州

Qi 祁
qianwan 千萬
Qiao 喬
Qiao 譙
Qin 秦
Qin Fu 秦福→秦宓
Qin Shihuang zhuan 秦始皇傳
Qinchuan 秦川
Qinglong 青龍
Qingzhou 青州
Qiwang (King of Qi) 齊王
Qizhou 祁州
quan 勸
Quanxiang pinghua Qian Hanshu xuji
全相平話前漢書續集
Quanxiang pinghua Wuwang fa Zhou shu
全相平話武王伐紂書
Quanxiang pinghua wuzhong
全相平話五種
Quanxiang pinghua Yue Yi
tu Qi qiguo chunqiu houji
全相平話樂毅圖齊七國春秋後集
Quanxiang Qin bing liuguo pinghua
全相秦併六國平話
queshuo 卻說

Ran Qing 冉卿
Ren 任
Rencheng 任城
Rongguo 戎國

San Qi wang (King of the Three Qi)
三齊王
Sanfen shilüe 三分事略
Sanguo 三國
Sanguozhi 三國志

Sanguozhi pinghua 三國志平話
Sanguozhi tongsu yanyi
三國志通俗演義
Sanlue 三略
Shandong 山東
shang 商
Shangsi 上巳
Shangyu 上虞
Shanxi 山西
Shanyang 山陽
Shaoxing 紹興
Shengzhou 勝州
shi bing da dao 使柄大刀
Shifang 石防
shihua 詩話
shiwan 十萬
Shiyuan 仕元
shou 壽
Shouchun 壽春
Shouting 壽亭
Shu 蜀
Shu xiang 蜀相
Shun 舜
shuo 説
Si 泗
Sichuan 四川
Sima Bao 司馬保
Sima Guang 司馬光
Sima Yi 司馬懿
Sima Zhongda 司馬仲達
Sima Zhongxiang 司馬仲相
Song Wenju 宋文舉
Su Dongpo 蘇東坡
Su Shi 蘇軾
Suishui 睢水
Suiyang 睢陽
Sun 孫
Sun Hao 孫皓
Sun Jian 孫堅
Sun Liang 孫亮
Sun Qian 孫虔
Sun Quan 孫權
Sun Wu 孫武
Sun Zhongmou 孫仲謀
Suzhou 蘇州

Taihang 太行
Taishan 太山→泰山
Taizhou 泰州
Tang 湯
Tao Qian 陶謙
Tiekou 帖口
Tong 潼
Tongjian gangmu 通鑑綱目

Wang Hun 王渾
Wang Jun 王浚
Wang Mang 王莽
Wang Ping 王平
Wang Qiang 王強
Wang Shouzhong 王守忠
Wang Shuang 王雙
Wang Yun 王允
Wang Zhan 王湛
Wei Long 危隆
Wei shui (Wei River) 渭水
Wei Yan 魏延
Weiyang 未央
wen 文
Wen 溫
Wen Chou 文醜
Wenchang 文長
Wenshu 文叔
Wentong 文通
wu 武
Wudaishi pinghua 五代史平話
Wudang 武蕩
Wudi (Jin) 晉武帝
Wu Fan 吳範→Lü Fan
Wu *gou* 吳鉤
Wu Sansi 武三思
Wu Zetian 武則天
Wu Zilan 吳子蘭
Wu Zixu 伍子胥
wulou 屋漏
wuzuo zhi chu 無坐之處

Xi Shi 西施
Xiahou Dun 夏侯敦
Xiakou 夏口
Xiandi (Han) 獻帝

Xiangyang 襄陽
Xiang Yu 項羽
Xiao He 蕭何
Xiaopei 小沛
xiao shimin 小市民
Xiapi 下邳
Xichang 西長
Xichuan 西川
Xieliang 解良
xiezhi 獬豸
Xiliang 西涼
Xiqing 昔慶→襲慶
Xindu 信都
Xinye 新野
Xingyang 滎陽
Xiong Kai 雄闓
Xiuwu 修武
Xu Chu 許褚
Xu Shu 徐庶
Xu You 許攸
Xuande 玄德
Xuanhe yishi 宣和遺事
Xuanyuan 軒轅
Xuchang 許昌
Xue Rengui yijin huanxiang
薛仁貴衣錦還鄉
Xue Rengui zheng Liao shilüe
薛仁貴征遼事略
Xuzhou 徐州

Yan 燕
Yan Liang 顏良
Yan Yan 嚴顏
Yang Feng 楊奉
Yanghou 羊后
Yang Xiu 楊修
Yang Yi 楊儀
Yangping 陽平
Yangzhou 揚州
Yanxi 延熙
Yanzhou 兗州
Yao 堯 (sage king)
Yao 姚
yaodi yi nanmian yizhu
邀帝倚南面翊杼

Ye 鄴
Yi 沂
Yi Ji 伊籍
Yide 翼德
Ying Bu 英布
Yizhou 益州
Yong Kai 雍闓
Yongle dadian 永樂大典
you 酉
Youzhou 幽州
Yu 禹 (sage king)
yu 羽
Yu 虞
yu buming 羽不鳴
Yu Chang 于昶
Yu Fan 于番
Yu Jin 于禁
Yu Zhang 豫章
Yuan Qiao 元嶠
Yuan Shao 袁紹
Yuan Shu 袁術
Yuan Tan 袁譚
Yuan Xiang 袁襄
Yuanqi 元起
Yuanxi 元熙
Yunchang 雲長
Yunmeng 雲夢
Yunnan 雲南
Yunzhou 鄆州
Yuzhou 豫州

zaixiang Wang Zhan 宰相王湛
zhanhou 占候
Zhang 張
Zhang Bangrui 張邦瑞
Zhang Bao 張寶
Zhang Ben 張本
Zhang Biao 張表
Zhang Da 張達
Zhang Fei 張飛
Zhang He 張合
Zhang Ji 張濟
Zhang Jue 張角
Zhang Liang 張良

Zhang Liao 張遼
Zhang Lu 張魯
Zhang Mao 張茂
Zhang Ren 張任
Zhang Shan 張山
Zhang Sheng 張升
Zhang Song 張松
Zhang Xiang 張項
Zhang Yi 張益
Zhang Zhao 張昭
Zhang Zhong 張忠
Zhangwu 章武
Zhao Fan 趙範
Zhao Gao 趙高
Zhao Shidao 趙師道
Zhao Wen 趙文
Zhao Yun 趙雲
Zhao Zhiwei 趙知微
Zhao Zilong 趙子龍
Zhen 鴆
Zhengshi 正始
Zhenhuai 鎮淮
zhi 徵
Zhong Hui 鐘會
Zhonglü 鐘呂
Zhongping 中平
Zhongshan 中山
Zhou 紂
Zhou Cang 周倉
Zhou Yu 周瑜
Zhu Xi 朱熹
Zhu Yuan 朱怨
Zhuge 諸葛
Zhuge Jin 諸葛瑾
Zhuge Liang 諸葛亮
zhugongdiao 諸宮調
Zhuo 涿
Zifang 子房
Zijing 子敬
Zilong 子龍
Ziwu 紫烏
Zizhi tongjian 資治通鑑
Zuoguo 左國